03/14
22.00

The **LEFT**
in British Columbia

D1603149

OTHER BOOKS BY GORDON HAK

Capital and Labour in the British
Columbia Forest Industry, 1934–1974
(UBC Press, 2007)

Turning Trees into Dollars: The British Columbia
Coastal Lumber Industry, 1858–1913
(University of Toronto Press, 2000)

The LEFT

in British Columbia

A HISTORY OF STRUGGLE

Withdrawn from Collection

Gordon Hak

RONSDALE PRESS

THE LEFT IN BRITISH COLUMBIA: A HISTORY OF STRUGGLE
Copyright © 2013 Gordon Hak

All rights reserved. No part of this publication may be reproduced, stored in a retrieval system, or transmitted, in any form or by any means, without prior written permission of the publisher, or, in Canada, in the case of photocopying or other reprographic copying, a licence from Access Copyright (the Canadian Copyright Licensing Agency).

RONSDALE PRESS
3350 West 21st Avenue
Vancouver, B.C. Canada V6S 1G7
www.ronsdalepress.com

Typesetting: Julie Cochrane, in Granjon 11.5 pt on 15
Cover Design: Julie Cochrane
Cover Photo: Art Kube, BC Federation of Labour president, surrounded by reporters, addressing Solidarity crowd at BC Legislature, Victoria, 1983. Photograph by Sean Griffin, *Pacific Tribune* Archive.
Paper: Ancient Forest Friendly Rolland Enviro Satin, FSC Recycled, 100% post-consumer waste, totally chlorine-free and acid-free.

Ronsdale Press wishes to thank the following for their support of its publishing program: the Canada Council for the Arts, the Government of Canada through the Canada Book Fund, the British Columbia Arts Council, and the Province of British Columbia through the British Columbia Book Publishing Tax Credit program.

Library and Archives Canada Cataloguing in Publication

Hak, Gordon H. (Gordon Hugh), author
    The left in British Columbia: a history of struggle / Gordon Hak.

Includes bibliographical references and index.
Issued in print and electronic formats.
ISBN 978-1-55380-256-3 (print)
ISBN 978-1-55380-257-0 (ebook) / ISBN 978-1-55380-258-7 (pdf)

    1. Right and left (Political science) — British Columbia — History.
2. Political parties — British Columbia — History. 3. British Columbia — Politics and government. I. Title.

JL439.A45H35 2013   324.2711'009   C2013-903231-2   C2013-903232-0

At Ronsdale Press we are committed to protecting the environment. To this end we are working with Canopy (formerly Markets Initiative) and printers to phase out our use of paper produced from ancient forests. This book is one step towards that goal.

Printed in Canada by Marquis Book Printing, Quebec

Contents

ILLUSTRATIONS

ACKNOWLEDGEMENTS

Many people contributed directly and indirectly to the writing of this book. Michael Atkinson, Patrick Dunae, Larry Hannant, Elizabeth Lamb, Frank Leonard, Keith Smith, and Anne Young helped shape my sense of the left. Timely aid, advice, and information came from Jean Barman, Tzeporah Berman, Clarence Bolt, Elaine Brière, Ros Davies, Meagan Dyer, Robin Folvik, Sean Griffin, Norman Hak, Joey Hartman, Dan Hawthorne, Christopher Hatch, the Labour Heritage Centre, Noah Moscovitz, the Pacific Northwest Labor History Association, Ross K. Rieder, and Deirdre Salisbury. Sam Young shared his knowledge of the left and the environmental movement of the past three decades, clarifying my perspective on many points. As editor and publisher, Ron Hatch demanded precision and focus, advice I heeded as best I could. Finally, Joanne Finnegan endured the ups and downs of the project, and, as always, her contribution was immense. Though they have been named, the above do not necessarily share the views found herein. Errors of fact and interpretation, of course, are my responsibility alone.

ABBREVIATIONS

ACCL	All-Canadian Congress of Labour
AFL	American Federation of Labor
BC FED	British Columbia Federation of Labour
BCFL	British Columbia Federation of Labour
BCGEU	British Columbia Government Employees Union
BCTF	BC Teachers' Federation
CBRE	Canadian Brotherhood of Railway Employees
CCF	Co-operative Commonwealth Federation
CCL	Canadian Congress of Labour
CCPA	Canadian Centre for Policy Alternatives
CIO	Congress of Industrial Organizations
CLC	Canadian Labour Congress
CLP	Canadian Labour Party
CPC	Communist Party of Canada
CPR	Canadian Pacific Railway
CSL	Canadian Socialist League
CUPE	Canadian Union of Public Employees
E&N	Esquimalt and Nanaimo Railway
FLP	Federated Labor Party
IBPSPMW	International Brotherhood of Pulp, Sulphite and Paper Mill Workers
ILP	Independent Labour Party
IWA	International Woodworkers of America
IWW	Industrial Workers of the World
LGBT	Lesbian, Gay, Bisexual, and Transgender People
LPP	Labour Progressive Party

LWIU	Lumber Workers Industrial Union
MMLPA	Miners' and Mine Labourers' Protective Association
NAC	National Action Committee on the Status of Women
NDP	New Democratic Party
OBU	One Big Union
ORN	Olympic Resistance Network
SDP	Social Democratic Party of Canada
SFU	Simon Fraser University
SLP	Socialist Labor Party
SPBC	Socialist Party of British Columbia
SPC	Socialist Party of Canada
SPEC	Society for Pollution and Environmental Control
TLC	Trades and Labour Congress of Canada
TUC	BC Trade Union Congress
UBRE	United Brotherhood of Railway Employees
UFAW	United Fishermen and Allied Workers
UMWA	United Mine Workers of America
USLP	United Socialist Labor Party
USSR	Union of Soviet Socialist Republics
USWA	United Steelworkers of America
VTLC	Vancouver Trades and Labour Council
WCWC	Western Canada Wilderness Committee
WFM	Western Federation of Miners
WIUC	Woodworkers Industrial Union of Canada
WUL	Workers Unity League

Introduction

BRITISH COLUMBIA IS A province with a long, vibrant leftist tradition, but like elsewhere in the world, the left has been under serious attack since the 1970s. Neither the hard-won institutions nor the ideals of the left have fared well. The density of union membership is declining, governments spend less enthusiastically on social programs, and competitive, private enterprise is advanced by influential voices as the best way to operate education, pension, and health care systems. The optimism of leftists that existed in BC as late as the 1980s — the feeling that history was moving in a positive direction — has dissipated. In the ongoing struggle among competing ideas and competing institutions to shape the future, the left is not setting the agenda.

Setbacks are not new to the left. The first significant stirrings of a left in BC came in the 1880s, when political and union activists mounted a challenge to the emerging industrial capitalist order, but the initiative was in retreat by the mid-1890s. In the first two decades of the twentieth century a new wave of militants and radicals, in an array of unions and political parties, confronted employers and governments, culminating in the great upheaval of the years from 1916 to 1920. Again hopes were dashed, defeated by business leaders and governments. The left rebuilt, and in the 1940s had sufficient legitimacy and influence to force a shift that produced three decades when history tracked leftward. In this era, the BC left cheered a government-run unemployment insurance program, legislation supporting collective bargaining rights for unionized workers, and hospitalization insurance. Pension payments became richer, and public-sector workers won full union rights. Medicare arrived in the 1960s.

The New Democratic Party (NDP) formed the government in BC in 1972, the first time that a leftist political party had been in power in the province. The traditional left also diversified, intersecting with radical university students, committed environmentalists, women seeking equality in the workplace, and lesbian and gay activists, all of whom created new social movements in the 1960s and 1970s. The broad-based Solidarity movement challenged the anti-left legislative agenda of the Social Credit government in 1983, when thousands of British Columbians took to the streets in towns and cities across the province.

Solidarity was an impressive, though temporary, mobilization of the left, but times were changing. In the 1980s the provincial left was increasingly on the defensive, and the neo-liberal right, which was ascendant across the western world, took a stronger hold. In 1987 the Alberta-based Reform Party, the most vigorous expression of the New Right sensibility in Canada, was formed at a Vancouver convention, and it would have much influence in BC. In the new political climate there were still successes — the New Democratic Party governed the province from 1991 to 2001, the human rights agenda was advanced for lesbian, gay, bisexual, and transgender (LGBT) people, and environmentalists made headway on some fronts — but overall the right was dominant, pulling the whole political spectrum rightward. The current NDP pursues a guarded course in difficult times.

The moderation of the NDP, the shrinking union movement, and the weak appeal of radical political expressions have led many to conclude that the traditional left, built by unions and political parties, is now irrelevant, its past only of interest to historians. With major political parties concentrated at the centre of the political spectrum, it is argued, variations in policies are minor. From this point of view, governance is merely about providing pragmatic solutions to problems in a liberal capitalist society. The market economy, though needing minor adjustments, is essentially seen as sound. Further, in the last forty years the most dynamic and interesting challenges to the entrenched order have come from social movements fighting for rights for LGBT individuals, for women, a healthy environment, and a new role for Indigenous peoples. These movements do not look to the unions or the NDP for guidance; indeed, relations between new social movements and the left are often testy.

It is also argued by some that the left–right political division in many modern societies is obsolete because the problems of the past that preoccupied the left — concerns about security and material well-being in a world where many people lacked basic goods, educational opportunities, protection at the workplace, and access to healthcare — have been largely solved. Citizens, especially younger people, in many affluent countries now subscribe to a post-materialist value system, it is claimed, searching for self-fulfillment, personal growth, enjoyment of the environment, and a rewarding lifestyle. As such, the concerns of an earlier era that focused on the economic plight of workers and their families are old-fashioned and unimportant.[1]

The dismissal of the left, however, is overdrawn for a number of reasons. For one, wage and salary labour remain at the core of our economic system; even when employees are called "associates," have university degrees, sport unconventional attire, or enjoy on-site gyms at work, there remain unequal power relations between employers and employees. Workers still need protection to ensure their rights are respected. Secondly, economic inequality remains in prosperous societies, and the gap between the wealthy elite and the rest is widening. Homelessness, poverty, and the working poor are continuing realities. In addition, the welfare state, which provides ordinary people access to education, healthcare, and insurance against loss of income, as well as financial security in old age, is not a given; it faces powerful enemies and needs constant defence. Another reason, as the years since 2008 have shown, is that liberal capitalism is fragile, and analyzing it and considering plausible alternatives — a major preoccupation of the left — remain important tasks. Further, there are questions about the limitations of capitalism, a system dedicated to profit-making, in achieving a secure, natural environment that benefits the people as a whole. Corporate strategies do not necessarily correspond to the interests of the environment or the larger population.

The left continues to distinguish itself from opponents that to varying degrees accept and even celebrate economic and social inequality, militarism, and a view of the world that puts the interests of business and the marketplace first. The left supports unionism, speaks to equality issues, and harbours the potential for more ambitious policy directions in a less difficult political time. Finally, the left remains relevant because it seeks a broad, alternative social vision, going beyond single issues and the resolution of particular grievances, integrating social, economic, and environmental themes. The history of the left in BC, then, is not just a discussion of a world gone by, it helps us understand current predicaments.[2]

Defining the left with precision is not straightforward.[3] For one thing, the left includes diverse values, ideas, strategies, and institutions. Social democracy and communism, reformers and revolutionaries, unions and radical women's groups have all found a home in the left. They are often in conflict. Revolutionaries attack reformers for lacking commitment and zeal, for being too close to the status quo, and for not being true leftists, while reformers write off revolutionaries as unrealistic dreamers.

Defining the left is also problematic because it had a different complexion in different historical periods. For example, neither LGBT rights nor climate change were in the minds of leftists in the first years of the twentieth century. In the 1930s, unlike today, communism in Canada had a prominent profile. One strategy to cope with the diversity and variability is to focus on one individual, event or institution — perhaps, a socialist politician, a particular strike, or a miners' union — and use this perspective to suggest aspects of the broader left. The goal in this book, however, is to be inclusive, to consider the sets of relationships that constitute the historical left over time rather than the details of one element in a defined period. This means accepting a vibrant, internally dynamic, changing, tension-ridden left, a conception of the left that is necessarily somewhat blurry and murky at times, where the various components are stumbling or marching, depending on the circumstances, in the same general historical direction.

Fuzziness has advantages. It recognizes the complexity of the left and highlights the fact that its meaning is contested, even by those who see themselves as part of the left. As is the case with many political concepts, such as democracy, liberalism, freedom, and socialism, the fact that the left is not clearly fixed makes it interesting, with different agents appropriating the notion for their own purposes. Embracing a multi-faceted left also encourages the perception of the left as living and changing, not a static dictionary entry. The left becomes a sensibility operating in the real world, where the idea of the left is a serviceable, heuristic guide to understanding the world and informing political action. This realm, where terms are sometimes unstable and meanings variable, is the politics of everyday life, living politics.

The left may be broad but it is still built around defining principles and ideals. Intertwined at the heart of the left are values related to equality and community, as well as physical, social and environmental security, human dignity, democracy, and a decent standard of living for all. None of these notions is uncomplicated. Does equality mean just racial equality, or does it include gender equality and economic equality? Does economic equality mean curbing the excesses of the wealthy, democracy in the operation of businesses, or an equal sharing of the rewards of the economic system? Obviously, equality has different connotations in different eras: the vision of equality constructed by white, male, skilled workers in the 1880s did not include gender or racial equality. Over time, however, the left has become more inclusive. Understandings of security, democracy, dignity, and a decent standard of living are also contestable. The elasticity of these terms should not cause consternation. The left project has been and continues to be about working out the limits and possibilities of these issues.

Critically, at the core of the left is the belief that many or even most injustices are rooted in the nature of the economic system, a system, it is argued, that rewards the few with wealth and power and creates wide disparities between those at the top and the rest of society. The goal of the left, representing the people, the working class, or the 99 percent, depending on circumstances and the era, is to wrest economic and political power from a group known variously as the interests, the bourgeoisie, monopolists, the establishment, or the 1 percent, again depending on circumstances and the era. The left in BC emerged as a response to a new capitalist order in the late nineteenth century, and it is attention to this economic dimension that helps distinguish leftists from progressives and liberal reformers, who largely accept the existing economic, political, and social order. Unlike leftists, they believe that a bit of tinkering, a few improved government policies, or a new business plan by a corporation, regarding the environment or LGBT rights, for example, can set things right. It is not that leftists are against progressive causes — they are usually major supporters, at least in the long run. The achievement of racial, gender, and sexual equality in mainstream liberal capitalist society is lauded, as are the struggles for a healthy environment, but inequalities linked to the economy, capitalism, and social class remain. Leftists, then, demand deeper and wider change. In the real world, though, which is messy and not amenable to simple classroom definitions, the division between the moderate left and progressive liberal reformers is not always precise, whether in the 1880s, the 1970s, or now.

This book focuses on institutions, especially unions and political associations, that attempted to implement leftist ideals and values. Unions are prominent in the history of the BC left. They are operated and controlled by working people, and, because of their crucial place in the production system, their actions have the potential to alter dramatically relations between employers and employees in the economy and thus transform society. All unions and unionists have not been notably leftist, of course, but overall the union movement was and is a major institution in the struggle for change. In British Columbia history, the health of unionism, particularly in the private sector, is a good measure of the general state of the left at any given time; when the left is vigorous it includes a demanding, growing union movement that challenges employers and their influence.

Political organizations, like unions, have come in different shapes and sizes, and because their ideologies and strategies varied, they often have been in conflict. Much of this text is about sorting out the relationships among political associations and unions in the left. A glossary of political and union terms at the end of the book offers help in keeping the players straight.

The core left has always had links with movements that focus on particular issues, most notably those committed to racial exclusion in the nineteenth century and the early twentieth century, and to anti-racism, women's and LGBT rights, environmental health, peace, and Canadian nationalism in the twentieth century. In some cases, new organizations were formed because unions, which focus on employed workers, and leftist political parties, which rely on compromise to serve the needs of a wide variety of interests, had proven unsatisfactory. The environmental and women's movements of the 1960s and 1970s did not fit neatly into earlier conceptions of the left, and many modern activists pushing progressive causes found a home within liberal or even conservative parties, created new organizations, or shunned party politics altogether. But all progressive movements contained a left contingent that pushed for more extensive social change. Leftist personnel and values flowed through these many organizations, even though the movements and groups retained their own integrity and travelled their own paths. At a deeper level, however, the left project is about subsuming social movements, about weaving economic, social, and environmental ideas and organizations into a larger whole in order to shift the direction of history leftward. Unions and political parties have traditionally been at the forefront of doing so, but in the future, other institutions, such as a refashioned environmental movement, may emerge to lead a leftist crusade.

The struggle continues for the left. As I write, workers' rights, having been eroded after years of Liberal government provincially and Conservative government federally, remain in jeopardy. Governments have also weakened environmental regulations and social welfare programs. Internationally, the economic collapse of 2008 cut deeply and temporarily reinvigorated discussions of corporate greed, the unfairness of economic disparity, the benefits of strict public management of financial and business institutions, and the positive role of government. On the streets and in public urban spaces across the province, protesters, often youthful, participated in the international Occupy demonstrations in the fall of 2011, attacking the inequities of the modern order. Proposed massive pipeline projects, linking Alberta oil fields and the Pacific coast, have faced broadly based protest, instigated by the environmental movement, the NDP, and First Nations. Just what future will be created, of course, remains to be seen.

CHAPTER 1

Unions and Politics:
1880s–1894

IN JUNE 1892, MRS. MATTIE A. BRIDGE, a professional lecturer from the United States, delivered three lectures in Northfield, a coal-mining community near Nanaimo, British Columbia. Her final talk was entitled "The Labor Problem." A spell-binding orator, she held forth on the political and economic problems of the republic, attacking the money kings, Wall Street gamblers, the cost of elections, the land monopoly, and foreign immigration. Her remedies for these ills included the gospel of brotherhood taught by Christ, the eight-hour working day, restricted immigration, the dispossession of foreign landlords, and the death of corporations and syndicates that controlled industries. She also discussed the means of bringing about change, beginning by saying that "it is not the time now, or in the future, to convert the workingman's sighs and heartaches and disappointments into clubs or stones to destroy capital." Instead she argued for unions and political action: "The first step . . . is

Labor Unions; the second the federation of these unions; the third the consolidation of the labor force at the ballot box, in the interests of wives and children and freedom."[1]

The speech is remarkable, in part because it was delivered by a woman in a time when female public participation in politics and unions was not common. That she was speaking in a coal-mining community is also noteworthy; miners, along with skilled tradesmen and small business people, played a prominent role in the British Columbia left of the 1880s and 1890s. In part, too, her talk showed that the urge for change in British Columbia was part of a larger phenomenon in the western world. Most significantly, Bridge effectively linked a broad range of interconnected criticisms, ideas, and goals into a whole. She articulated a sense of the people and the possibility for change. Beyond specific policies and issues, then, there was a suggestion of a web that interlaced the individual concerns and actions into something broader — a left.

In 1892 the realization of Mattie Bridge's vision seemed possible to many in BC. A recent upsurge in union activity and worker political action had not yet abated. The construction of the Canadian Pacific Railway (CPR), completed in 1885, had spawned an economic boom and led to the establishment of Vancouver, which rapidly grew to a population of 13,685 by 1891. Carpenters, masons, painters, and lathers flooded into the province to work in the construction sector. Other towns also expanded over the course of the 1880s. The population of New Westminster quadrupled, while Nanaimo and Victoria tripled in size.[2] Tradesmen and small businessmen mingled in these communities, dreaming of a society where equality prevailed and the hard work of ordinary people was rewarded. Large-scale capitalists operated coal mines on Vancouver Island, fish canneries along the Fraser River, iron works in Victoria, and sawmills in Vancouver, and strong unions, appeals to reason, and the effective use of democratic institutions, it was thought, would keep them under control.

Establishing permanent organizations to represent the interests of workers over the long term, as Bridge noted, was essential, but it was also difficult. Vancouver Island miners set up the Miners Mutual Protective

Victoria workers, 1885, John Kurtz's Cigar Manufactory. Vancouver Public Library 6380.

Society in 1877. It survived for a few years but defeat in a major strike in 1883 caused its dissolution. Other workers had also organized. Bakers in Victoria established a short-lived association in 1859, and the Victoria Typographical Union and the Shipwrights and Caulkers Union were both in existence by 1863. A more ambitious project brought Victoria workers together in the Workingman's Protective Association in 1878. However, this institution, which also established a branch in New Westminster, lasted less than one year as a formal organization.[3]

In the 1880s, the union movement put down firmer roots. The Knights of Labor, an American-based organization that spread through North America in the early 1880s, established themselves in BC. The Knights were committed to a society based on cooperation and the interests of ordinary people. Men and women, skilled and unskilled, native and immigrant, were to be represented in one organization. The Knights were massively successful across the continent in the mid-1880s. In 1883 and

1884, workers and allies in Victoria, New Westminster, Nanaimo, and Wellington formed Knights locals, which were called assemblies. Two years later in Vancouver they established two assemblies. The Knights of Labor were also active in the railway towns of Kamloops and Yale, as well as the mining communities of Rossland and North Wellington.

Perhaps twelve local assemblies existed in British Columbia in the 1880s, although not necessarily at the same time. In 1887 six local assemblies met in New Westminster to form District Assembly 203. According to Paul Phillips, membership in the District Assembly peaked in the spring of 1888 at 459 members.[4] Then came disarray. Employers in the United States ruthlessly crushed strikes and undermined organizational activities. The Knights were also demoralized by internal disputes. Skilled workers, who because of their skill and standing in the community had more clout in dealing with employers, felt that they could better achieve their aims by acting independently without the drag of unskilled labourers diluting their influence.

For their part, skilled workers built craft-based unions, often connected to American organizations. They were especially active from 1889 to 1892. Tabulations from newspaper records show that the years from 1886 through 1888 had been lean years for organization, while the years 1889 through 1891 witnessed an abrupt increase. In the Victoria, New Westminster, Vancouver, and Nanaimo areas, thirteen unions were formed in 1889, sixteen in 1890, and eleven in 1891. Perhaps most telling was the creation of city Trades and Labour Councils, evidence of sufficient stable unions to sustain a larger organizational structure. Activists formed Trades and Labour Councils in Vancouver in December 1889, in Victoria and New Westminster in 1890, and in Nanaimo in 1891.[5] Labour organizations, a key pillar of the left, were beginning to take shape.

Like unionism, protests and strikes were part of the work world. A small party of Scottish coal miners, who arrived at Fort Rupert on Vancouver Island in 1849, brought the custom with them, engaging in a job action shortly after beginning work. Wages and living conditions, as well as dismay that their skills were being ignored by an employer that expected them to do mere labourers' work, were the reasons for the strike.[6] In 1855 coal miners in Nanaimo struck. Further strikes occurred on Vancouver Island in 1861, 1865, 1877, 1880, 1881 and 1883 over wages, working conditions, and safety in the mines. Also of note was the notorious anti-labour stance of Robert Dunsmuir, an immigrant miner, who had uncovered a rich coal seam in 1869, and who ruthlessly refused to recognize employee grievances and unions. Non-miners also took job action. The Knights were involved in the first known strike in a coastal sawmill in April 1886, when workers struck the Hastings Sawmill in Vancouver. After 1885 tradesmen increasingly struck. Overall there were eight strikes in the years 1885–1888 and thirty-four strikes in the years 1889–1892. Increased wage rates were a primary goal. Other issues included employer acceptance of the union and all-union work sites.

Limiting the hours worked was a major objective in the era, reflecting an international trend. In the United States and Europe the demand was for the eight-hour system; in British Columbia the goals were more limited. Sawmill workers demanded that their working day be reduced from 11.5 hours to 10 hours, while trades persons wanted to work nine hours per day rather than the traditional ten. A shorter working day was a straightforward demand that was easy to monitor and it appealed to many. Independent, healthy workers needed sufficient time away from work, it was argued, to develop their intellectual and political capacities in order to build a better society. More time off meant, said the workers, that they would be more productive when on the job.

Store clerks, who at times toiled for fourteen hours per day, six days a week, also sought to reduce working hours, often with the support of employers. In Vancouver, the Early Closing movement spread in the spring of 1889, the real estate agents having "fallen into line with the hardware merchants, and boot and shoe dealers."[7] In early May 1890, Victoria real estate offices and shoe stores closed on Saturday afternoons, and blacksmiths decided to follow suit at the middle of the month. In June a majority of Nanaimo businesses declared a half holiday on Thursday afternoons.[8] But unity was impossible to maintain in a competitive business environment; by the end of July the Nanaimo experiment had collapsed, with some storekeepers complaining that "they prefer to give their clerks a holiday when needed rather than close their stores and let others who refuse to reap the benefits."[9]

Activism continued, and 1891 witnessed the most concerted drives. In New Westminster the secretary of the half-holiday closing movement reported that as of 2 July the furniture, jewellery, shoe, harness, and hardware stores had agreed to close from one to six on Saturdays, that the dry goods and gentlemen's furnishings stores were undecided, and that the grocery stores were still being canvassed. The committee was also working on behalf of mill hands, carpenters, bricklayers, and other mechanics and labourers.[10] Keeping the firms in line, however, was difficult. In Vancouver the push in April and May of 1891 for a store closing on Wednesday afternoons was abandoned, and activists began seeking a standard 7:00 p.m. closing time instead.[11] In Victoria the Saturday half-holiday lasted only through the summer of 1891.[12] Nanaimo jewellers concocted an elaborate agreement to bring about early closing in April 1892. They agreed that from the 2nd of May until the 1st of October they would close at 6:30 p.m., except on Saturdays, or on the evenings before holidays and days on which there were excursions visiting, when they would close at ten p.m. Any complaints could be taken to a committee of two members of the Jewellers' Association, and anyone breaking the rules would be fined five dollars, the money being donated to the local hospital.[13] The fate of the pact is unknown.

The demand for shorter hours resonated through society. In July 1890, the newly formed Victoria Trades and Labour Council challenged the local clergy to endorse the movement for shorter hours. They drew up a long resolution, which recognized the influence of the churches on the masses and portrayed Christ as the first labour reformer who "did infinitely more than all other agencies since combined towards the amelioration of the conditions of oppressed humanity — breaking their shackles and proclaiming them free men." Shorter hours, argued the resolution, would allow workers more time devoted to Christian enlightenment, and supporting shorter hours would draw people closer to the churches, "stamping out forever the calumnious doctrine which infidels would propagate — that Christianity has always arrayed itself on the side of the merciless plutocracy, and in direct opposition to the interests and aspirations of the wage earners."[14]

Group of men, including clerks, at R.V. Winch Grocery Store, Vancouver, 1890.
Studio: Bailey Brothers/Dominion Photo Co. Vancouver Public Library 19839.

Having been flushed out, Victoria clergy delivered sermons on the labour question during the summer of 1890. Nanaimo ministers did the same.[15] Ministers also took the occasion to go beyond the movement to reduce working hours to discuss unions, relations between capital and labour, socialism, and strikes. All endorsed the movement for shorter hours, but the degree of their commitments varied. A few worried about what workers would do with the idle time, envisioning more time for working men in saloons, but the majority felt that workers would act appropriately and improve themselves. Reverend Jenns of Victoria opined that he favoured shorter hours, but argued that this was not the time, that in a new country long labour was necessary to develop God's resources and sustain a good standard of living. In Nanaimo, Reverend Baer, offering a radical Christian position, argued that the conflicts between "Capital and Labor have their roots far below the difficulties reached by the eight-hour system. . . . I believe the ultimate ground of settlement will be much higher than the adoption of an eight hour system." In the summer of 1890, then, BC churches, despite their diversity of opinion, were forced to engage the question about relations between capital and labour and were forced to acknowledge the justice of the workers' perspective.

For some, however, such as free thinker John Leslie, who submitted the following poem to a local newspaper, the responses of the churches to the problems of the working man were far from satisfactory:

> Learn to labor and to wait,
> This the precept, the mandate,
> From the church and from the state,
> From each perch of high estate;
> (From each tyrant and ingrate,
> Who on labor's shoulders sate,
> E'er since Adam, *oft bevate* [berate],
> At Eve's deceptive bidding ate,
> Work them early, work them late,
> Leave no time to contemplate,
> No time with our's such life to rate,
> Keep the gap the difference great,
> Twixt our refined — their beastly state;
> Prove by Scripture 'tis their fate —
> Thus stood the church and thus the state —
>
> What must be done? Why, agitate,
> Let union give our ballot weight,
> Let wisdom point and keep it straight;
> For men well pledged to legislate
> The hours of labor down to eight.[16]

There were workplace struggles. The most dramatic strike of the era occurred in the Wellington coal fields, just outside Nanaimo.[17] On 1 February 1890, Nanaimo and Wellington miners, facing a wage cut, formed a union, the Miners' and Mine Labourers' Protective Association (MMLPA). In May they struck the Wellington colliery owned by Robert

Coal miners at Wellington, Vancouver Island, 1890. British Columbia Archives F-07452.

Dunsmuir & Sons. On 18 May 1890, eight hundred miners, representing all four area MMLPA lodges, held a mass meeting near the No. 6 Wellington shaft in a demonstration of strength and resolve.[18] The Dunsmuir company refused to recognize the miners' strike, hiring strikebreakers and evicting strikers from company-owned homes. In early August, soldiers marched into Wellington, ostensibly to maintain the peace, although there was little in the way of disturbances. Supported financially by workers throughout British Columbia, as well as by Washington coal miners and the three other area MMLPA lodges, the Wellington miners held out for three aims: an eight-hour working day from surface to surface, acknowledgement of the miners' union as the legitimate representative of the workers, and recognition of pit committees to arbitrate disputes between the miners and foremen. The company conceded the first but was totally unprepared to admit the last two.[19]

The strike continued into 1891, and in August of that year the striking miners voted 342 to 80 in favour of remaining out.[20] On 13 November 1891, just three days short of being on strike for eighteen months, the MMLPA conceded, calling the strike off. While the union was not accepted, strikers were allowed to return to work for the company. Throughout the ordeal, the strikers had been cared for by the union, which spent "the enormous sum of $84,000," largely raised by an assessment on MMLPA miners working in other Nanaimo area mines, during the strike.[21]

Often workers won gains without a strike. In February 1889, Victoria bricklayers, stonemasons, and stonecutters met employers, demanding the nine-hour working day. Contractors agreed to the scheme, effective April 1, with the exception of the Royal Jubilee Hospital construction site, which, due to time deadlines, would not adopt the nine-hour system until May 1. The workers were pleased with the arrangement.[22] In the spring of 1890, Victoria's fifty unionized tailors enforced a new scale of prices without a strike, and tinsmiths inaugurated the nine-hour system with no response from employers.[23] In June 1892, Victoria plasterers secured the eight-hour working day without a strike.[24]

In the Nanaimo coalfields, too, unionization and the potential for job action forced negotiations and satisfactory settlements for workers. The Dunsmuir Company smashed the unions in their operations, but the New Vancouver Coal Mining and Land Company, managed by Samuel Robins, recognized the authority of the MMLPA, and negotiated in good faith. In an agreement between the MMLPA and the company dated 24 July 1891, the company agreed to employ union members only and not to dismiss any worker without reasonable cause, while the union agreed not to strike before "exhausting all other means of conciliation available."[25]

In March 1892 a committee of the Northfield Lodge of the MMLPA met Superintendent Robins to discuss a change in the method of mining. The meeting was satisfactory, and the union delegation accepted Robins' changes. Robins added that while "the Company retained the right of managing and changing the management of the mines as they saw fit, should any change in the management cause a reduction of wages; the Company would be willing not only to meet the miners, but would be pleased to give them all redress that was possible."[26] Robins personally negotiated with Northfield, East Wellington, and Nanaimo miners when, due to sagging United States markets, wage reductions were imposed in late 1892 and 1893, ensuring that workers remained in their homes and that mines continued operating.[27] There were short work stoppages as well, but, as one miner noted at a public meeting, Robins was still respected: "Never in my experience on labor questions have I known a superintendent of a large company like this to meet the men in such an unselfish manner. . . ."[28]

Unions educated workers about local labour conditions. During the 1890–1891 Wellington coal strike the union encouraged a coal boycott in the important San Francisco market. The MMLPA sent delegates to San Francisco to speak before the Council of Federated Trades, achieving an endorsement for the coal boycott.[29] Union-to-union representation also quickly spread information about local strikes, labour market conditions, and union label campaigns. Immigrants were seen as a threat, especially Italians, who were notorious as strikebreakers: "What between wet weather, being laid off, dear living and Italian competition, it is a hard struggle. . . ."[30] But even solid unionists could be a problem if they arrived in town, lured by rumours of prosperity, and glutted the market with workers, opening up the possibility for wage cuts and union busting.

The cooperative principle also informed calls for worker-run operations, especially during disputes with employers. In March 1884, unionized Victoria carpenters met to discuss going into business for themselves, either by setting up a labour bureau or becoming contractors: "After some discussion the sense of the meeting was that it was not advisable at present to take the work out of the employers' hands, but if they refused to come to terms in a few days the carpenters would be obliged to protect themselves by forming a co-operative association to take contracts and general work."[31] In 1890, again during a labour dispute, Victoria members of the United Brotherhood of Carpenters and Joiners proposed "to start a sash and door factory, to be run on the co-operative system."[32] A group of Nanaimo union tailors reached a settlement in 1893 after giving notice of having "taken a store with the intention of running a union establishment."[33] In September 1893, Vancouver striking tailors established the Tailors' Co-operative Store at 312 Homer Street.[34] When plasterers began taking contracts during an 1891 strike, one commentator suggested that contractors were unnecessary in the house-building industry, arguing that carpenters, plasterers, and painters, through their unions, were sufficiently competent to take contracts themselves and that "the contract element for the ordinary purposes of house building might be eliminated altogether."[35]

Despite some defeats, the unions had achieved much by the early 1890s. The nine-hour working day was the norm:

> In the building trades, as in the majority of occupations, in both Vancouver and Victoria, nine hours constitutes a day's work. Employers conceded to reductions without much protest, believing that, on the whole, they would get as much work done in nine hours as they formerly did in ten. There has been no complaint about the nine hour system, and apparently there is no desire to return to the ten hour plan.[36]

Some employers still chafed, as one bricklayer noted in a rather inelegant phrase, trying to make workers "re-swallow the vomited 10 hour system,"[37] but optimism prevailed.

The left also existed in politics. BC was peculiar at this time in that there were no Liberal and Conservative parties at the provincial level. Rather, there was a Government party and an Opposition, as well as Independents. The Government party, largely politicians with links to the federal Conservatives, was in power through the 1880s and 1890s. The Opposition faction was largely made up of federal Liberal supporters. There was also a more nebulous leftist orientation that must be distinguished from the Opposition (in this chapter, when the first letter of Opposition is capitalized it refers to the political organization active in provincial elections, while opposition with a lower case "o" refers to a broader left.) The leftist orientation in the politics of the late nineteenth century was found in many areas, including the themes of greater economic equality, workers' rights, worker representation in government, and more control by the people of natural resources.

The leftist opposition built on the ideals of the Knights of Labor. In June 1886, a series of meetings of Victoria workingmen presided over by J.M. Duval, a local Knights of Labor leader, coordinated the role of labour for the upcoming provincial election. At the first meeting, Byron West, a

shoemaker with a small company, set out the workers' platform in a resolution that began: "the legislature of the country has been directed mainly
by the wealthier part of the community and that the time has come when
the toiling masses should have representatives on the floor of the house
of assembly." The resolution condemned the government's policy of alien-
ating large areas of public land to private individuals and corporations. It
also decried the legislative protection given the legal, dental, and medical
professions, called for shorter hours of work, and sought legislation to
produce safer working conditions for miners. Moreover, the platform
called for legislation to allow the recall of unsatisfactory members: "that
provision be made by pledge if not by law for the enforced resignation of
any member whose line of conduct may render him distasteful to the
majority of his constituents."[38]

A few days later, a meeting of workingmen created a fifteen-member
committee to seek out candidates for the legislature. A 16 June meeting
chose two candidates, one of whom was Duval, to run in the next provincial election on a ticket with two Opposition nominees. All would vie for
the four seats in the Victoria riding.[39] The Vancouver Knights of Labor
put forward a platform in November 1886 for the civic election that candidates were expected to support; it called for curtailment of corporate
control of the city waterfront, citizen discussion of all proposed tax increases, and the establishment of a public library.[40]

From 1887 to early 1889 working-class involvement ebbed, but in late
1889 all parties and candidates catered to and claimed to represent the
working man. At the provincial level, Government, Opposition, and
Independent candidates sought the workingman's vote, and in federal
politics the Liberals and Conservatives did the same. Some issues were
designated particularly relevant to working men, but the way to deal with
the problems varied, and questions became obscured in legal complica-
tions, economic rationalizations, employer strategies, political delay and
obfuscation. A working-class constituency had been created, but it was
fragmented politically.

For labour activists, political action held perils. Direct political involvement, either in running candidates or forming a political organization,
was financially costly. While discussing running an independent labour
candidate in an impending federal by-election, Tully Boyce, a prominent

MMLPA leader, reminded a mass gathering of Nanaimo area miners in 1892 of the difficulties: "While in favor of a labor candidate he did not believe that the workingmen would be willing to give him [the candidate] financial support. It was necessary therefore to find some one to represent them who was able to pay his own expenses."[41]

Unionists also feared the internal divisiveness that might be occasioned by too close involvement in politics, as their organizations contained good trade unionists of both the Liberal and Conservative persuasion. The Vancouver 1889 civic election exposed the difficulties. Both mayoralty candidates claimed to represent the working man, and garnered endorsements from prominent trade union leaders. A union carpenter, however, protested the actions of his union president, who endorsed one candidate. The critic disagreed with the choice, arguing that the union leader had "usurped his position," and, furthermore, was disingenuous because most carpenters, longshoremen, and workers generally supported the other candidate.[42]

The June 1890 provincial election campaign witnessed a major push from the emerging opposition. A meeting of some one thousand members of the MMLPA on Saturday, 17 May 1890, at Wellington, nominated two candidates, Thomas W. Forster and T. Keith, to run as Independents.[43] Later, a third candidate, C.C. McKenzie, was put forward as the workers' Independent candidate. None of the candidates was at the time a miner. On that same Saturday a large meeting was held in Hart's Opera House in Vancouver "to honestly see what could be done to have their class, during the next parliament, represented." Prominent union leaders, including Duncan McRae, George Pollay, J.M. Duval, and George Bartley, were among the participants. The meeting endorsed a platform and, after a vote, two candidates.[44]

The Vancouver and Nanaimo platforms were formed from the same template, and the influence of the social and moral principles of the Knights of Labor was notable. Indeed, the Nanaimo manifesto drew directly on that of the Knights:

> Believing that the first principles of representative Government should be to accomplish the greatest good for the greatest number, to secure the workers the full enjoyment of the wealth they create, sufficient leisure in which to develop their intellectual, moral and social faculties, in a word,

to enable them to share in the gains and honors of advancing civilization; to secure these objects we must have men to advance our causes on the floor of the Legislative Hall of our Province. . . .[45]

The Government party retained control of the legislature in 1890, but Opposition and Independent candidates did well, winning the three Nanaimo area seats, New Westminster City, two Vancouver seats, and three of the four Victoria City seats.[46]

Entwined with the early left of unionism and labour politics was the Single Tax crusade. Prominent in BC after 1889, the Single Tax movement was a product of the writing and activism of American Henry George. The phenomenon swept North America and Britain in the 1880s. At the core of George's analysis was land, which, he argued, when held in an unimproved state while still increasing in value, undermined the efforts of capital and labour to produce society's necessary goods. Landholders did nothing to increase the value of their properties; they just waited upon the industriousness of others, who created economic activity, to raise property values. The wealth generated by true producers was sucked up by the parasitic class through increased rents and rising property values. George's notion of land included natural resources and, like air and water, land was seen as a gift of nature that should not be privately owned. The solution was the Single Tax, a tax on all unimproved land and property to its full value, which would replace all other taxes, such as excise taxes, property taxes, and the most galling tax, that on property improvement.[47]

George's ideas were set out in his 1879 book *Poverty and Progress*, as well as a number of pamphlets and speeches. In his thought, the so-called productive elements — workers and industrial capitalists engaged in useful enterprises — shared interests, as well as a legitimate hostility against a segment of the capitalist class that held private legal rights to natural resources and speculators. Its radicalism was in its challenge to the unfettered rights of private property. According to historian Ramsay Cook, many feared that "once established ideas about the economic order were questioned, especially those concerning property, a large hole was opened in the established order. There was no reason to believe that the

'Single Tax' would be the stopping place."[48] British Columbia critics of the Single Tax deemed it socialism and communism, arguing that it was outright confiscation of private property that would engender a levelling of the social order whereby all would be equal, a belief in direct contradiction of human nature, God's will, and common sense.

In the mid-1880s George's ideas were not yet prominent in British Columbia. One Victoria commentator discussed George's 1886 lecture tour in Ontario, noting that his lack of appeal was due to the fact that "Canadians take no stock in socialism."[49] Two years later the same voice predicted the demise of George's popularity: "His converts in the United States and Canada are comparatively few and it would seem that they are becoming less zealous as well as diminishing in number."[50] However, the George era in British Columbia was just beginning.

Byron H. West was a key figure. He was an active thinker and speaker, almost certainly a member of the Knights of Labor, who had been discussing issues of interest to the working class for years. In 1889 the Single Tax solution became increasingly prominent in his addresses. He spoke at a Nanaimo Knights of Labor meeting in January 1889. After endorsing labour organization, temperance, and anti-Chinese legislation, he spent the bulk of his time on the land question, a topic that "was greeted with loud applause." West said that in British Columbia, land was falling into the hands of a few wealthy landowners and corporations: "The United States, Canada and British Columbia, and even Nanaimo, were building up an aristocracy as grievous as ever existed." The result was that the labouring classes, cajoled by "an unholy, unjust and detrimental law," were forced to pay tribute to a few. The solution was Henry George's Single Tax system. Speaking during a coal-mining dispute, West said that if the Single Tax society came to be, there would be no strikes, because no longer would the few men who controlled the land or what was under it be able to dictate terms to the labouring man. West concluded by saying that "he had more faith in the principles advanced by Henry George than any since the days of Jesus Christ."[51]

In May 1889, West spoke again in Nanaimo, and during the meeting the Nanaimo Reform League was formed.[52] In October 1889, Walter Roos, a political activist with the federal Liberals, spoke publicly in defence of the Single Tax.[53] Thomas Forster, elected to the provincial legislature to represent Nanaimo in June 1890, was a longtime Single Taxer who was given the nomination by the miners "because they knew he was a single tax man."[54]

The land question was relevant in BC. Hostility to speculators and government favours in the granting of public lands had been a theme since the colonial era. In granting early timber rights in the 1860s, colonial governments were keen to keep away land speculators, and stipulations for the actual construction of sawmills in order to be given access to government timber were specified. Despite this concern in granting timber-cutting rights, people still worried. In the 1870s and 1880s, there were complaints about the amount of timberland that was falling into private hands, the poor financial return that the government received for the people's timber, and wasteful logging practices.[55] The coal lands were also in the hands of a few, most notoriously the Dunsmuir family. The land grants for the railway construction projects of the 1880s also prompted criticism. Robert Dunsmuir was given some two million acres of land rich in coal and timber in 1884 in return for constructing a rail line from Nanaimo to Esquimalt, near Victoria, a line that was completed in 1887. This land grant, the Esquimalt & Nanaimo Belt, made up almost one-third of Vancouver Island. Byron West called Dunsmuir "the Uncrowned King of Vancouver's Island."

Single Tax fever was widespread. Thomas Turnbull, a Liberal federally, published the *Single Tax Advocate* in New Westminster.[56] In June 1890, a New Westminster Single Tax meeting, where Byron West spoke, attracted five hundred people.[57] In February 1892, New Westminster City Council passed a by-law, proposed by an alderman who was a member of the Single Tax movement, exempting improvements from taxation. The local Single Taxers were jubilant.[58] In late September 1889, the Vancouver Single Tax Club was formed, based on the following principles:

Whereas, this meeting being of the opinion that the evils arising from the present system of making land, on which all men must live, the exclusive property of some, thereby creating a monopoly upon which all other monopolies rest, and recognizing that in countries widely separated, differing in forms of government tariffs, industrial development and religious belief, the tendencies and effects of this system are everywhere the same, causing greater inequalities of the distribution of wealth as the population increases, and land becomes more valuable, and Whereas, the single tax on land values advocated by Henry George is the simplest, surest and most effectual remedy for the removal of these evils, therefore be it Resolved, that this meeting do organize a Single Tax Club. . . .[59]

Long-time unionist and Knights of Labor activist George Pollay was the president. In the fall of 1890, a Vancouver alderman, Dr. J.T. Carroll, was pressing for the city to adopt the Single Tax. He was an unabashed Single Taxer in his run for the mayoralty the next year.[60]

The Single Tax Club organization in Vancouver faltered, but in December 1891 the Club was reorganized, still under the guidance of George Pollay, making the Single Tax a major public issue in the city in early 1892. Robert Macpherson, a carpenter, unionist, and new president of the Vancouver Single Tax Club, along with Pollay, were the main advocates and defenders of the cause.[61] In 1892 they organized a series of eleven lectures over three months to consider the ramifications of the Single Tax.[62] During the civic elections in late 1892 the Vancouver Trades and Labour Council and the Single Tax Club cooperated, each putting forward candidates in the various wards. The Trades and Labour Council endorsed the Single Tax.[63]

In Victoria, at a public meeting in late May 1890, in the run-up to the provincial election, hundreds filled a Victoria theatre to hear a debate on the Single Tax. Speakers in favour of the Single Tax included Byron West, his business partner, R. Jackson, Edward Bragg, a workingman and alderman, and J. A. Cohen, a printer.[64] A Single Tax Club was formed in July 1890.[65] The influence of the Single Taxers in Victoria was such that the entire Opposition slate vying for the four Victoria seats in the provincial legislature came out in favour of the Single Tax, which in Victoria was the major issue of the campaign. In June 1892, Victoria Single Taxers began publishing the *Single Tax*, and in October they were trying to bring the Victoria, Nanaimo, Vancouver, and New Westminster clubs together in one provincial body.[66] In December of 1892 they organized the Progressive Party to put forward candidates in elections.[67]

Although the Single Tax was associated with unionists and labour politicians, it had supporters across the political spectrum. Reform liberals, especially, were attracted to the Single Tax. In 1889 the *Daily Times* in Victoria came out in favour of the Single Tax. The paper also vociferously supported the federal Liberal Party and the provincial Oppositionists, as well as free trade, and a prominent role for unions in the economy and society as a whole. The other main paper, the *Daily Colonist*, was apoplectic in its criticism of the Single Tax, branding it socialism and simple confiscation of property owned by others. The *Daily Colonist* was the organ of the federal Conservatives and supported the provincial Government party. It also extolled the virtues of the Dunsmuir interests, defended the merits of large corporations, and barely tolerated the right of workingmen to form unions, and only then as long as these unions were not allowed to interfere in the management of companies, question the absolute rights of private property, or challenge employers, who were seen as overwhelmingly beneficent and the kingpins in development.[68]

Despite the flurry of activity regarding the Single Tax and its interconnection with other goals, it was a short-lived phenomenon, and as the 1890s progressed it became an increasingly minor strain in political thought. Radical socialists opposed the Single Tax solution because its focus on land and rent missed what they saw as the crux of the problem, the capitalist exploitation of labour. All capitalists, not just major landholders and resource controllers, held sway over the lives of workers. As British Columbia became more and more industrialized, with more workers in factory settings, the weakness of the Single Tax became clearer. The Single Tax survived in municipal politics, and the mayor of Vancouver championed the cause in the years just before World War I. But now the Single Tax was no longer a vehicle to transform society, but rather a tactic to encourage investment. The Single Tax did not disappear completely on the left. Bob Williams, a prominent cabinet minister in the BC NDP government of the 1970s, had a university degree in economics and took the ideas of Henry George seriously.[69]

The leftist activists of the 1880s and 1890s were white, and despite appeals to equality and fairness, their version of who constituted the people was restricted. Anti-Asian sentiment helped unite white workers and stimulated political action. Chinese immigrants had begun arriving in significant numbers during the gold rushes of the late 1850s and early 1860s. As well as establishing themselves in the gold fields, they settled in Victoria, where they provided wage labour and engaged in business. By 1867 there were Chinese workers in the Vancouver Island coalfields, and the numbers grew steadily: "Almost immediately after their introduction Chinese workers constituted nearly half the workforce of the mines, and in the individual mines at the end of selected years — Harewood in 1877, Wellington in 1881 and 1887, and Union/Cumberland in 1888, 1889, and 1890 — Chinese mine workers outnumbered whites."[70]

A further influx of Chinese workers occurred in the 1880s with the construction of the CPR. By the summer of 1882, some twelve thousand Chinese lived in BC, and about half were employed on the railway. In the end, over fifteen thousand Chinese workers were imported on contracts to build the grade in the British Columbia section, although many did not stay long. The end of CPR construction meant that thousands of Chinese labourers lost their jobs. Most left the province. Others spread through BC, working on farms and construction crews, toiling in coal mines, tailor shops and cigar manufacturing operations, and serving time as house servants. In 1881 the Chinese made up an estimated 18 percent of the non-native population, and though their numbers in BC rose from 4,300 to 8,910 over the course of the decade, their proportion of the non-native population had dropped to 13 percent by 1891.[71]

In this era, white union leaders and politicians spoke the language of fear, mixing racist assumptions and economic concerns.[72] They worried that Chinese contract labour was a new form of slavery that, given an opportunity, would be favoured by capitalists and undermine the rights of free British subjects. Slavery had only recently been defeated in the United States.[73] The use of Chinese contract workers by employers such as CPR contractors and the Dunsmuirs suggested that employee rights at the workplace were in peril. The Chinese worked for lower wages and competed directly with unskilled white workers, small business people, and farmers. They were also seen as a threat to skilled white workers. There were Chinese tailors, cigar makers, longshoremen, laundry workers, coalmine workers, and shoemakers. The concern about Chinese workers taking on traditionally white jobs was so high that BC newspapers reported when a Chinese carpenter was seen working in Victoria at a private residence and when three Chinese printing shops opened in San Francisco.[74]

Most strikes in the coal industry included a demand from workers calling for the elimination of Chinese labour. Urban tradesman sought to keep construction worksites free from Chinese workers. In late 1889, for example, Victoria stonemasons and bricklayers resolved not to work with any Chinese hod carriers and mortar mixers who had exclusively performed these tasks for a number of years on construction sites, serving notice that this embargo would take effect on 1 April 1890. On the morning of 1 April, without a strike, only white labourers worked on the new buildings in the city, though "one contractor, who had employed a faithful Celestial for six years, felt a pang of sorrow at parting with the old hand."[75]

There were peaks and valleys in the anti-Chinese agitation, depending on labour market conditions. In 1885, with the construction of the Canadian Pacific Railway coming to a conclusion, Chinese construction workers moved to Victoria in increased numbers. A downturn in the economy and a federal inquiry into the Chinese question, the Chapleau Commission, pushed anti-Chinese sentiment to a feverish level over the winter of 1885–1886. The report of the two-man committee, which came out in March 1885, was deemed unsatisfactory because it did not go far enough in eliminating the Chinese population, prompting indignation meetings, and threats of secession from Canada.

In Victoria, anti-Chinese citizens assembled on the night of 21 May 1885, some two thousand strong according to one report and, with torches burning, paraded through the streets of Victoria bearing banners that read: "Boycott the Chinese Employers," "They that are not with us are against us," "No yellow slave shall eat our children's bread," and "Let B.C. be a home for men only."[76] The Knights of Labor vociferously called for halting the influx of Chinese.[77] In June the newly formed Victoria Anti-Chinese Association, an organization in which Knights of Labor leaders such as J.M. Duval, Byron West, and W. Tuckfield were prominent, launched a boycott against all individuals and firms engaging Chinese workers in any capacity.[78] In the next months petitions demanded that the immigration of Chinese be halted, that the immigration of white domestics be encouraged, and that governments make it difficult for Chinese to work in the province, thus forcing them to return to China.

By late 1886, anti-Chinese agitation in Victoria had subsided. In the new, rapidly growing Vancouver, however, it worsened. In November 1886, the Vancouver Knights of Labor circulated a card telling consumers not to purchase goods from stores with an X painted on the sidewalk in front of them, as they employed Chinese labour.[79] Two months later the Vancouver Vigilance Committee posted notices saying that all Chinese found within the city after 16 January "will be forcibly ejected."[80] White citizens were especially alarmed because some 250 Chinese workers were being brought in from Victoria to clear land. On the 2nd of February an Anti-Chinese League was formed; George Pollay was on the organizing committee. Violence against Chinese ensued and in late February a mob of whites initiated a full-blown riot, forcing Chinese workers from their dwellings and burning their camp down.[81]

While street harassment continued, and although there was ongoing pressure from individual unions and the occasional public rally, in fact concentrated, organized anti-Chinese agitation largely waned, until a slipping economy helped generate a flurry of activity in 1892. On 3 February 1892 some one thousand people gathered in the Market Hall, Vancouver, intending to revive the "anti-Chinese agitation of five years ago." The meeting organized a branch of the Canadian Anti-Chinese League, and George Pollay and George Bartley, unionists from Vancouver, as well as C.C. Steuart, president of the New Westminster Trades and Labour Council, played prominent roles.[82] The next evening Steuart organized a branch of the League in New Westminster.[83]

After April 1892, the Victoria Trades and Labour Council aggressively sought anti-Chinese legislation.[84] In September 1892, a Vancouver meeting called for restricted Chinese immigration, an increase in the head tax on Chinese entering British Columbia to $500, and the imposition of an annual head tax of $50 on Chinese living in BC.[85] British Columbia was to be the preserve of the white race. The left's hostility to Chinese settlers, which it shared with almost all of non-Asian British Columbia, brought together white workers, contributing to the growth of the union movement. But it also divided the working class between Asians and non-Asians and furthered pernicious racist doctrines.

First Nations interests were also beyond the scope of the early left. By 1891, due to the rapid rise in the number of white settlers and declining First Nations numbers, the Indigenous population of 27,305 constituted only 28 percent of the provincial population.[86] Increasing numbers of First Nations people engaged in wage labour as miners, farm labourers, cannery workers, longshoremen, loggers, and sawmill labourers, and they were integral in early industrial capitalism.[87] But leftists, who spoke of justice and equality, ignored calls for respect, dignity, and fair land settlements that came from Indigenous peoples. Leftists shared the racist conceits of the nineteenth century with the larger society.

The world-wide economic depression, which set in during late 1892 on the West Coast and dragged on until the last years of the decade, deflated the economy, caused rampant unemployment, and ultimately sapped the vigour of the left. In January 1893, the government launched public works projects near New Westminster and Vancouver to provide work for unemployed labourers.[88] In March 1893, three hundred men attended a rally of unemployed men at Victoria city hall. A resolution demanded relief in the form of public works to provide jobs. The resolution blamed the "unjust system of land laws," which rewarded speculators and drove up real estate values as the major reason for the depression. It also condemned the practice of recruiting workers from easterly sections of Canada into a sated labour market, as well as the weak laws restricting Chinese immigration.[89]

Nanaimo miners suffered from a weak coal market, and in Vancouver, according to an August 1893 report by the Vancouver Trades and Labour Council statistician, stone cutters faced unemployment, many having been forced into the interior to "work for Chinese wages"; half of the union bricklayers were unemployed; and two-thirds of union steamship men and one-third of union carpenters were unemployed.[90] Already in September 1892 the Vancouver Trades and Labour Council reported that over the past year three of its unions had disbanded, and that overall "the membership was slowly but surely becoming less because of removal, and the number of unemployed workmen steadily increasing."[91] In New Westminster, the printers', painters', and bricklayers' unions had gone under by the end of 1893, and by February 1894 the Trades and Labour Council had ceased to exist.[92] The economic downturn also had an impact on political associations. In June 1894, the *Single Tax*, the organ of the Victoria Single Tax Club, ended publication, blaming tough economic times.[93]

But the depression of the 1890s was not the only factor that confronted workers and unions. Printers faced new technology in the form of the Mergenthaler Linotype Typesetting machine, which meant employers were able to use fewer skilled workers and lower rates.[94] Tailors faced the threat from central Canadian manufactories sending their goods into the British Columbia market. Wage cuts and unemployment were the result.[95] Unions, cash starved at the best of times, also became entangled in administrative duties and government red tape, leaving little time for organizing or building alliances. Throughout 1893, proposed provincial legislation to set up an industrial disputes system and a government labour bureau took up much time and energy. Complicated and lengthy, it was hardly the stuff to put a fire in the belly of most workers. Unionists discussed the issues, argued, protested, met government officials, and attended meetings. The Government, for its part, delayed, obfuscated, watered down the legislation, and played union workers off against non-unionized workers.[96] Tully Boyce, a miners' representative from Nanaimo, was blunt in his opinion of a provincial labour conference that brought together worker representatives and the government: "The conference was worse than a failure; it was a screaming farce."[97]

The legal system also worked to undermine unionism. During the 1890–1891 Wellington coal strike, six union miners were charged with intimidating Joseph B. Hugo, a miner who was both against the strike and the union, by following him through the streets of Nanaimo. The six were also charged with "besetting and watching." The charge read that the six, "who wrongfully and without lawful authority, with a view to compel Jos. Hugo, a workman working for Dunsmuir & Sons, colliery owners, in the colliery, did beset and watch the place where the said Jos.

Hugo works, to wit No. 5 shaft of the Wellington collieries. . . ."[98] The case was much-publicized on Vancouver Island, warranting full transcripts of the proceedings in newspapers. The trial dragged on into March of 1891.[99] In Vancouver, George Irvine, vice-president of the Vancouver Trades and Labour Council, was chosen in January 1891 as walking delegate for the building trades. His job was to ensure that all workers at union sites carried a union card. In the summer of 1891, while carrying out his duties, Irvine was charged with "watching and besetting," ostensibly intimidating workers at a construction site to persuade them to join the union. It became a test case to establish just what a labour organizer would be allowed to do on behalf of a union.[100]

In both cases the union men lost. Among union coal miners the Nanaimo six became martyrs, imprisoned for six weeks for the principles of organized labour. Nevertheless, the guilty miners were upbeat about their impending prison terms, and before departing by train to serve their sentences, they weighed themselves on the railway scales to calculate how much weight they would lose during their incarceration. An observer noted: "the men went cheerfully to their sentence, feeling that their imprisonment was not only an honor, but that it was undeniably not called for."[101] Chief Justice Matthew Baillie Begbie, in sentencing the miners, stated that "freedom of action should be allowed in every case."[102] Clearly, the freedom to operate democratic unions made up of all workers at a worksite, when endorsed by the majority, was given a lower priority.

The waning clout of unionism was evident in the fall of 1893 when Victoria union bricklayers demanded that the School Board fire the construction superintendents and hire "practical" bricklayers instead. They also wanted Victoria City Council to dismiss the building inspector, a carpenter by trade, in favour of a bricklayer. The unionists threatened to strike, effective 25 September 1893. This intrusion into the hiring policies of elected bodies was met with ridicule, not fear. "Let them strike," said the chair of the school board. City aldermen were equally unconcerned. One alderman opined that the union was going too far, another that it was preposterous that a union should dictate to the council, and another that strikebreakers should be employed, stating jocularly, "Get the dagos [sic]."[103] The bricklayers did strike, but after a few days, returned to work without having won their point.[104] They had overestimated their influence and power.

As has been seen, the incipient left of the 1880s and early 1890s drew on diverse ideas and was woven through a number of institutions and actions. Union principles, anti-monopoly sentiment, cultural assumptions about Asians, Single Tax economics, the role of government, and broad reflections on the meaning of social and material relations stimulated debate, while unions, political parties, leagues, and associations, using electoral activities, strikes, and even riots, gave them historical resonance. Individual activists often participated in many causes and organizations. Byron West, the Victoria Single Taxer, spoke out against Chinese workers, participated in union affairs, and was committed to shorter working hours.[105] Committed unionists such as George Pollay, George Bartley, and C.C. Steuart debated the Single Tax, free trade, and monopoly, while working to restrict Chinese immigrants in the work force and to shorten the daily hours of work.

Skilled workers in unions and small producers were at the core of the leftist opposition in this era, interconnected by a common commitment to the value of productive labour, by similar standing in the community, and by similar levels of wealth. Indeed, the distinction between a shoemaker who owned a small shop and a journeyman employee was not that great, and there was movement between these classes. Joseph Dixon, a Vancouver carpenter and prominent unionist, for example, started working as a contractor in the 1890s and opened a carpentry-joiner shop in 1902.[106] Labour was seen as the producer of wealth and, as such, workers were key parts of the economy and society. The accepted view was that capitalists and owners had legitimate roles, and happy relations between employers and employees could be secured by honest, fair dealings. Upright men working together in unions and active in politics could control bad employers and speculators, tame unfair governments, and create the good society. But the future development of industrial capitalism brought new circumstances, and with the new circumstances came new responses from the left.

CHAPTER 2

Rising Radicalism and Militancy: 1895–1920

AFTER THE DEPRESSION of the 1890s, the left rebounded in the booming, expanding economy of the new century, but now, because socialists,
influenced by Marxism, became prominent, it had a sharper edge. In the
late nineteenth century, socialist ideas, which had long been present in
Europe and North America, constituted a line of thought that was critical of the individualistic liberalism of developing industrial capitalism,
supporting instead societies run by the people for the good of the people,
rather than just the wealthy, and celebrating cooperation in society and
economic activities. The scope was broad and allowed many perspectives
and actions to be considered socialist. In BC during the first decades of
the twentieth century some socialists were radical, even revolutionary,
while others were more moderate in their ideas and behaviours.

The socialist intellectual world included Marxism, a system of thought
and a critique of capitalist society developed by European thinker and

writer Karl Marx in the middle years of the nineteenth century. Marxism
sought to understand the workings of capitalism and looked to the time
when this system of producing goods and services would be completely
replaced. Marxist socialists referred specifically to the technical ideas, concepts and theories found in Marx's works, though they interpreted his
work in different ways. Whereas the left of previous decades had generally encouraged workers and good employers to work out sensible, mutu-
ally satisfactory arrangements to solve issues, Marxists labelled all capitalists and owners of productive facilities as exploiters. It did not matter
whether the owner was a "morally" good fellow; capitalism to Marxists
was about the capitalist expropriating the "surplus value" that the worker produced. From this insight flowed an understanding of the economy
and society. Political parties, the courts, government, the education system, and other influential parts of society were controlled by the capitalists, or at least served their interests. This led to the belief that the whole
system had to go. Only a classless society, where one class did not exploit
the other, said Marxists, would create the context for the good life. United by their circumstances as employees and organized into political and
union organizations, workers were the agents of change, representing
ordinary people against the capitalist minority.

Marxist-influenced socialism was hardly unproblematic, and a few
preliminary comments on early Marxism in BC are worth noting here.
First, even armed with Marxist analysis, the road to the future was not
easily mapped. Marxists debated whether capitalism would collapse on
its own because of inherent tensions or because the tendency of capitalists
to replace workers with machines to reduce labour costs would eventually lead to the disappearance of consumers and the collapse of the system.
Was it necessary to do anything or did history need a helping hand? If
action by leftists could help usher in the new order, what was to be done?
Some Marxists stressed educating people to vote for a classless society,
while others emphasized unions and strikes to destabilize and undermine
the system. Second, living Marxism in the real world did not exist separate
from society. Ethnic, gender, regional, occupational and religious identities
remained and intertwined with Marxist understandings.[1]

A third problem, and following from the last one, is trying to understand how Marxism played among the foot soldiers of the left, how the

ideas were understood and used in everyday life by those in socialist organizations. Did central European immigrant workers belong to a radical, revolutionary union led by skilled, competent, intelligent Marxist organizers because of a commitment to the program of the union, or was their participation part of a longing for dignity, respect and a decent standard of living? Did voting for a revolutionary socialist party in Nanaimo mean a commitment to the classless post-revolutionary society? Or was the vote merely a wish for hours-of-work laws and the public ownership of a few key industries? It is probably impossible to know this. In fact, there probably was no firm position. Leftist class rhetoric embodied and symbolized many things. At one level it was condensed into notions of hope and optimism for a better future, while at another level it was an intricate explanation of the workings of the material world in history. This leads to a final point: Marxist analysis did not completely displace the leftist ideas of an earlier era, and evil capitalists, fair play, just society, rights, honesty, independence, and equality, among others, were notions that resonated in all leftist arguments.

The twists and turns of early socialist organizations in BC are complex.[2] In late 1898, twenty-two Vancouverites formed the province's first local of the Socialist Labor Party (SLP). The SLP, a North American party, was dominated by Daniel De Leon, an American Marxist theoretician. The party understood the world in terms of an ongoing class struggle, sought the unity of the working class, and envisaged the achievement of a new socialist order. A trade union arm of the SLP, established in Vancouver in 1899, was small and served only as an irritant to the established unions. The SLP, with its rigid interpretation of Marxist principles, also alienated other political radicals in the province. Still, during 1899 the party was expanding and making inroads on Vancouver Island. However, internal disputes in the United States spilled over into Canada, and in 1899 a group of British Columbian members of the SLP, led by Will McClain, left the party and established the United Socialist Labor Party (USLP) in the spring of 1900. USLP leaders such as McClain and Frank Rogers were active in union affairs. In 1900 McClain ran as the first socialist candidate in a provincial election, losing but still polling 684 votes, 4.46 percent of the votes cast in the riding.

In this lively socialist world, Christian socialism was also evident. The

Canadian Socialist League (CSL), a central-Canadian association rooted in a moral socialism based on the teachings of Christ, had a seventeen-point platform that made no mention of class struggle, a cornerstone of Marxist thought. By 1901 the CSL had a presence in Port Moody, Vancouver, and Revelstoke, and members of the CSL and the USLP were meeting together. In the fall of 1901, British Columbia socialists convened and they formed the Socialist Party of British Columbia (SPBC). A leading light in the new organization was Ernest Burns. Burns was born in England and while a young man was influenced by the writings of Henry George. In the mid-1880s he joined the Marxist Socialist Democratic Federation. He emigrated to Victoria, but quickly moved on to Washington State in 1890, where he became involved with the Knights of Labor and the Populist Party. In the late 1890s he returned to British Columbia, and was soon president of the fishermen's union in Vancouver and secretary of the Vancouver branch of the CSL. Burns initiated the creation of a province-wide body to represent socialists. Burns was a gradualist, believing that the inherent weaknesses of capitalism predestined its eventual collapse and that the role of activists was to ameliorate the conditions of the working class and perhaps give tottering capitalism a push.

Beyond Vancouver, the Socialist Party of British Columbia was strong in the Kootenays, where radical politics intertwined with militant unionism.[3] The exploitation of major deposits of silver, copper, lead, and gold began at a small-scale level in the Kootenay region in the 1880s. In 1890 the Le Roi operation at what would become Rossland began, and the famous Sullivan mine at Kimberley opened in 1892. Ore was transported to facilities in the United States around Spokane to be smelted, and smelters were also built in the Kootenays, most notably at Trail. Many workers came from the United States. The Western Federation of Miners (WFM), an American union, organized Kootenay hard-rock miners in the mid-1890s, but there was little notable radicalism. After political and union action met uncompromising responses, Kootenay miners, linked organizationally to the radical WFM locals in the Spokane area, became increasingly susceptible to socialist ideas. In 1899 the American socialist Eugene Debs addressed two mass meetings in Rossland. R. Parm Pettipiece, editor of the *Lardeau Eagle*, was a leading spokesman for the new radicalism.

He was from Ontario and in 1900 organized a branch of the Canadian Socialist League in the Kootenays.

If experience had guided the radicalization of Kootenay constituents, so too had the experience of many Vancouver Island coal miners. The strong anti-union actions of the Dunsmuir family gave credence to a class-based revolutionary understanding of the social and political order. To drive home the point of the close connection between business and the state, James Dunsmuir served as premier of the province from 1900 to 1902. Marxist ideas and institutions were present in Nanaimo in the first years of the twentieth century, and in April 1902 Nanaimo radical social-ists formed the Revolutionary Socialist Party of Canada. The Nanaimo Marxists had initially refused to join the SPBC, decrying its moderation and gradualism. The Revolutionary Socialist Party of Canada was point-edly radical, analyzing the world in terms of class conflict and demanding

Local 119 of the Western Federation of Miners, Lardeau, West Kootenay, 1901.
Vancouver Public Library 100.

collective ownership of the means of production and industrial democracy. The voice of the vanguard of Nanaimo revolutionary thought was E.T. Kingsley, recruited by Nanaimo miners to serve as their propagandist. In an industrial accident in California, Kingsley had lost both of his legs, and during his recuperation in hospital he read the work of Marx. He joined the SLP in Oakland, but split with De Leon over the issue of the primacy of political versus union action.

Kingsley, who remained skeptical of the efficacy of trade unionism to bring about change, was adamant that political action was the only way to bring about a new social order. Meaningful reforms of the capitalist system were impossible; trade union achievements and wage hikes merely served to undermine the revolutionary ardour of the working class. This so-called impossibilist position was evident in the platform of the Revolutionary Socialist Party of Canada. It called for the total destruction of capitalism and stated that "the pathway leading to our emancipation from the chains of wage slavery is uncompromising political warfare against the capitalist class, with no quarter and no surrender."[4] In the fall of 1902, there were again talks of uniting the socialist left, and at a unity convention in November this was achieved under the banner of the Socialist Party of British Columbia. Officially, the impossibilist views of Kingsley prevailed, but in reality most socialists retained close ties to unions and fought for immediate gains in the lives of working people.

In the October 1903 provincial election, the Socialist Party of British Columbia ran ten candidates, winning a remarkable 9 percent of the popular vote. In Vancouver the socialist candidates won over 1,100 votes each. On Vancouver Island two SPBC standard bearers won their ridings. James W. Hawthornthwaite had served as the labour MLA for Nanaimo but joined the Revolutionary Socialist Party in the early autumn of 1902. Born in Ireland and educated in England, the outspoken and politically astute Hawthornthwaite, who married into a prominent coal-mining family, worked as a real-estate agent, journalist, and night watchman before achieving political success. The other elected socialist was Parker Williams, a Welsh-born coal miner from the Ladysmith area. William Davidson, a miner from the Kootenays, was elected on the labour ticket in 1903, but once in the legislature worked closely with the SPBC members.

The small socialist core had influence in the legislature because the ruling Conservatives needed their support to sustain a majority. Indeed, there was a talk of a Socialist–Conservative alliance. Despite the impossibilist platform, the SPBC members also fought for female suffrage, old-age pensions, the weekly payment of wages, the eight-hour workday for all workers, and anti-Asian legislation.[5] The success of the SPBC also had national implications. After negotiations with Manitoba and Ontario socialists, delegates at the December 1904 SPBC convention amended their platform and constitution to give it national relevance. As such, the SPBC disappeared and the Socialist Party of Canada (SPC) was born.

In the 1907 provincial election, the SPC fielded twenty-two candidates, including a full slate of five in Vancouver. But despite the optimism of activists, only Hawthornthwaite, Williams, and John McInnis, the president of the Phoenix Miners' Union, who represented the Kootenay riding of Grand Forks, were elected. The 1909 provincial election was similar. The party ran nineteen candidates and doubled the number of voters that it had attracted in 1907, but returned only two party members, Hawthornthwaite and Williams. The party was stagnating. Indeed the votes for leftist candidates generally, socialist and labour, had peaked in 1903 at 15.9 percent of the popular vote. In 1907 they received 14 percent and in 1909, 11.1 percent.

The lack of success and the dominance of a Conservative majority government, which reduced the influence of the socialists, accentuated developing internal disputes in the BC section of the SPC. In December 1906, Ernest Burns was expelled from the SPC. Sixty other SPC members joined him and they established the Social Democratic Party (SDP) of British Columbia in 1907. More reformist, more committed to healthy relations with the union movement, and wary of being zealously theoretical, the Vancouver group joined with a number of Manitoba locals to form the Social Democratic Party in 1911.

In the 1912 provincial election, socialists again returned two candidates, and again they were both from the coal-mining areas of Vancouver Island. Parker Williams was victorious as an SPC candidate and Jack Place was elected running on the SDP ticket. Left candidates won 11.1 percent of the popular vote. Only four SPCers and one SDPer ran in the 1916 election, polling fewer than two thousand votes. Three candidates (John McInnis, Herbert Skinner, and Parker Williams) running as Independent Socialists, former members of the SPC, garnered a further 1,300 votes. Williams was again elected to represent the Vancouver Island riding of Newcastle. These results compared unfavourably to 1909, when twelve thousand votes were cast for the SPC alone. In 1916 leftists won just over 4 percent of the popular vote.

Political action in socialist parties was not the only leftist option. Some leftists tried to create perfect societies outside the dominant social and economic order. Already in the 1890s in the Fraser Valley a utopian experiment was launched. Short-lived and understudied, the community of Ruskin was based on the ideas of British social thinker, John Ruskin. More prominent and better known was the community established by Finns on Malcolm Island. It was called Sointula and was located off Vancouver Island near the Vancouver Island settlements of Alert Bay and Port McNeill. The project began with a group of disgruntled, activist Finnish coal miners working in Nanaimo. They recruited a well-known Finnish radical, Matti Kurikka, to spearhead their adventure. At the time, Kurikka was in Australia, but he took up the call, arriving in Nanaimo in the fall of 1900. The group set up the Kalevan Kansa Colonization Company and secured property on Malcolm Island. By the summer of 1902 the colony numbered 127 adults. The colonists' main source of income was taking out logs for the Industrial Power Company. Kurikka, who advocated "a society formed on the power of love, justice and humanity," was also a champion of women's rights, promoting freedom in the area of sexual relations.[6]

On the night of 30 January 1903 a fire ravaged the community, leaving many destitute and prompting some to move away. Interpersonal tension caused by controversial sexual liaisons created division in the community. Then a poor business decision to take on a contract at much too low a price to build a bridge near Vancouver proved financially disastrous. Kurikka left the colony in October 1904, taking about half of the colonists with him. For a brief time, the remaining group tried to sustain the settlement as a commune, but failed. On 27 May 1905, the assets of the commune were divided up and distributed to individuals. Leftist ideals remained but the communal years were over. In the late 1960s and early 1970s, young people who were part of the back-to-the-land movement revived the communal vision.[7]

Many unionists and reformers, it should be said, were indifferent to utopian projects and hostile to revolutionary Marxism. Heirs to the leftist tradition of the 1880s and 1890s, they lived at the progressive edge of the Liberal Party after the establishment of traditional party lines in BC politics in 1903. These activists drew on trends in British politics, especially the liberalism of William Gladstone, who served as prime minister four separate times between 1868 and 1894. Current views on nineteenth-century liberalism are often distorted, having been reduced to a simplistic notion of no government and free reign in the marketplace for business. But Gladstone's liberalism embodied a much broader social vision, one that celebrated the independence and self-reliance of workers, and contained a deep concern about government power. This aversion to government did not reflect commitment to abstract economic *laissez-faire* but rather reflected fear of the consequences of close links between economic elites and government. Sobriety, frugality, duty, and worker respectability in the social order were also part of the liberal package. Farmers, small employers, independent artisans, tradesmen, and organized workers were at its core, while the privileged aristocrats and monopolists were excluded. The appeal of popular or radical liberalism to trade union leaders and to the working class generally in Britain was immense.[8] In politics they sat in the British House of Commons as Labour members, but they were strong Gladstonian Liberals.[9] They were Lib-Labs, and tended to be union officials who adhered to notions of localism, extended political democratic rights, cooperation, and self-help.

This sensibility was evident in BC, and many political activists straddled the liberal-left border. Three men were particularly prominent in representing workers and their concerns within liberalism. George Maxwell, the son of a Scottish miner, became an ordained minister of the

Church of Scotland in 1880. He moved to Canada in 1885 and assumed responsibilities at the First Presbyterian Church in Vancouver in late 1890. In 1896 Vancouver Liberals put forward Maxwell as a candidate to challenge the Conservatives in the Burrard riding, which he narrowly won. The issues that he took up were leftist: union rights, fair wages, public ownership of utilities, and further restrictions on Asian immigration.[10]

Christopher Foley was also active in the liberal-left borderland. He was born in Toronto in 1848, spent a number of years as a miner in the United States, and settled in Vancouver in 1886, working as a contractor and accumulating real-estate holdings. He was wiped out financially by the depression of the 1890s and moved to Rossland, in the Kootenays, in 1895, working again as a miner. He was quickly active in the union, the Western Federation of Miners. He was chosen by Nelson unionists to run as an Independent Labour candidate in the 1900 federal election, but during the election Foley called himself a Liberal, and was seen in fact as a Liberal. In the end, the vote was split and the Tory candidate was victorious.

Two years after the federal election, in 1902, Foley participated in the formation of a new political party. After a meeting of delegates from Canadian WFM locals in Kamloops, the Provincial Progressive Party was formed. Foley was elected president. Despite its independence from the Liberal Party, it was moderate and reform-oriented, representing the perspective of the liberal-labour alliance. The party only lasted a few months. Foley returned to Vancouver, and during the summer of 1902 was defending the independent labour approach in the face of the rising socialist trend. After losing in a bid to replace George Maxwell as a federal MP in a February 1903 by-election, Foley saw his public profile decline.[11]

Ralph Smith was the most prominent British Columbian in the Lib-Lab world, active in unionism and politics. Smith worked in a Nanaimo coal mine, served as a Methodist minister and was elected general secretary of the local miners' union, the Miners' and Mine Labourers' Protective Association, before winning a seat in the provincial legislature in 1898. He remained active in the union world and was vice-president of the Trades and Labour Congress of Canada (TLC) in 1896 and president from 1898 to 1902. His national activities solidified his ties with the Laurier Liberal Party and his position as a Lib-Lab. He continued to be politically active and worked hard to tighten ties between unions and the Liberal Party in order to fend off the socialists. Defeated in the 1911 federal election, he returned to provincial politics, serving as president of the Vancouver Liberal Association and vice-president of the provincial Liberal association.[12]

After 1912, the provincial Liberal Party successfully mobilized as a party of reform. Richard McBride, who had become the Conservative premier of the province in 1903, retired in 1915. By the last years of his tenure, scandals, allegations of corruption, and the economic downturn tarnished the Conservative standard, and his replacement, William Bowser, was unable to refurbish the party before the November 1916 election. The Liberals took advantage of the Conservative misfortune, calling on all progressive British Columbians to vote Liberal in order to throw out the Tory scoundrels. They effectively catered to reform elements and many people who had previously voted for leftist parties. The Liberals secured a majority government with thirty-six members elected on 50 percent of the popular vote. The Conservatives were reduced to nine members and took 40.52 percent of the popular vote. Thus began a Liberal era in provincial politics that lasted until 1952.[13]

In this era, perhaps even more important to the left than political action was the union struggle for economic and social justice. These were years of rapid population growth and, up to 1913, economic prosperity. Mine owners, lumbermen, building contractors, and cannery operators made money; workers pressed for a greater share of the wealth, as well as better working conditions and recognition of their important place in the social order. In order to achieve these goals, they established democratic unions and fought for recognition. Union recognition was critical. At this time, before the government legally obliged companies to negotiate with elected representatives of their workers who had associated in a union, employers could just refuse to recognize unions and their representatives. Strikes were then necessary to force union recognition.

Miners were notably militant. Kootenay hard-rock miners, organized in the Western Federation of Miners, fought employers on a number of issues after the first local was established in 1895, including working conditions, safety, wages, Asian workers, the contract system, and union recognition. The issues were not satisfactorily resolved in the short run, prompting a spurt of organization in 1898 and 1899, when thirteen new WFM locals were established in the Kootenays. More were added in the next few years. Strikes were called from September 1899 into February 1900 at area mines, but the hard-line employers prevailed, forcing workers to accept their compromise wage offer. In July 1901, Rossland miners struck, and while smaller operations settled, the major firms held out against their workers, prompting a visit from a federal government mediator, William Lyon Mackenzie King, in November 1901. But there was no settlement and the strike petered out over the next months. Workers had little to show for their efforts. Despite the loss, the WFM expanded in the Kootenays, taking in Crow's Nest Pass coal miners in 1902, and in 1903, immediately leading them out on strike.[14]

On Vancouver Island, too, miners led the charge for rights and dignity as well as improved material conditions. In 1911 Vancouver Island Collieries employed 4,600 men and produced a record amount of coal for Canadian and American markets. Issues had long been festering, especially in the mines owned by the Dunsmuir family, and problems continued after the Dunsmuirs exited the industry in 1910. Wages, the use of Chinese workers, union recognition, and safety conditions in the mines were constant concerns for workers and their families. Vancouver Island mines were very unsafe, among the most dangerous in the industrialized world, and when disaster hit, it left a deep scar. On 5 October 1909, for example, in an explosion at Extensions' No. 2 mine, near Ladysmith, "thirty-two men lost their lives, thirteen women were widowed, and thirty-eight children, only two of whom were of an age to provide for themselves, lost their fathers."[15]

Workers struggled to maintain a union. In 1902, the Miners' and Mine Labourers' Protective Association voted to join the WFM. A 1903 strike was unsuccessful, and the WFM disappeared from Island coalfields. Over the next years, this body was replaced by the major American union for coal miners, the United Mine Workers of America (UMWA), which formed UMWA District 28 in December 1911. Employers were implacably hostile to the UMWA.

Then, in September 1912, Oscar Mottishaw, a miner and UMWA activist, was dismissed from his job in the Union mines at Cumberland. In previous work at Extension, Mottishaw had been extremely critical of company safety procedures regarding the presence of gas in the mines. Workers felt that Mottishaw was being discriminated against, setting off a chain of events that led to the "Great Strike." Under the terms of the federal Industrial Disputes Regulation Act of 1907 the strike was illegal. The main issue became union recognition. On 12 August 1913, some four hundred frustrated Ladysmith, Extension and Nanaimo miners, who were enduring company spies in their midst and the presence of a provincial special police force that had arrived a year earlier, engaged in a public protest. Of special concern was the introduction of strikebreakers into the mines, all with the protection of the special constables. There was confrontation and violence, though no deaths. Within days more troops were dispatched to the area. By the end of August, 128 men had been arrested. The strike continued, but on 19 August 1914, just weeks after the outbreak of World War I, the miners capitulated.

Railway workers were also willing to fight. The United Brotherhood of Railway Employees (UBRE), an American union, entered British Columbia, forming locals in Vancouver, Revelstoke and Nelson in the first years of the twentieth century. The UBRE sought to bring all railway workers into one union. The union began with CPR clerks but soon included trainmen, freight handlers, machinists, trainmen, and maintenance-of-way men. In February 1903, the Vancouver local struck the CPR, demanding union recognition. They received support from Nelson and Revelstoke workers, as well as the Western Federation of Miners in the Kootenays, who refused to supply the railway with coal. Vancouver longshoremen and teamsters struck in sympathy with the railway employees. In Vancouver, the CPR took a hard stand, bringing in strikebreakers, and breaking the union as well as the strike within four months. During the strike, Frank Rogers, a socialist and labour leader, while visiting a gathering of strikers at the CPR yards in Vancouver, was killed after the crowd was fired upon. While many believed that a strikebreaker or special constable was responsible, a logical supposition, the inquest reached no firm conclusion.[16]

The leftist struggle to establish unionism went beyond railway workers

Laying sidewalks on Georgia Street, Vancouver, 1910.
Photographer: Philip Timms. Vancouver Public Library 7728.

and resource industries. Vancouver boasted some seventy-seven union locals in 1911, representing over seven thousand workers, about 22 percent of the city's wage earners. Semi-skilled and unskilled workers such as shingle weavers, mill workers, laundry workers, and general labourers were union members as were some women, who joined either mixed unions with men, such as the tailors, or single-sex unions for waitresses, home and domestic employees, and garment workers. In the pre-war decade, painters, telephone operators, carpenters, machinists, longshoremen, and sheet-metal workers engaged in significant strikes.

Reflecting the provincial pattern, James Conley notes two periods of exceptional strike activity, 1900 to 1903 and 1910 to 1913. Both time frames were periods of a booming local economy and a tight labour market. The city's largest labour conflict of the era involved four thousand building trades workers. Carpenters went on strike demanding a fifty-cent per day wage increase, and when the Master Builders' Association declared an open shop, the strike became a battle for the union shop. Building labourers and electricians also went out and then, after five weeks, there was a general shutdown that was respected by even non-unionists. In the end, aided by an influx of construction workers, the employers won out, although some of the stronger unions were able to keep their closed-shop agreements. The carpenters settled for $4.75 per day, the same rate that they had achieved in 1907.[17]

Strikes were also part of industrial life in New Westminster. Telephone workers, carpenters, iron moulders, bakery workers, and deck hands engaged in job action. Asian workers, too, struck. In 1903 Japanese mill workers struck to protest the discharge of a foreman, and in 1907 Sikh mill workers struck over wages.[18] The province-wide nature of labour activism led to the founding of the BC Federation of Labour in 1910, an institution that eclipsed the Vancouver Trades and Labour Council (VTLC) as the largest representative labour body in the province. The labour uprising of the first decade of the century was tamed by the depression that began in 1913.[19] Workers feared for their jobs and endured wage cuts and unemployment. It was not a propitious time for union organizers.

With Canada's entry into the Great War in 1914 the economy began to improve. Moreover, with men going overseas, the need for workers rose. In 1911, according to Department of Labour statistics, 22,600 workers belonged to unions in British Columbia, representing some 12.4 percent of the non-agricultural labour force. By 1915 this had dropped to 10,750 workers, 5.9 percent of the workforce. But in 1916 the trend reversed. There were 11,600 unionized workers in 1916 (6.3 percent of the labour force), 21,220 in 1917 (11.6 percent), 27,216 in 1918 (14.8 percent), and 40,000 in 1919 (21.8 percent). Workers were also emboldened in the new circumstances to go on strike. Issues abounded. Wartime inflation raised the cost of living, and workers sought wage increases just to sustain their standard of living. Hours of work, rate standardization, camp conditions, wages, and union recognition remained key issues. In 1915 there were only five recorded strikes or lockouts in British Columbia. In the following year there were ten, then twenty-seven in 1917, and twenty-six in 1918. In 1919 there were forty-one. The number of people involved in industrial disputes tells the same story: 1915 (896), 1916 (9,835), 1917

Ginger Goodwin, 1916. Cumberland Museum and
Archives C110-002.

(14,026), 1918 (16,164), and 1919 (12,706).[20] The labour revolt after 1916 was widespread. In the Kootenays, District 18 of the United Mine Workers of America nearly doubled its membership in the Crow's Nest Pass district between 1914 and 1919, rising from 3,500 to over 6,700. These miners engaged in strikes in 1917 and 1918, as did smelter workers in Trail and gold miners in Rossland.[21] In Vancouver, shipyard workers, waitresses, laundry workers, and shingle weavers engaged in job action.

On 2 August 1918, Vancouver workers, with the overwhelming support of the Vancouver Trades and Labour Council, engaged in a one-day general strike to protest the shooting of labour activist Albert (Ginger) Goodwin. Goodwin, a socialist who was active with the smelter workers in Trail, was called up for active military service, under the terms of the new federal conscription law. Prime Minister Robert Borden introduced conscription in the spring of 1917. This controversial legislation forced young men to serve in the army. It met resistance from militant unionists in the Vancouver and Victoria labour councils. Goodwin, who suffered from tuberculosis, went into hiding near Comox on Vancouver Island. Late in July, Goodwin was found in the woods by a number of Dominion police officers. In the encounter that followed, Goodwin was shot. Labour leaders believed that he had been killed for his union activities and his opposition to conscription.

Goodwin quickly became a martyr for the trade union movement. At his funeral in the small community of Cumberland, the townspeople organized a mile-long parade led by the city band. In Vancouver the call for a general strike was heard enthusiastically. Longshoremen, street railway workers, building trades workers, and metal workers gave full support. Only a few groups of workers — telephone workers, printers and teamsters — remained on the job. Some returned soldiers took issue with the protest. A contingent of approximately three hundred soldiers advanced on the Vancouver Labour Temple in the mid-afternoon, gained entrance, and ransacked the building. The secretary of the VTLC, Vic Midgely, was captured, beaten, threatened with being thrown out of a second-storey window, and forced to kiss the Union Jack.[22] These soldiers saw Britishness and radical unionism as incompatible.

The rising militancy of British Columbia workers was not just a

Ginger Goodwin funeral procession, Cumberland, 2 August 1918.
Cumberland Museum and Archives C110-001.

product of the peculiar circumstances of the war. While the hothouse
atmosphere of war heightened tension, accelerated capitalist industrial
development, and put issues such as conscription and imperialism front
and centre, workers sought the same goals that they had in the first decade
of the century: wage security, respect, and some control over their work
life. The post-1916 militancy was a continuation of the class struggle that
had roots in the nineteenth century.

Nor was the rising militancy unique to British Columbia. The British
Columbia experience echoed patterns across the western world. There
were worker uprisings across Canada, in the United States, and in Europe.
The Russian Revolution of 1917 represented the most radical rupture,
and to many activists in North America it appeared to be the harbinger
of a new age. While Canadians knew little of the details of the complicated creation of the Union of Soviet Socialist Republics, it appeared that
workers were coming into their own, that a just and humane society that
treated workers and their families fairly was indeed possible. If the nine-

teenth century had been the era of the middle class and the bourgeoisie, the twentieth century, in this progressive vision, would belong to the working class. The struggle for unionism, a decent standard of living, and basic worker rights was infused with the ideal of a better future, a sensibility that could be refracted through socialist or reform lenses to contribute to solidarity.

The national dimension of the worker revolt was exposed most fully in 1919. From coast to coast Canadian workers engaged in job action. Best remembered is the six-week Winnipeg General Strike of 1919. At 11:00 a.m. on 15 May some thirty-five thousand workers refused to work, shutting down the city of Winnipeg. The Strike Committee decided what was and what was not an essential service, allowing, for example, bread and milk delivery. The strike was remarkable for bringing together workers from different trades, skilled and unskilled, union and non-union, immigrant and native born, and men and women. At the heart of the struggle was the demand for union recognition and the right to bargain collectively with employers. The core goal spawned sympathy strikes across Canada in the spring of 1919. By 31 May 1919, there were seventy-five thousand workers on strike from Rossland to Amherst, Nova Scotia.[23] In Prince Rupert, New Westminster, the railway community of McBride, and Victoria, workers responded, but the fullest response came in Vancouver.[24]

As in other strikes associated with the Winnipeg General Strike, workers in Vancouver mixed local concerns with their statement of solidarity with Winnipeg strikers. After Winnipeg postal workers had been dismissed for striking, the Vancouver Trades and Labour Council endorsed a sympathy strike. On 30 May the council set out its demands, which included the resolution of immediate points of contention as well as broader issues. Calling for the immediate reinstatement of Winnipeg postal workers and settlement of their grievances, the list included demands for the six-hour work day, pensions for soldiers and their dependents, and a $2,000 gratuity for all who had served overseas. The council also called for nationalization of cold storage plants, abattoirs, and grain elevators, and crucially, "the right of collective bargaining through any organization that workers deem most suited to their needs."[25] When the strike in Vancouver commenced on 3 June, metal trade, shipyard, street railway, and dock workers were at the forefront. The strike ended in early July, one week after the end of the Winnipeg General Strike, and by this time some forty-five Vancouver unions had engaged in job action. Still, the Vancouver strike was not as complete as the Winnipeg strike, and the vote to go out had been very close, 3,305 to 2,499. The victorious side represented 57 percent of voters but only 40 percent of the Vancouver Trades and Labour Council members.[26]

By the end of 1919, job action had declined across Canada and in most industries in British Columbia, but there was one exception. This was the logging industry. In the decade after 1900 the lumber industry surpassed mining as the most significant industry in the province. The logging-off of forestlands in the American Midwest created new interest in the timber of the Pacific Northwest and British Columbia. Moreover, for British Columbia lumbermen, the rapid settlement and economic development of the Prairie West during the Laurier years created a protected market and this, coupled with the local building boom, led to buoyant times. Some of the manufacturing facilities were large. In the New Westminster and Fraser Valley area in 1910, for example, the Fraser River Lumber Company employed 550 workers, Royal City Planing Mills employed 280 workers, and Brunette Sawmills employed 242.[27] Large woods operations supplied logs to the mills.

Nevertheless, despite the danger of the jobs and the factory-like settings in the woods and the mills, unionism had not taken hold. In the mills, race and skill intersected, dividing the work force. A survey of major sawmills in Vancouver in 1908 identified 2,443 workers, comprising 1,067 whites, 802 Japanese, 399 Chinese, and 175 East Indians. White workers held the most secure, most skilled, highest paying jobs, while workers of Asian descent laboured in lesser jobs. Despite organizational drives, results had been minimal. In the logging camps, race was not an issue — loggers were largely white. But the dispersion of the workforce in isolated camps made unionization difficult.[28]

Beginning in early 1919, a new organization, which became known as the Lumber Workers Industrial Union (LWIU), achieved remarkable success, bringing some 70 percent of provincial loggers into the union by 1920. Remarkably, the LWIU had a provincial presence, and included Kootenay and Northern Interior, as well as coastal, loggers in its ranks. The loggers were militant. There were no recorded strikes in either 1917 or 1918, but there were thirty-one strikes in 1919 and fifty in 1920. Improved conditions in the remote camps, where sanitary and health conditions were abysmal, as well as recognition of union camp committees, were behind the job actions. Workers wanted to be treated like humans, not beasts. The LWIU had fifteen thousand members by late 1919.[29]

Across Canada, however, the labour uprising from 1916 to 1920 was defeated. In Winnipeg most strikers achieved nothing. The coalition of governments and employers crushed the attempt to achieve basic collective bargaining rights and union recognition. The federal government used immigration law, arrests, and the presence of troops to cow workers. In Vancouver the city council threatened to dismiss striking workers who did not return to work, and changed the law to allow private vehicles to carry passengers, thus undermining the resolve of striking street railway workers. Employers were adamant, refusing to recognize unions and give any meaningful role to employees in their companies. A few firms embraced corporate welfare programs to keep independent unions at bay. At Imperial Oil's Ioco refinery near Vancouver, the company set up employer-dominated employee-manager councils to address shop floor grievances: it put in place an array of welfare programs, such as a pension system and sports teams, to buy loyalty and increase control over workers' lives; and it implemented a plan to allow employees to purchase company shares. These were part of a national campaign by Imperial Oil that began in January 1919. Ioco was not unionized until 1946.[30]

Other employers used the stick rather than the carrot to keep out elected unions. In the coastal logging industry, camp conditions improved as a result of the 1919–1920 upheaval, but the companies also launched a well-orchestrated open-shop campaign. Coastal logging operators banded together to create a hiring hall in Vancouver. This hiring hall dispatched workers to coastal camps, but only if it was clear that those workers would toe the line and remain aloof from any union activities. This effective blacklist strangled unionism in the coastal woods for the next decade and a half. The labour defeat of the post-war years was so pronounced that the BC Federation of Labour disbanded in 1920, not to be revived until 1944. The depression, which began in 1920 and lasted much of the first half of the 1920s, further ensured the demise of a vibrant union movement. Layoffs, wage cuts, and job security were not conducive to unionism, especially in the aftermath of a major defeat. The loggers union had all but disappeared by 1922.

Left politics and workplace action were tightly intertwined in the upsurge of the late 1910s, as the history of the One Big Union (OBU) shows. When the national TLC refused to challenge conscription, western Canadian militants felt frustrated. Moreover, these unionists were more committed to organizing all workers in one industry rather than individual trades into separate unions, the position of the brass in the central-Canadian-dominated TLC. In March 1919, the BC Federation of Labour held its conference in Calgary so that delegates could participate in the Western Labour Conference of the Trades and Labour Congress, a body representing disgruntled workers from the four western provinces. The result was the call to form a new organization to represent the more radical, militant stance of the western labour body.

Over the next months, workers in western Canada voted on whether or not to join the fledgling One Big Union. The OBU, as it tried to sort out an identity in a chaotic climate, reflected a mélange of socialist and industrial union ideas rooted in a Marxist vision of class conflict and revolutionary change. In British Columbia the new organization received significant support from workers in shipbuilding, mining and smelting, and the lumber industry. BC support was hardly absolute, but according to Allen Seager and David Roth, "the OBU was theoretically capable of mobilizing a majority of British Columbia unionists."[31] The OBU, however, was unable to withstand internal and external pressure. It disintegrated rapidly in the early 1920s.

The BC Federation of Labour was active in the provincial political arena, reviving the political left after the war. With support for socialist parties waning, as was evident in the 1916 election, the Federation dissolved its ties to the Socialist Party of Canada, creating a new party, the Federated Labor Party (FLP) in 1918. The FLP was socialist, but hoped to broaden its appeal. Most SPCers, including E.T. Kingsley, joined the new FLP, and even those who remained loyal to the purity of the SPC agreed not to contest single-member ridings where there was an FLP candidate running. In the 1920 provincial election the Federated Labor Party ran fourteen candidates, five of whom ran in the six-member riding of Vancouver. The party won just over 9 percent of the popular vote province-wide. The coal-mining regions remained most committed to leftist politics. Two of the three elected FLP candidates, Tom Uphill in Fernie and Sam Guthrie on Vancouver Island, came from these regions. The other elected FLPer was a typographer, Harry Neelands, in the South Vancouver riding.[32] Overall, leftist candidates won roughly 16 percent of the popular vote. The victorious Liberals won twenty-five seats and 38 percent of the provincial vote.

One notable leftist organization of the early twentieth century did not fit comfortably with other groups and raises issues that continue to animate discussions on the left. The Industrial Workers of the World (IWW) was formed in Chicago in 1905 by delegates from across North America, including the Kootenays. The IWW quickly organized workers, often workers who had been ignored by established unions: agricultural labourers in the prairies and Midwest, loggers in the Pacific Northwest, and workers on railway construction grades. By 1907 there were five locals in the Kootenay region and at least three in Vancouver. The Wobblies, as IWW members were called, are best known in BC for organizing construction workers on the Canadian Northern and Grand Trunk Pacific lines. In late March and early April 1912, some four thousand workers between Hope and Kamloops went on strike to protest wages and poor sanitary conditions in the camps. In July, workers on the Grand Trunk Pacific line also went out. Despite the early solidarity of workers, the companies had more lasting power. Work resumed on the Canadian Northern line by July and on the Grand Trunk Pacific line by September. There were also strikes in 1913 but they lacked the punch of the 1912 offensive.[33] Wobblies organized unemployed workers in the pre-World War I depression and were active in the loggers' organization of 1919 and 1920. In the 1920s they retreated to lumber locals in the Kootenays, and by the end of the decade were a marginal group in the province.

The IWW was Marxist inspired, but, unlike other left organizations such as the SPC and SDP, which focused on political action, developing political parties and running election campaigns, as well as supporting established trade unionism, the IWW took a different tack. Political action was seen as pointless. Elections were a sham controlled by moneyed interests and manipulated by the wire pullers. The road to socialism was not through electoral politics or waiting for the inevitable collapse of the capitalist system, but rather through organizing all workers into One Big Union. With the perfection of total unionization, the theory (known as syndicalism) indicated that workers could force capitalists to capitulate and usher in the classless socialist society. The focus on job action reflected the experience of many of its supporters, poor immigrant and transient workers with no permanent home address and thus no voting rights.

The IWW was at odds with the province's Marxist socialist politicians. The reminiscences of one Wobbly, who had participated in the Vancouver Island Coal strike of 1912–1914, reek of contempt for the behaviour of some socialists who "stood apart, draped in their 'pure socialist' mantle. They would not become contaminated by participation in purely economic struggles!"[34] IWW unionism was industrial unionism. All workers in a particular industry would belong to the same organization, a section of the One Big Union. Wobblies were different in another sense, as well. Trade unions had long struggled to achieve union recognition in order to negotiate binding contracts with their employers. The Wobblies, on the other hand, distrusted time-bound contracts because it suspended the ability of workers to use their only weapon, the strike, to solve issues.[35]

The IWW was anti-bureaucracy. In the IWW critique, the socialist political parties were run by an elite that was too aloof from everyday workers. The IWW also scorned the organizational structure of other unions, seeing them as similar to public corporations, in that a few members managed these unions in the same way that corporate executives managed the business of a public company." Union members paid dues. Officials were elected to represent the interests of the workers and to manage the day-to-day affairs of the membership. Officials were paid to work in union offices and not on the shop floor. Periodically, disgruntled members had the opportunity in an election to throw out a disagreeable union executive.

Over time, as Mark Leier has shown in a careful study of the Vancouver union leadership before World War I, a small group came to control the expertise involved in managing a union and thus the overall affairs of individual unions, as well as the Vancouver Trades and Labour Council. This group also hired others to work directly for the union as organizers and business agents. In essence, this cadre became a group of labour professionals. This labour bureaucracy emerged in both radical socialist and reformist labour organizations.[36] Traditional unionists, labourists, and socialist political activists were all committed to perfecting organizational structures that had elected presidents, vice-presidents and secretaries. The executive controlled members' dues, hired organizers and specialists, and decided whether or not to release strike funds.

The IWW, on the other hand, supported direct democracy, whereby the workers on the job would control all aspects of union life. The Wobblies eschewed representative democracy, seeing it as leading to hierarchy, bureaucracy, oligarchy, centralization, and rule by the few. The IWW was decentralized. All members were equal. All members served as organizers. Any group of members could decide to go on strike. There could then be no professional elite to at a distance from the membership.

The question of organization was and remains important. The argument in favour of a well-disciplined, hierarchical union is that it is stronger and more permanent and thus able to take on companies in a more effective manner. The loss in democracy is compensated for by the ability to wield more power on behalf of workers. The gains are measured in higher wages and better contracts. On the other hand, if the goal of the left is to build better organizations and allow for a fuller life experience, men and women must learn to control and manage their own affairs, to become full participants in their own lives. The IWW's vision has much to offer here. In British Columbia the touch of the IWW was slight in terms of membership numbers and influence in the broader union movement, but it offered an alternative, radical left-wing perspective. This perspective did not disappear. Similar sentiments informed the new social movements of the 1960s and 1970s, including the women's movement, the student movement, and the environmental movement, as well as the more recent anti-globalization and Occupy movements.

The race question continued to animate the left in the new century, and anti-Asian sentiment continued unabated. The white activists of British descent almost all sought to halt immigration from India, Japan and China, and to restrict the opportunities for Asians already in British Columbia. Pressure from British Columbia labour leaders and left politicians contributed to the passage of federal laws that increased the head tax on Chinese immigrants in 1903 and 1905; to the negotiation of a Gentlemen's Agreement with Japan in 1907 whereby Japan "voluntarily" curtailed emigration to Canada to four hundred labourers and servants per year; and to the institution of the "continuous journey" regulation in 1908 which made it mandatory for all immigrants to come on one ticket from their country of origin to Canada at a time when there was no shipping company that directly linked Canada and India. Unionists participated in organizations that harassed and harangued Asians in British Columbia, and figured prominently in the Vancouver anti-Asian riots of 1907, when gangs of whites wreaked havoc, destroying parts of the Chinese and Japanese areas in the city. They were also part of the mobs that crowded the shores of Burrard Inlet in 1914 and cheered when a Canadian gunboat escorted the *Komagata Maru* out of Vancouver, forcing the Indian passengers on board to return to Calcutta. After the war, anti-Asian sentiment increased again, culminating in the Asian Exclusion Act of 1923, an Act that essentially curtailed Chinese immigration for the next twenty-four years.

Prejudice was also rampant against the thousands of immigrant workers from central and southern Europe who had entered British Columbia in the years after the turn of the century. Labour leaders constantly sought to restrict the numbers of immigrants coming to Canada, but to no avail. Unskilled and unable to speak English, these immigrants often lived on the edge of society, stuck in work camps in the bush or along isolated railway lines, segregated by language from the dominant society, and perceived as too often engaging in suspect male pastimes of drinking, gambling, and visiting houses of ill repute. There were exceptions. Marxist class discourse challenged traditional racial and ethnic exclusions. The IWW set out to organize all workers, arguing that class was a more important identity than one's ethnic or racial group. As one Prince Rupert Wobbly declared: "when the factory whistle blows it does not call us to work as Irishmen, Germans, Americans, Russians, Greeks, Poles, Negroes or Mexicans. It calls us to work as wage workers, regardless of the country in which we were born or the color of our skins."[37]

Gillian Creese has shown that at times of heightened white labour radicalism and active Asian labour militancy, when the language of class had greater currency, pockets of solidarity between white and Asian workers, albeit temporary, were evident. In 1918 and 1919, for example, Chinese workers in the lumber industry went on strike, participated in some white unions, and organized their own unions. In March 1919, some twelve hundred Asian shingle workers, mostly Chinese, struck some fifty shingle mills in the Lower Mainland to protest a wage reduction. At the same time a Vancouver labour newspaper noted that "it is time that all workers in Canada realized that the 'Chink' is as much part of this country as the Scotchman [sic]; that the 'Bohunk' is as necessary as the Englishman; that all of us are exploited by a master-class who cares not what nationality we are so long as we remain willing slaves."[38]

The first decades of the twentieth century were the era of the great temperance and women's movements, but while the left participated, the causes, driven by middle-class initiative, transcended the left-right divide. Union leaders often supported temperance or prohibition, believing that the consumption of alcohol sapped the vigour of workers, wasted their time, and undercut their commitment to union and political action. But many employers also supported prohibition. They especially wanted to keep alcohol out of logging and mining camps, as well as other work sites, because its consumption undermined productivity. Workers, for their part, often saw drinking alcohol in terms of camaraderie, pleasure, and escape from the memories of unpleasant, dangerous work environments. The achievement of prohibition both federally and provincially during World War I was the result of a massive mobilization of people by temperance and prohibition groups, but it intersected awkwardly with the left.[39] It did little to ameliorate the social and economic distance between the haves and have-nots.

The other great crusade was the women's movement, and it too had supporters and detractors across the political spectrum. In the 1880s already, eleven bills had been presented in the BC legislature calling for political rights for women, but they were easily defeated. An 1899 bill put forward by the Lib-Lab Ralph Smith came closer, but it too was defeated on second reading. In the early twentieth century the socialists James Hawthornthwaite and Parker Williams supported female suffrage in the legislature, and in 1912 the BC Federation of Labour endorsed the vote for women. In 1916, a Nanaimo socialist, Jack Place, played a prominent role in the legislature during the politicking between the Conservative and Liberals over female suffrage.[40] After a referendum on the issue in 1916, British Columbia women were eligible to vote provincially. In January 1918, running as an Independent in a by-election to contest the seat made vacant by her husband Ralph's death, Mary Ellen Smith became BC's first woman member of the legislature. In 1918 white women were able to vote in federal elections, and in 1919 they were eligible to stand as candidates. Whereas the left suffered a setback in the post-war years, the movement led by middle-class women achieved gains.

Women on the left, of course, participated in the suffrage movement, and despite difficulties, they also participated in unions and acted as organizers. In the first decade of the century, domestics organized unions. Laundrywomen also organized and struck in 1918. In 1919 female telephone operators in Vancouver stayed away from work for two weeks after the general strike had been called off. Men, though, were usually the union organizers and leaders.[41] There were exceptions, but they enrich the main story rather than change it. Helena Gutteridge, for example,

was born in England in 1879, and arrived in Vancouver in 1911. A journeyman tailor, she was the only woman on the Vancouver Trades and
Labour Council. In 1918 and 1919 she was a moderate leftist, at odds with
the push for socialist solutions and general strikes.[42] She was also active
in the struggle for the vote for women, founding the BC Women's Suffrage League in 1913. Gutteridge worked with Conservative and Liberal
women to win women their political rights. Full equality, though, was a
project for the future, and women's equality would remain a conundrum
for the left, as it would for the broader society.

The new radicalism and militancy of the left in the first decades of the
twentieth century created turbulent times. The left carved out a niche in
the political arena, and unions challenged owners to give working people
greater input and control over their lives. Workers wanted more democracy at work, recognition of their elected unions representatives, and a
decent, secure standard of living. The struggle by ordinary people to participate more fully in the economic and political life of the province
would continue in the next decades, despite the defeat of 1919–1920. More
effective political vehicles would complement the union struggle, and
greater attention would focus on using government and the state to
achieve leftist goals.

CHAPTER 3

Communists and the Co-operative Commonwealth Federation in the Interwar Years

IN THE 1920S AND 1930S LEFT activists established two new political parties in British Columbia. The Communist Party of Canada (CPC) was formed in 1921. Aligned with the international communist movement, the CPC sought to harness the power of the working class in order to effect radical change in BC, Canada, and the world. It wanted to build on and expand the experiment in the Soviet Union, a society that was being developed based on a particular interpretation of Marxism. The goal was a communist society, seen in Marxism as an advanced phase of socialism. The other party, the Co-operative Commonwealth Federation (CCF), was established in 1932. It drew together much of the left that was not communist, including non-communist Marxists, and promoted government planning and regulation in the social and economic life of the province, as well as an eventual transformation to socialism. Both were left parties, but the CPC and CCF engaged in fierce competition with each other.

Economically, the interwar years divide into the 1920s and 1930s. In the early 1920s, reflecting what was happening throughout the Western world, the provincial economy sank into a depression. By 1924 this turned around and there was general growth throughout the rest of the decade. Then the Wall Street stock market crash of 24 October 1929 exposed the weakness of the western economic system. The ensuing panic drove the west into a downward economic spiral. The Great Depression in British Columbia bottomed out in the winter of 1932–1933. Unemployment rates topped 30 percent of the workforce. The general economic malaise in British Columbia was exacerbated by American protectionist policies; the 1930 Smoot-Hawley tariff placed a duty against imports coming into the United States. The British Columbia forest industry, which relied heavily on the US market, was devastated. A slow recovery was evident by the mid-1930s, a result of the general economic turnaround internationally, as well as the fruits of a Canada-Great Britain trade agreement in 1932 that facilitated the entry of provincial resources into the British market. The agreement was a godsend for many resource industries, and by 1934 there was already evidence of cautious expansion by forestry companies in the coastal region. Logging camps reopened and new sawmills were built. The farming and fishing industries also received a boost. In 1936, too, American reductions in tariffs against Canadian imports rekindled trade ties between BC and the United States. Nevertheless, only after the outbreak of the Second World War in September 1939 did production in BC return to levels experienced in the late 1920s.[1]

The left politics of the 1920s are too often ignored in the rush to move from the upheaval of 1919 to the creation of the Co-operative Commonwealth Federation in 1932. But the twists and turns of the 1920s, and especially the entrenchment of the Communist Party of Canada, set the stage not only for the early 1930s but also for future decades.

The Russian Revolution of 1917 brought Lenin and the communists to power, leading to the creation of the Soviet Union. The impact was immense, even in British Columbia. The working class, it seemed, as predicted by generations of socialists, was coming into its own: first the Soviet Union and then the rest of the world. To further the interests of the international socialist cause, the Communist International (Comintern) was established in 1919. The Comintern, dominated by Moscow, coordinated the worldwide communist crusade, and soon had representation in countries around the globe.

The Communist Party of Canada, founded in Ontario in 1921, belonged to the Comintern. For leftists, in the wake of the upheaval of 1919 and 1920, the CPC was an alternative that offered hope. The One Big Union (OBU) was in disarray, the Socialist Party of Canada (SPC) had no momentum, and the Industrial Workers of the World (IWW) had strength only in a few pockets of hinterland resource workers. These organizations were soon eclipsed by the CPC, which built on a successful revolution, provided a concrete institutional structure, and exuded the promise of a new international order.

In the fall of 1921, a meeting in Vancouver brought together Jack Kavanagh of the OBU, William Bennett of the SPC, J.M. Clark of the Lumber Workers Industrial Union, A.S. Wells of the Federated Labor Party (FLP), and members of the IWW. They formed a provincial branch of the Workers' Party. The Workers' Party was the public name of the CPC in Canada at the time, and it was affiliated to the Comintern.[2] The party's strategy throughout most of the 1920s was known as "boring from within." This entailed aggressively participating in the activities of established unions and left political parties with a view to winning them over to communism. In early 1923, a Vancouver branch of the Trade Union Education League, linked to the Communist Party of Canada, was set up. The established unions were not amused. A statement by the mainstream Trades and Labour Congress of Canada (TLC) executive committee in 1922 was blunt: "The intention of the Workers' Party of Canada and the Workers' Education League, is not to improve the usefulness of trade unions, but, by first destroying confidence in the methods established through years of experience, to utilize them to bring the workers of Canada under the control of the Red Trade Union International of Moscow."[3]

Another political expression of the left in the early 1920s, the Canadian Labour Party (CLP), was a national party ushered into being with the help of the Trades and Labour Congress of Canada. The CLP, which absorbed the Federated Labor Party that had been formed in 1918, was intended to be the political arm of the labour movement. A BC wing was established, and Tom Richardson of the Federated Labor party represented the province at the first national Canadian Labour Party convention. The CLP was largely a copy of the Federated Labor Party. The influence of socialism was evident in the call for a complete change in the economic and social system. Internationalism was reflected in a celebration of solidarity with workers the world over. Immediate policy demands included unemployment insurance, nationalization of the banking system, public ownership of utilities, old age and disability pensions, and international disarmament.[4]

In the spring of 1924, a convention was held to establish a BC section of the Canadian Labour Party. In attendance were ninety-six delegates representing twenty-eight Vancouver unions, the Vancouver Trades and Labour Council, three branches of the FLP and two branches of the Workers' Party. The participating groups retained their organizational integrity but agreed to cooperate in running candidates during elections. The BC section of the CLP was very much a union operation. The first executive consisted of active union people, including Angus MacInnis, W.H. Cottrell, and Harry Neelands. A number of Vancouver unions affiliated to the party.[5]

In the 1924 provincial election, the Canadian Labour Party ran sixteen candidates. Three were elected: Harry Neelands in Vancouver, Tom Uphill in Fernie, and Francis Aubrey Browne in Burnaby.[6] The CLP garnered 11.3 percent of the provincial popular vote. Tension between communists and non-communists within the Canadian Labour Party led in 1926 to the establishment of the Independent Labour Party (ILP) in British Columbia, with the intent of aligning the anti-communist left. Thereafter the ILP and the CPC battled for control of the CLP. The communists remained influential, despite their smaller numbers. What finally split the CLP in early 1928 was communist support for the enfranchisement of Asians. The ILP and affiliated unions voted against extending the franchise to Asians, leading to their withdrawal from the CLP. Thereafter the CLP collapsed. However, as Paul Phillips argues, the enfranchisement issue was merely the culmination of a series of disputes. It was the aggressive communist actions that were at the core, undermining the unity of left politics in the mid-1920s.[7] In the July 1928 provincial election, the ILP ran only nine candidates, four of whom were from Vancouver Island and four from Vancouver and Burnaby. Only Tom Uphill in Fernie was elected. The party secured a mere 4.95 percent of the popular vote.

For organized labour, too, the 1920s were lean years. In 1919 there were some 263 union locals in the province. This dropped to 235 in 1922, but thereafter the number rose, and there were over 270 union locals in the province in 1929. Membership numbers, however, were less healthy. In 1919 an estimated forty thousand workers in BC belonged to unions. In 1920 this had dropped to nineteen thousand. The nadir was reached in 1924 when a mere 16,500 workers were unionized, some 8 percent of the workforce. It had been over 20 percent of the workforce in 1919.[8] Militancy also waned. In 1918 an estimated 16,164 BC employees were involved in strikes, and in 1919 this number dipped to 12,706. In 1920, however, only 4,910 were involved in job actions, most scattered throughout the province in small logging camps. Over the rest of the decade the number of strikes in the province fluctuated between seven and fourteen, and the number of workers involved each year between 691 and 4,152. As Paul Phillips notes: "By the end of 1925, B.C.'s once strong labour movement had been reduced to a core centred in Vancouver and district. This area held almost 80 percent of B.C. unionists and the only cohesive and central union organization."[9]

The moderate left retained links with the progressive wing of liberalism in the 1920s. The provincial Liberal Party under the leadership of John Oliver won a majority government in 1920, with twenty-five seats and 37.89 percent of the popular vote, and a minority government in 1924, with twenty-three seats and 31.34 percent of the vote in what was now a forty-eight-seat legislature.[10] Oliver died in 1927. His replacement was unable to win the 1928 election; the Liberals won only twelve seats and 40.04 percent of the vote. The Oliver Liberals were in tune with the growing reform sentiment that solidified in the second decade of the century.

Making cookies at the National Biscuit and Confection Company, 1926.
Studio: Dominion Photo Co. Vancouver Public Library 22207.

Prohibition, mothers' pensions, and anti-patronage legislation were brought in. The BC Liberals also reflected the face of reform put forward by the federal Liberal Party. In 1919, a Liberal convention in Ottawa made William Lyon Mackenzie King national party leader and adopted a new platform. This new program for liberalism endorsed minimum wage laws, government-run health insurance and pension schemes, and unemployment insurance. Twentieth-century Canadian liberalism was taking shape, adopting a commitment to government social programs. Pressure from the left, increasing urban and factory problems, the chaotic nature of capitalist production, and evident class conflict prompted the new Liberal agenda.[11]

For moderate leftists hostile to the revolutionary Communist Party of Canada and aware of the weakness of other leftist parties, reform liberalism was appealing. In Prince George, for example, John McInnis, a left activist, supported the Liberal candidate throughout the 1920s. McInnis had been elected on the Socialist Party of Canada ticket to represent a Kootenay riding in 1907. Defeated in the 1909 election and finding himself blacklisted from the Kootenay mines, he moved to the Northern Interior in 1910. He went into business as a building contractor, and established an SPC local in the region in 1911. In 1916 McInnis ran as an Independent Socialist. He appealed to a broad swath of voters, including local farmers, who were a significant factor, and was at odds with the official policy of the Socialist Party of Canada. McInnis scoffed at the idea of government-owned coal mines, and argued, invoking the law of supply and demand, "that if the profit in fuel was so large there would be more capital invested in this industry and the normal price would be ultimately reached."[12] A saw-off was arranged and no Liberal candidate contested the seat. But despite much Liberal support, McInnis could not best the high-profile Conservative candidate. In 1918 McInnis played a prominent role in founding a local of the Federated Labor Party in Prince George and it quickly had twenty-five members. However, the party did not last in the area, and most activists, including McInnis, left to support the Liberals. Nevertheless, McInnis himself was not a Liberal. In the 1930s he would again support a socialist party, campaigning against the Liberal Party.

The case of R.J. Burde also shows the fluidity of personal political allegiances, as well as the difficulty in distinguishing clearly between the left and the non-left. Burde won the Alberni Valley riding on Vancouver Island in 1920 and 1928, but he had already undergone a remarkable political journey. Prior to World War I he was a staunch Conservative, but after serving overseas, his ideas changed. In a 1919 by-election he won a seat in the provincial legislature under the Independent-Soldier banner, and in 1920 he won as an Independent. In the legislature he was an outspoken advocate of pro-labour legislation, leading the battle to secure an eight-hour day in BC lumber mills and a minimum wage law. When the Liberal government postponed implementing the legislation because of pressure from sawmill owners, Burde argued that employees would see the delay as a tightening of the "grasp of the capitalist hand upon the throats of the worker."[13] Publicly, Burde adamantly declared that he would have no truck with either of the old-line parties, but behind the scenes the Independent leftist and the Liberals cooperated. This was not unusual. In the mid-1920s, the federal Liberal party approached the Canadian Labour Party to arrange a saw-off of seats. The CLP refused, but this did not help its fortunes in federal elections.[14]

If the 1920s were lethargic years for the left, the 1930s offered both anxiety and hope. For some, the collapse of the economy bred concern and fear about the future, a clinging to old ideas, and a desperate desire to revive the more prosperous past. But for others, the economic malaise suggested that capitalism as a system was in free fall and that change was not only desirable but necessary. The communists, especially in the first half of the decade, were particularly dynamic in organizing for change. Their behaviour, though, is not only explained by the depths of the economic crisis, which suggested the communist analysis of capitalism was correct, but also by changes in international communism.

After the death of Lenin in 1924, competing heirs vied to assume the mantle of leadership in the Soviet Union. In the end, Joseph Stalin prevailed, purging his opponents and putting his stamp on the Soviet Union and the Comintern. Throughout the world communist parties adopted the Stalinist line. At the 1928 meeting of the Comintern the future was outlined. Capitalism was about to enter a period of crisis. To take advantage of this instability and further the goals of international communism, communists were to withdraw from participation in leftist organizations, such as political parties and unions, to create independent communist organizations. Communists were no longer to work with or cooperate with the broader left. Indeed, social democrats were labelled "patsies" of the capitalists, and, in language similar to the impossibilist critique of an earlier era, the minor reforms that they achieved with regard to hours of work or wages were portrayed as undermining the revolutionary fervour of the masses. Social democrats, as well as capitalists, were the enemy. The goal was to prepare the international working class for struggle. It was to be class against class, with the communist parties organizing and leading the working class. International communist activities had a long-term goal, but in the short run it was expected that they would destabilize western economies and help shore up the security of the Soviet Union. In Stalinist thought, the Soviet Union was the motherland of the international revolution, and the first goal was to ensure the viability of the Soviet Union, feeling increasingly threatened by western democracies and rising fascist states. This era, which lasted from 1928 to 1935, is known as the "Third Period" in the history of the Comintern.

British Columbia communists, who adhered to the Stalinist line, have been much maligned by many on the left. First, taking the Comintern line seriously, the communists, it was and is argued, put the interests of the Soviet Union ahead of the interests of British Columbians. This alienated potential leftists who might otherwise have joined a union or a political party. Moreover, it played into the hands of employers who portrayed unions led by communists as puppets of Soviet foreign policy. In the 1930s, there were constant rumours, ill-founded, of "Moscow gold," financial aid being provided to BC communist unionists solely for the purpose of disrupting the provincial economy. Second, the "class against class" strategy isolated communists within the broader left, and splintered the left at a time when unity would have furthered the socialist project. The energy and time spent fighting others on the left would more beneficially have been used to achieve helpful changes for working-class families. Third, the Stalinist agenda stifled other, more democratic Marxist options. Whereas the 1920s, the argument goes, was rich with discussion about the appropriateness of various Marxist options, the Trotskyist model being put forward most prominently, Stalinization blunted discussion, and hence creativity, and ensured the future ossification of revolutionary Marxism in British Columbia. In other words, from this point of view, Stalinism in the late 1920s and early 1930s was a major reason for the weakness of the revolutionary left in Canada for the rest of the twentieth century.

From the perspective of British Columbia communists, however, the world looked different. The Soviet Union was a noble experiment at the forefront of history. Many leftists looked with favour on the Soviet Union and its attempt to reformulate a social order. The Soviet Union also saw the world in international terms. Capitalism was international and so should be the socialist counterattack. Most leftists concurred that socialist responses had to pay heed to international events, even if they were less

Communist Party march, Vancouver, 1930s. Vancouver Public Library 8787.

enthusiastic about the USSR. Internationalism was common currency on the left in the 1930s. Stalinization could also be defended by arguing that the left needed order and discipline to achieve its goals. The upending of capitalism demanded a core of dedicated soldiers prepared to work in unison for a better world. The debate about the place of BC communists in the left of the early 1930s raises interesting and important issues about tactics, the search for unity, and the question of ideological purity, but in the longer historical perspective it is just as important to appreciate the communists as key components in a diverse left that was charting, in a rough, often awkward fashion, a new historical course.

In 1935, the Comintern changed strategies. In Europe the rise of Mussolini, Hitler, and Franco made fascism enemy number one. Fascists were strongly anti-communist. In Germany the rise of Hitler was based in part on anti-communist rhetoric. Moreover, the bitter division on the left between the communists and the social democrats in Europe had weakened the opposition to fascism. Communists were now to work together with all anti-fascist groups. The survival of the Soviet Union in the face of rising fascist sentiment was the primary goal. In the Comintern analysis, social democrats and even liberals were now to be embraced in the struggle against fascism. In Canada the Conservative Party was the party deemed to have fascist tendencies, and all other parties were to unite to keep it from power.

Communists were the most vigorous union organizers in the 1930s. The Depression was a difficult time for the established union movement, and little energy was expended organizing new members. The unions hunkered down to weather the storm. The communists were the exception. First, they actually organized workers in the 1930s, a feat in itself. Second, they organized semi-skilled and unskilled industrial workers, workers who had for the most part been ignored by the craft unions. Third, they were at the forefront in organizing the forest industry, the largest industry in the province and an industry that was not yet unionized.

In late 1929, Canadian communists established the Workers Unity League (WUL), a new labour congress to represent communist-led unions. It was a competitor to the Trades and Labour Congress of Canada. Since communists had been active within the traditional union movement until 1928, there were not many independent communist unions. There was a small forest industry union, the Lumber Workers Industrial Union (LWIU), an offshoot of the communist woods union in Ontario, in the late 1920s. By 1931 the communists were able to get a toehold in the provincial mining industry, with the Mine Workers' Union of Canada, and on the waterfront, with the Marine Workers' Industrial Union. All were affiliated to the Workers Unity League. In 1933 the Workers Union League launched the Fishermen's and Cannery Workers' Industrial Union, a competitor to the BC Fishermen's Protective Association, establishing locals in Port Alberni, Prince Rupert, Sointula, and Vancouver.[15]

Communists led prominent strikes in the 1930s. In 1931, at Fraser Mills in the Fraser Valley, the communist Lumber Workers Industrial Union led a strike that began on 17 September to challenge wage cuts, gain union recognition and a closed shop, and reinstate workers who had been fired for refusing to work overtime. Overtime work, it was argued, took jobs away from the unemployed. Remarkably, at the end of the strike on 20 November, the workers made gains in the compromise agreement, no mean feat in the worst time of the Depression.[16] In 1934 the LWIU led a strike by loggers on Vancouver Island. Loggers had endured unemployment and wage cuts, and now wanted a share of the evident newfound prosperity of their employers. In late January, a strike wave began, sweeping across Vancouver Island. Campbell River and Port Alberni were the focal points of the strike, but many striking loggers were also based in Vancouver, the distribution point for loggers throughout the coastal region. After weeks on the picket line, striking loggers voted to end the strike in early May. Workers were able to improve their wages, but the companies refused to recognize the union or even elected camp committees.

The communist ties of the union leadership were important in the strike. Employers portrayed the strikers as dupes of Moscow, as did the provincial government. Non-communist union leaders were critical of the LWIU leadership:

The "Workers Unity League" of which the LWIU is an offspring, is not a "Bona Fide" labour movement, but rather the instrument of a foreign controlled revolutionary party, whose primary object is not to improve the lot of the workers but to keep industry in a state of turmoil by carrying on a campaign of guerilla warfare by pulling strikes on the slightest provocation, wherever and whenever they find workers who will listen to their nefarious propaganda.[17]

The public, though hardly supportive of communism, was sympathetic to the strikers in light of the improved economic conditions in the industry.

In 1935, Vancouver longshoremen struck. A number of unions represented dock workers on the Vancouver waterfront, including the Seafarers' Industrial Union, an affiliate of the Workers Unity League, and they came together to present a united front in April of 1934. There were festering issues, including wages and control of the hiring hall, and after a number of local disputes, a general waterfront strike began in May. At a major confrontation on 18 June, one thousand strikers marched on Vancouver's Ballantyne Pier and were met by a force of police. A melee ensued: twenty-eight people were hurt and one bystander was shot by police with a sawed-off shotgun. There was much public support for the strikers, and it seemed that there would be a satisfactory conclusion. However, a federal government investigator blamed left-wing union leadership for the dispute, stiffening the resolve of the companies. Union leaders were arrested. On December 6 the strike ended in failure.[18]

If the communists were prominent in a few large-scale labour disputes in the first half of the 1930s, they achieved little in the way of establishing solid, viable union structures. The lumber industry remained largely unorganized, the longshoremen's union was in disarray, and their other industrial unions were little beyond shells. Perhaps their greatest achievement was exposing the lethargy of non-communist unions in the period.

The 1935 change in Comintern policy had implications for BC unionists. Communists were now to work harmoniously with the broader left. In Canada, the Workers Unity League was duly disbanded, as were its constituent unions. In British Columbia, for example, Lumber Workers Industrial Union delegates from coastal sawmills and logging camps met in Vancouver on 29 December 1935 and endorsed a resolution favouring a merger with the Lumber and Sawmill Workers Union, an international, American-based union that was affiliated to the United Brotherhood of Carpenters and Joiners. In March the LWIU membership voted on the proposal and it passed by an overwhelming margin. However, the larger trade union movement was not enthusiastic about the new, improved communist strategy. The Vancouver Trades and Labour Council fought to restrict the representation of the Lumber and Sawmill Workers Union in their assembly, fearing the spread of the communist influence.

The Brotherhood of Carpenters and Joiners also had reservations. The carpenters, because they worked with wood, had jurisdiction over the lumber workers in North America. They had two concerns. First there was the issue of communism. Second there was much hostility to allowing semi-skilled and unskilled workers into the ranks of the skilled craftsmen. At their convention in Florida in late 1936, the carpenters voted to maintain the craft nature of their organization and refused to grant voting rights to the unskilled and semi-skilled lumber workers. The Lumber and Sawmill Workers Union was relegated to second-class status within the carpenters' brotherhood. In the spring of 1937, the vice-president of the United Brotherhood dismissed the lumber and sawmill workers as a "bunch of communists," and the large craft union ordered several Lumber and Sawmill Workers Union locals to turn over members such as painters, truck drivers, and engineers to the appropriate craft unions. The lumber workers recognized that their presence within the carpenters' brotherhood was untenable and began meeting amongst themselves to discuss disaffiliating from the two organizations. Due to changing circumstances, in 1937 they had another option.

A new organization had been created due to a long-standing division in the North American union movement, and because of the importance of unions in the left, it deserves comment. Most unionists of the day were craft unionists who believed that their skills gave them power in negotiating with employers. As the lumber worker example makes clear, these craft workers looked down on those that they deemed unskilled, and they were unwilling to support organizing drives in the growing mass-production industries and among unskilled workers generally. There was a bitter dispute in the United States between those in favour and those against committing to organize unskilled and semi-skilled industrial workers. The result was the establishment of a new labour body, the Congress of Industrial Organizations (CIO), formed in 1935. The CIO, in opposition to the American Federation of Labor, represented and helped organize industrial workers. In July 1937, lumber worker union delegates from British Columbia and the American Pacific Northwest voted to affiliate with the CIO, a decision that was later ratified by the membership. The new CIO union was called the International Woodworkers of America (IWA) and British Columbia was District 1 in the international union.[19] It was led by communists.

Despite the creation of the Congress of Industrial Organizations, the union movement in BC was in the doldrums. In the forest industry, the province's main industry, there was no union presence in the Interior and the hold in the coastal region was tentative. In 1937 the lumber workers' union became involved in a six-week strike at Blubber Bay on Texada Island against wage reductions. After a favourable settlement for the union, however, the company refused to live up to the agreement and engaged in questionable hiring practices to keep out pro-union workers. A major strike ensued, beginning in June 1938. It lasted eleven months and included violence, evictions from company houses, and arrests. Ultimately the company won. For the IWA, the loss was very costly in terms of both money and energy, leaving it a spent force at the onset of the Second World War.[20]

The Blubber Bay failure highlighted for the left the necessity of both strong political and union action. The provincial Liberal government, elected in 1933, had been active in updating labour law, partly as a result of strikes, partly as an attempt to forestall the arrival of more militant Congress of Industrial Organizations unionism in the province, partly due to political pressure from the left, and partly to meet liberal notions of fairness. The Industrial Disputes Conciliation and Arbitration Act, passed in December 1937, echoed developments in the United States, where the Wagner Act of 1935 had given some government support to unions. However, the enthusiasm of unionists was short lived. A June 1938 strike of 650 men at two Alberni Valley sawmills failed because the Minister of Labour, George Pearson, refused to get involved, even though the union argued that it had signed up over 50 percent of the workforce.[21] Blubber Bay further drove home the weakness of the legislation when the government refused to recognize the IWA, which had the overwhelming support of the workers, as the legitimate representative of the men, and allowed the company to run roughshod over its workers.

At the outbreak of World War II the provincial union movement was weak. A slight surge in union membership after 1935 reflected the forays of union activists, often communist, into unorganized industries, especially the forest sector, and the acceptance by many of the efficacy of industrial unions. In 1930 an estimated 10.7 percent of the workforce was unionized, a figure that dropped to 7.2 percent in 1934. In 1937 some 12.9 percent of the workforce was organized, though it dropped to 12.7 percent in 1939.[22] There was still no significant government legislation that supported unions, restricted employer anti-union tactics, or supervised effective collective bargaining.

The plight of single, unemployed young men was a prominent issue for the left in the 1930s. Early in the Depression the provinces, including British Columbia, established camps to house unemployed single young men. These were far from urban centres, and the province provided funds for work projects such as road building or airport runway construction. But as the Depression progressed, the make-work aspect became more difficult. For one thing, the financially strapped province could not afford to provide materials for the projects. Moreover, private contractors, who were also feeling the financial pinch, complained that these government projects took work from them. In 1932, the federal government took control of the relief-camp system across Canada. A large number of the camps were in British Columbia. The Department of National Defence ran the camps. The reason for the federal coordination of the program was not solely the poor financial situation of the provinces. The federal government was concerned about the growing numbers of restless young men congregating in urban centres. They were prey to the appeals of radical orators, especially communists. The goal was to remove these young men to isolated camps. The flaw in the plan, of course, was that agitators found their way to the camps. Furthermore, the grievances of the men in the camps were real and increasingly understood by the population at large.

The Relief Camp Workers' Union and the National Unemployed Workers Association, affiliates of the communist Workers Unity League, were active among the unemployed and from an early date they launched protests in the camps. They demanded abolition of the camps, a government-run unemployment insurance program, and meaningful work. In December 1934, over a thousand relief-camp workers abandoned the camps to congregate in Vancouver and protest conditions in the camps. A few months later the protest became more formidable when some four thousand men converged on Vancouver demanding "work and wages." The strike dragged on from April through May. Many Vancouverites feared the large gatherings of militant young men. The communist leadership of the strike also faced a problem: how to sustain interest in the protest, especially when it was becoming clear that neither the province nor the federal government was willing to offer anything meaningful.

An idea was put forward to take the protest to Ottawa; on 3 June 1935 about one thousand men boarded boxcars leaving Vancouver. The On-to-Ottawa Trek was led by Arthur "Slim" Evans. As the trek headed east more men joined. By the time the group arrived in Regina they were twenty-five hundred strong. Moreover, in Manitoba more men were waiting to join the trek, and in Ontario and the Maritimes contingents were also moving towards the national capital. The federal government of R.B. Bennett decided to halt the trek before it reached Ottawa. On 1 July the Royal Canadian Mounted Police broke up a meeting of the unemployed in downtown Regina, setting off what became known as the Regina Riot. One policeman died, many trekkers were injured, and some one hundred arrests were made. Thereafter the trekkers were dispersed across Canada.

The federal Liberal government, elected in October 1935, disbanded the unpopular relief camps. The Liberal government also offered new temporary forms of assistance and started railway construction projects. A slight improvement in the economy, too, undermined further protest. Left-wing agitation also weakened when many activists went to Spain where they participated in the war to defeat fascism. In the Spanish Civil

War, fought from 1936 to 1939, leftists from around the world rallied to try to stop General Francisco Franco from imposing a fascist dictatorship.

Nevertheless, direct action in BC was not dead. Unemployed workers continued to make their way to British Columbia, some to work in provincial forestry projects. Much to the concern of government officials, the numbers kept rising, reaching six thousand in 1938. The province decided to cut relief payments and offered free transportation back to the prairies for unemployed workers. Leftists mobilized, organizing tag days and marches. On 11 May they escalated the Vancouver protest: "1,600 men, formed into compact, orderly brigades, with group leaders for each ten men, marched into the Art Gallery, the Post Office and the Hotel Georgia."[23] The group at the Hotel Georgia was persuaded to leave after ten days, but the other occupations lasted until 20 June, when the "sit-downers" were forcibly removed by federal and provincial police.

Despite protests against unemployment, a few major strikes, and the zeal of the communists, the major long-term achievement of the left in the 1930s was the creation of the Co-operative Commonwealth Federation, a party that quickly took on a prominent role in BC politics. The party was founded in Calgary in 1932, and it brought together diverse individuals and organizations. In the summer of 1933, unionists, radical farmers, members of the Socialist Party of Canada, which was the new name of BC's Independent Labour Party, and young academics from Toronto and Montreal in the League for Social Reconstruction, among others, congregated in Regina. Also evident was the influence of the Social Gospel movement that had sprung up in the late nineteenth century in the Protestant churches of English Canada, a movement committed to social change and the creation of a heaven on earth. This religious connection gave reform and progressive change a degree of legitimacy in some circles, and although the Social Gospel movement waned after the First World War, socially conscious Christians still were evident in the left in the 1930s. The delegates at Regina articulated the goals of the new party in the Regina Manifesto, a document that guided the party for the next two decades.

Citizens Protest Police Terror.

Protest against police actions, Vancouver, 1938. British Columbia Archives C-07949.

The Regina Manifesto drew together leftist ideas from the past three decades, offering both guiding principles and concrete policies. The socialist orientation was clear in the first sentence of the manifesto: "The CCF is a federation of organizations whose purpose is the establishment in Canada of a Co-operative Commonwealth in which the principle regulating production, distribution and exchange will be the supplying of human needs and not the making of profits." The capitalist system was seen as disintegrating in the early 1930s, and CCFers envisioned that the exploitation of one class by another would be eliminated. Society and the economy were now to be planned and managed, "not by a small group of capitalists [acting] in their own interests, but by public servants acting in the public interest and responsible to the people as whole." The manifesto ended with the clarion call: "No CCF Government will rest content until it has eradicated capitalism and put into operation the full programme of socialized planning which will lead to the establishment in Canada of the Co-operative Commonwealth."

Concrete policies in the platform included the nationalization of the banks, and public ownership of transportation, communication, and electric power services. Further, the mining and pulp and paper industries, and the distribution of milk, bread, coal, and gasoline were deemed too important to be run by private companies. There was not to be outright confiscation, but overall the "welfare of the community must take supremacy over the claims of private wealth." The new party also promised to improve the lot of farmers and to provide unemployment insurance and better pensions for urban workers. Unions were to be encouraged. Health, hospital and medical services were to be publicly organized.[24]

British Columbians, who were notably radical in the national CCF, achieved quick success at home. In an election held on 2 November 1933, the provincial CCF fielded forty-six candidates, one shy of running in every riding. CCF candidates included long-time labourists and socialists Sam Guthrie in Cowichan-Newcastle, Wallis Lefeaux in Vancouver Centre, Bill Pritchard in Vancouver-Point-Grey, Ernest Winch in Vancouver East, and Victor Midgely in Victoria City. The CCF won seven seats, far behind the victorious Liberals who won thirty-four seats, but still sufficient to have the second-highest number of seats in the legislature, partly a result of the implosion and disintegration of the provincial Conservative party. Most remarkably, the CCF won 31.53 percent of the popular vote (the Liberals garnered 41.74 percent of the popular vote). Almost one-third of British Columbians had chosen a socialist option. As might be imagined, the BC CCF appealed to a number of constituencies, ranging from class-conscious, revolutionary Vancouver Marxists to frustrated Kamloops left-populists deeply concerned about the economic and political situation. Nevertheless, despite the diversity, the party in BC was built around class analysis and a core socialist commitment to fundamental change.

Internal diversity meant that the CCF, nationally and provincially, faced the difficulty of maintaining unity. Nationally, the depth of the Depression and the strong presence of J.S. Woodsworth, the first CCF leader, were crucial in sustaining the party. Provincially, the Depression and the possibility of actually holding office imposed some discipline on competing internal organizations and individuals. But, as in all political parties, there were divisions and dissension. In the early years there were moderate and radical wings of the CCF in the BC legislature. The moderates congregated around Reverend Robert Connell, an Anglican minister from Victoria who came from the Social Gospel tradition. He became the CCF House Leader in November 1933, and his supporters included Victor Midgely, Ernest Bakewell, John Price, and Robert Swailes. The more militant group, including Lyle Telford, Wallis Lefeaux, and Dorothy Steeves, supported Ernest Winch, a secular Marxist and unionist who had cut his political teeth in the 1910s and early 1920s as a member of the earlier Socialist Party of Canada and as leader of the short-lived Lumber Workers Industrial Union. The clash in the CCF came to a head in 1936, and Connell was squeezed from the party. He and a few supporters created a new political party, the Social Constructives, which disappeared after the 1937 provincial election.[25]

The CCF defined itself and was defined in relation to the Communist Party of Canada and the Liberal Party. Distinctions were not cut and dried. Some CCFers, such as Connell, were willing to work with the Liberal Party, feeling comfortable with progressive liberalism. Others, such as Winch, were more comfortable with communists. There were members of the CCF in the 1930s, such as A.M. Stephen and Rod Young, who were close to the CPC. Angus MacInnis, on the other hand, thought that cooperation with the communists was a dead end. In a July 1937 speech to CCFers discussing the possibility of a united front proposed by the communists, he noted: "If you want another year of hell, carry out the united front idea. I suggest you throw the Communists on the dungheap where they belong."[26]

The CCF was born at the time when the Communist Party of Canada was guided by the Comintern's "Third Period" policy, when communists smeared non-communist leftists as reformist lackeys whose policies served only to prop up the capitalist system. CCFers spent much time and energy distinguishing themselves from communists. Relations were hostile. On 25 August 1933, a contingent of communists attended a CCF meeting in the Princess theatre in Prince George. There was a capacity crowd, with Dr. J. Lyle Telford, a prominent CCFer, the speaker. The communists in the audience disrupted the meeting by booing Telford, making disparag-

ing remarks about J.S. Woodsworth, and singing the "Red Flag." The
local paper noted: "The outstanding feature of the evening was the demonstration that there is no immediate connection between this phase of
communism and the CCF."[27] When the Communist Party line changed
in 1935, promising a united left to defeat fascism, CCFers were understandably skeptical about the sincerity of the CPC and about embracing
these brothers and sisters on the left. Some radical CCFers even felt that
the CPC was diluting its revolutionary fervour by calling for a broadly
based coalition against fascism.[28]

Nevertheless, a focus on the tension between the CCF and the CPC
obscures the similarities. Both shared a commitment to the betterment of
the working class and to giving workers and their families dignity, a
decent share of society's material rewards, and the opportunity to shape
public policy. Both wholeheartedly supported unionism and demanded
government support for unions and collective bargaining. Both attacked
the government's treatment of the unemployed. Both abhorred fascism.
Both wanted the relief camps abolished and demanded an unemployment
insurance system. Both saw the Liberals and Conservatives as unduly
dominated by the business class. On the ground in causes such as defending the civil liberties of union activists, abolishing relief camps, supporting
striking loggers, and attacking anti-left laws, CCFers and communists
often worked together.[29]

Neither the CPC nor the CCF was a labour party. That is, neither was
the political arm of organized labour, primarily representing the interests
of the unions in the political arena. While trade union people as individuals participated in the formation and early years of the CCF, no union
initially affiliated to the CCF. Nor was the CPC a labour party. When the
CPC established unions and set up the Workers Unity League, the party
had a place of importance, and ultimately the unions were to serve the
goals of the party. On the other hand, unionists were often wary of direct
political involvement. Union officials had a range of political stances.
Some were Liberals, others were social democrats, others were communists, others were unaligned Marxists, and some were apolitical. Political
ties to one party had the potential to divide the union. Further, independent, aggressive political action held perils in that involvement in the

political process would unnecessarily antagonize the government of day, which was unlikely to be leftist, and thus make the achievement of immediate legislative goals more difficult. So in the 1930s, except in the communist-created unions, unions remained wary of direct political involvement.

The CCF participated fully in parliamentary democracy, believing that expanding the power of ordinary people in the political process would lead to an equitable, just social order. If ordinary, right-thinking people, including farmers and the working class, used their electoral clout to elect a socialist government, the path to socialism was clear. The CPC was a lesser presence in electoral politics, using campaigns to spread their ideas, agitate against the system, and prepare for a revolutionary struggle. In the 1933 provincial election, the communists, running under the United Front Party banner, put up nineteen candidates and secured 1.20 percent of the popular vote. In 1937, after the Comintern policy change, the Communist Party of Canada offered only one candidate for office. He won 567 votes, less than 1 percent of the popular vote provincially.

One other distinction between the CCF and CPC was that the CPC was branded as foreign by the both the right and even some on the left. The CPC's membership in the Moscow-dominated Comintern, and its celebration of the Soviet experiment contributed to this image. Moreover, the CPC had strong contingents of supporters in the immigrant communities, especially among Jews, Finns, and Ukrainians. It also operated most visibly among the unemployed and in outlying resource industries, the constituency of the almost dead IWW. In the first half of the 1930s, unemployed workers launched a series of protests in Prince George under the leadership of the communists. Many of the protesters were Russians, Yugoslavs, Scandinavians and Poles, recent immigrants in unskilled poorly paid occupations who were outside the mainstream society.

On Empire Day, 24 May 1935, the local population found an opportunity to show their rejection of the growing communist influence in protests, wrapping their sentiments in the cloak of patriotism and the British traditions. A large parade was organized and 1,300 people marched through the streets of Prince George. At the end of the parade the Union Jack was run up amid cheers, and the school inspector delivered the flag address. The crowd then joined in singing "God Save the King." The editor of the local paper pointedly outlined the significance of the Empire Day demonstration, arguing that communism was foreign to the British, Canadian way of life and that "the parade of the citizens of Prince George on Friday should carry its lesson to the men who have been persistently fomenting trouble, supposedly in the interests of the unemployed."[30] In comparison to the communists, the CCF was much more British in terms of its tradition, image, and supporters. Indeed, according to John Richards, the CCF was among the most British of Canadian institutions.[31]

The Conservative Party, which had won the 1928 provincial election, had no solutions for the economic problems of the 1930s, and the party disintegrated in the run-up to the 1933 provincial election. The new Liberal government was headed by Duff Pattullo. Pattullo was a reform liberal. He had campaigned on the slogan of "Work and Wages," and promised government action to deal with the Depression. In power, the Liberals launched a number of public works, including the construction of the Pattullo Bridge across the Fraser River at New Westminster, to give work to construction companies and workers. There was also support for marketing boards, a minimum wage, hours-of-work laws, and government control of the prices of gas and oil. Pattullo linked his program to the popular "New Deal" experiment of Franklin D. Roosevelt in the United States, claiming that Roosevelt copied his government's agenda. Boldly, in 1936 the BC Liberals promised a comprehensive health insurance scheme, an initiative that had not been tried elsewhere in Canada. The program was to cover all employees earning less than $2,400 per year and would put doctors on a salary. The idea was popular with the public: in a 1937 plebiscite 59 percent of voters endorsed the proposal. In this instance, the threat from the left, changing public opinion, the circumstances of the Depression, and a reformist element in liberalism pushed the Liberal Party leftward.[32]

Pattullo's apparent reformism did not silence the left. After outrage from the doctors and the business community, Pattullo backed down, abandoning the hospitalization program in 1938.[33] Anemic labour legislation did provincial workers little good, unemployment and welfare programs were largely talk, the unemployed were ignored, and the voice of business dominated. The CCF again elected seven members in the 1937 election, although their popular vote fell off to 28.57 percent, partly as a result of a rejuvenated Conservative party, which won 28.60 percent of the popular vote and elected eight members. (The Liberals secured thirty-one seats and 37.34 percent of the popular vote.) Still, the CCF was a legitimate party and hopes for forming a government were not mere pipe dreams.[34]

Already by the 1920s First Nations had been corralled and marginalized by the white settler society. In 1927 the federal government, with the support of the BC government, passed legislation that made it illegal for First Nation bands to raise money to fight for land claims, thus squelching the Aboriginal protest against the lack of treaty settlements in the province. There was no outcry from the left, nor from virtually anyone else in the white community. Everyday racist discrimination by British Columbians of British descent persisted against central and eastern Europeans, too, although there were no legal prohibitions.

The main focus of politically debated racial discrimination remained the Asian community and Asian immigration. In 1939 the Asian Exclusion Act of 1923 was still in effect and would remain so until 1947. In Ottawa, British Columbia members of parliament, irrespective of party, were overwhelmingly united against Asian immigration.[35] Legal restrictions had been accumulating. British Columbia legislation barred Asians from working on Crown lands. A minimum-hours-of-work law in 1923 pertained to lumber and shingle mills; it was specifically calculated to reduce the number of Asian workers in the forest industry. A minimum wage law followed in 1925. The logic was that if forced to pay a decent wage, employers would hire ostensibly more productive white workers rather than Asians. There were also restrictions against Asians in the coal mining, restaurant, and fishing industries.

There were some anti-racist voices within the left. In 1927, for example, the New Westminster Trades and Labour Council admitted the Mill and Camp Workers Union, which was made up of seven hundred Japanese workers, but the decision generated much conflict within the union movement.[36] In a number of lumber and shingle strikes during the 1930s, notably led by communists, Asian and white workers cooperated. J.S. Woodsworth, too, spoke out, arguing that Asian workers should be encouraged to join white unions in order to eliminate the wage differentials between whites and Asians that employers exploited, and thus to enhance the power of labour. In 1934 the federal CCF leader endorsed the vote for Asians in BC, and was supported by his son-in-law, the prominent BC CCF MP Angus MacInnis, who argued that Asians in BC should be elevated to the economic level of white Canadians and that they should have full citizenship, including the right to vote.[37] However, there was political fallout as the Liberals and Conservatives exploited the issue, and the CCF waffled, preferring that the issue remain out of the public eye.[38]

In one area, however, there was change. The achievement of the vote for women allowed for greater female participation in electoral politics, and women were active quickly as candidates, though in far fewer numbers and with less success than men. The Canadian Labour Party fielded two female candidates in the 1924 provincial election. In 1933 two CCF women ran and three communist women ran under the United Front banner. In 1937, CCFer Dorothy Gretchen Steeves was elected provincially. Women on the left also took to the streets, participating in rallies, organizing workers, walking picket lines, and supporting striking family members. In the middle years of the 1930s, left-wing Vancouver women launched the Mothers' Council, a body dedicated to influencing government policy on the unemployed. Growing out of an established women's organization, initially formed in 1916 to facilitate women's political action in electoral politics, the Mothers' Council brought together activist women from a number of organizations in 1935. Leadership came from the CCF Women's Central Group and the CPC's Women's Labour League. The women raised money with tag days, organized and participated in marches, and lobbied the government. The women stressed that they were mothers, but they were mothers with a sense of class and a radical leftist agenda.[39]

On the left, the woman question was much debated. In the CCF, for example, some women called for separate women's groups to deal with women's issues within the party. Laura Jamieson, a university-educated

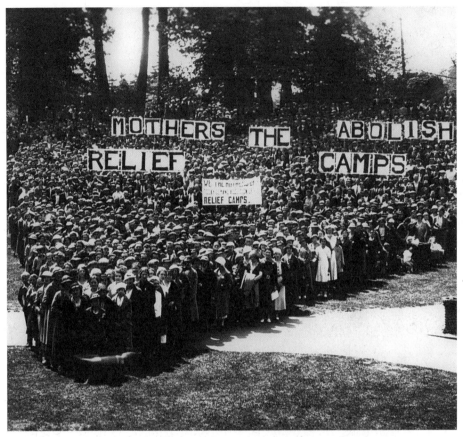

Mothers protest the Relief Camps, Malkin Bowl, Vancouver, May 1935.
Glenbow Museum NA-3634-10 and *Pacific Tribune* Archive.

teacher and a social worker before she married a BC judge, argued that
women's family and domestic concerns gave them a particular outlook
on politics that deserved a special place, while others, such as Dorothy
Steeves and Grace MacInnis, felt that women should be equal, full participants in the party.[40] For many men, equality was a difficult notion.
Union men had struggled for decades for a decent family wage, a single
wage for the male breadwinner that would allow him to support his wife
and children. The masculine identity and understanding of self was
wrapped up in this notion of being independently able to support one's
own family. Indeed, government social programs were constructed to
maintain the position of male breadwinners in a patriarchal society.[41] A

Helena Gutteridge, 1938. Vancouver Public Library 13333.

more egalitarian society, class-free even, could be envisaged, but it would still be one based on a fundamental division between the roles and powers of men and women. In politics, where issues were defined by men, economics were paramount, and so-called women's issues, such as equal pay, were secondary, though some hoped that class equality in the economic arena would be a prelude to full gender equality.

The left was out in front on one issue. Both CCF and CPC women were active in the contraception and birth control campaign of the era. It has been estimated that "between 1920 and 1950 probably close to five hundred women in British Columbia died as a result of abortion-related deaths."[42] Even providing contraceptives was a breach of the Criminal Code, and would remain so, at least technically, until 1969. In 1923, after a visit to Vancouver by American birth control advocate Margaret Sanger, the Canadian birth control movement in Canada was launched. Sanger spoke on 2 July, and it was very much a leftist women's affair. Laura E. Jamieson, representing the Vancouver branch of the Women's International League for Peace and Freedom, and Helena Gutteridge, representing the Vancouver Trades and Labour Council, organized the talk that was attended by 350 people. Sanger stressed the need for available, effective contraception to limit family size. The Canadian Birth Control League was formed shortly thereafter. In the 1920s and 1930s, the campaign for birth control, though sporadic, was largely a project of socialists and socialist feminists, such as A.M. Stephen, Dr. Lyle Telford, Dorothy Steeves, and Laura Jamieson, though others were also involved. The question was controversial; some, especially communists, worried that the birth control issue detracted from the more important issue of class struggle.[43]

At the end of the 1930s capitalism had not collapsed. Nor had the leftist agenda been noticeably advanced. Division remained the order of the day, with two political organizations competing for the allegiance of working people and their families. Yet there were points of agreement and, in the next decade, Liberal-dominated governments would put into practice ideas that had been part of the leftist agenda for decades. The 1940s also produced a winner in the political battle between the CPC and the CCF.

CHAPTER 4

Favourable Winds:
1939–1953

WORLD WAR II WAS GOOD for business in British Columbia. Production accelerated as lumber from provincial forests, fish from the Pacific Ocean and local rivers, minerals from Kootenay mines, and vessels from Vancouver shipyards were in great demand. The economy boomed. This surge continued into the post-war era. During the 1940s the real domestic product of British Columbia almost doubled.[1]

The war was also good for workers and unions. By 1941 the provincial economy was again running all out. With mills and factories operating at full capacity, labour was in demand. At the same time, many men and women were in the armed forces and immigration was at a standstill. Workers thus had the confidence to join unions without fear of being fired. They were also increasingly willing to go on strike; they could readily find a job elsewhere if they were fired for union activism. By 1945 an estimated 25.5 percent of the provincial workforce belonged to a union.

In 1942 and 1943 a strike wave swept through British Columbia, approaching numbers that had not been seen since 1919 and 1920.[2] The strength and confidence of labour was such that a new congress, taking the name of the BC Federation of Labour, was established by the industrial unions in the fall of 1944. It, in turn, was affiliated with the national Canadian Congress of Labour (CCL), which had been formed in 1940 to represent industrial unions.

Militant unions forced government action. The example of the United States, where the Wagner Act of 1935 continued to provide a legislative umbrella that benefited American workers more than any Canadian labour legislation of the day, served as a model for Canadian workers. In early 1943, after lobbying by BC unionists, the BC government amended the Industrial Conciliation and Arbitration Act, bolstering the rights of unions. The new legislation clarified the status of unions, provided for compulsory recognition of unions, and restricted the rights of employers to interfere in union activities. At the time "the BC legislation was the most advanced in Canada."[3]

Shortly thereafter, in February 1944, the federal government brought in an order to govern unionization and collective bargaining. Since BC industries, such as forestry and ship building, were under federal jurisdiction due to the exigencies of war, the famous federal order, known as PC 1003, was important to the province. PC 1003 represented a new approach to collective bargaining in Canada, ushering in the modern era of industrial relations. PC 1003 set up procedures for organizing unions, and if these rules were followed, unions would be certified, meaning that they would enjoy government support in forcing recognition by employers and in negotiating contracts with employers. Union recognition was now to be settled in government-supervised votes. The government also would set up administrative machinery to monitor the activities of unions and employers to ensure that they adhered to labour law. These administrative units were Labour Relations Boards, and they settled disputes about union jurisdiction, investigated complaints about "unfair labour practices," and reprimanded companies for failing to bargain in good faith. PC 1003 had great reach because of the range of the emergency war-time powers of the government.

At the end of the World War I, employers and governments had worked together to crush the union movement. Now, in World War II, the government accommodated organized labour, recognizing its legitimacy, treating it as a significant element in society and in the economy. The government now took on an interventionist role, mediating between employers and the elected representatives of employees. Employers naturally chafed in the new labour relations environment. Some sought advantage at the expense of unions and tried to defeat certification drives. There were still big strikes, but the framework for working out class conflict at the workplace had fundamentally changed. This was seen as a victory by most unionists — social democrats, communists, and liberals alike — a culmination of the struggle for trade union and collective bargaining legitimacy that had been underway for a century.[4]

The breakthrough in the forest industry, the province's most important industry, gives a sense of the changing circumstances. Logger strikes at Lake Cowichan and Ladysmith on Vancouver Island over issues of seniority, leaves of absences, and union recognition were successful in 1941 and 1942. The main focal point, however, was Haida Gwaii (the Queen Charlotte Islands). By the summer of 1941, the International Woodworkers of America (IWA) had a presence in eight logging camps on the Islands. When employers refused to recognize the union, the federal government became involved. With no progress, the loggers struck in October 1943, winning union recognition from employers and setting the pattern for the rest of the woods industry. In December a contract was signed that covered about eight thousand workers in coastal logging camps. The IWA was also making headway in coastal sawmill operations. In the pulp and paper mills, employers had been largely able to keep the International Brotherhood of Pulp, Sulphite and Paper Mill Workers at bay during the Depression. There were only weak locals at Powell River and Ocean Falls at the outbreak of the war, but by 1945 there were locals at all five mills on the coast and they had achieved union recognition.[5]

At the end of the war, employers struck back, trying to undermine the unions once the special circumstances of the war had disappeared. But workers held firm. A massive IWA strike in 1946 involved some thirty-seven thousand workers, and after thirty-seven days on the picket line they won a wage increase, a shorter work week, and provisions for pay for overtime work. Most importantly, the strike affirmed the presence of the IWA on the coast. In the Interior of the province the IWA had more years of struggle; a bitter strike in 1953 finally put the union on firmer ground. Other unions also had successes. Workers at the Cominco smelter in Trail won union recognition for their Mine Mill union in the summer of 1944. Across the province new unions won gains and established unions expanded. By 1953 about 54 percent of BC wage workers, according to federal government data, belonged to unions.[6]

Governments also shored up the legal support for collective bargaining. PC 1003, the federal legislation passed as a wartime measure, expired in 1947. The federal parliament passed the Industrial Relations and Disputes Investigation Act in 1948, a measure patterned on PC 1003, which applied

International Woodworkers of America Ladies' Auxiliary march, 1946. Courtesy of Mona Morgan and the Trade Union Research Bureau. Pacific Northwest Labor History Association Collection.

to federal workers. At the provincial level, British Columbia brought in the Industrial Conciliation and Arbitration Act of 1947, and though unions questioned particulars in the legislation, the general thrust was seen as providing security for workers and their elected representatives.

The union struggle was abetted by political pressure from the CCF, which emerged as a major political presence in the 1940s. In the 1941 BC provincial election, the CCF increased its share of the popular vote to 33.6 percent, electing fourteen MLAs, the second greatest number in the assembly, making the CCF the Official Opposition. The election of Tom Uphill, a non-CCF leftist in Fernie running under the Labour banner, meant that there were fifteen leftists in the assembly and that the leftist popular vote was even higher than the CCF tally. Prominent elected CCFers included Grace MacInnis, Wallis Lefeaux, Ernest Winch, and Harold Winch. Remarkably, the CCF won more of the popular vote than either the Liberals, who won twenty-one seats with 32.94 percent of the vote, or the Conservatives, who won twelve seats with 30.91 percent of the vote. The CCF held its solid base of support in the 1940s. In the 1945 provincial election, the CCF won 37.62 percent of the popular vote and elected ten members. The non-CCF left elected one member — Tom Uphill in Fernie — and won 4.48 percent of the popular vote. In the 1949 provincial election, CCF fortunes slipped slightly, but the party elected seven members on the strength of 35.10 percent of the popular vote. Uphill, on the Labour ticket, was again elected.

While CCF support was buoyant, the CPC struggled in the late 1940s. The fortunes of provincial communists were linked to international events. In August 1939, the Soviet Union entered into a non-aggression pact with Nazi Germany, and when war broke out in September, the Soviet Union proceeded to gobble up parts of Poland. For international communists, who had spent the previous four years building anti-fascist organizations, this was indeed a stunning reversal. Labelling the war an imperialist, capitalist adventure was not totally persuasive, especially as most British Columbians heeded the call of Empire and prepared to support the war effort. In June 1940, the Canadian government declared the CPC illegal, an organization undermining the war effort. Prominent communists were arrested across the land and sent to internment camps. The CPC was on the wrong side of history in Canada.

This situation was, however, short-lived. On 22 June 1941, Hitler invaded the Soviet Union, and German troops moved toward Moscow. The Soviet Union became Canada's ally in the fight against Nazism. Communists now became enthusiastic supporters of the Allied war effort, buying Victory bonds, discouraging strikes to maintain full war production, and enlisting in large numbers to go overseas. The Soviet Union, the home of a worldwide revolution, had to be saved. The role of communist activists in Canada and the sacrifices of the Soviet Union in the fight against Hitler made it much more difficult to attack the CPC. The federal government released communists who had been put into internment camps because of their anti-war stance, under the condition that they engage in no political activities. Canadian communists responded by establishing a new political party in 1943, the Labour Progressive Party (LPP).

Committed to a total victory over fascism and anticipating harmonious relations between the Soviet Union and the West after the successful conclusion of the war, the CPC/LPP eschewed revolutionary rhetoric, gave full support to the war effort, and offered to work productively with the CCF. The CCF was reluctant to cooperate and was now damned by the communists for fomenting class divisions and strikes. The communist hope for continuing harmonious relations between Canada and the Soviet Union was such that in the 1945 federal election the LPP supported the Liberal Party in ridings where there was no communist candidate. In the 1945 BC election, the LPP ran twenty-one candidates and won 16,479 votes, 3.52 percent of the provincial total. Candidates included Harold Pritchett, Nigel Morgan, Maurice Rush, Tom McEwen, and Bruce Mickleburgh, who won 14.31 percent of the vote in Prince Rupert.

The post-war era did not unfold as Canadian communists expected. The Cold War divided East against West. The West, led by the United States, moved to stop the spread of Soviet influence around the world. Moreover, there was a battle of ideologies: religion versus atheism, democracy versus dictatorship, capitalism versus socialism. In North America, the Cold War became increasingly intense, as Canadian and American governments cracked down on communists, portraying them as agents of a foreign power bent on overturning the North American way of life. Following the 1945 defection of a Soviet cipher clerk, Igor Gouzenko, in Ottawa, eighteen Canadian communists were arrested and tried for espionage, including Fred Rose, an elected member of parliament from a Quebec riding. Rose was sentenced to six years in prison and served most of his term.

It was difficult being a communist in Canada after 1945. In the 1949 provincial election, the BC section of the LPP ran only two candidates, Nigel Morgan in the Alberni Valley and Viola May Bianco in Vancouver East. They won only 1,660 votes, a meagre 0.24 percent of the provincial popular vote. In 1952, the LPP candidates in four ridings (Alberni, Nanaimo, North Vancouver, and Vancouver East, where they ran two candidates) won 0.33 percent of the popular vote on the first ballot. Other anti-CCF leftists included Tom Uphill in Fernie, running as a Labour candidate and winning, Emil Bjarnason, running as an Independent in Vancouver-Burrard, and Orville Braaten, running under the auspices of the Labour Representation Committee in Vancouver Centre. In 1953, twenty-five candidates earned 1.03 percent of the popular vote on the first ballot. Clearly the LPP was still not a contender in the battle to represent the left in provincial politics.

The communists, however, were powerful in union politics. Dedication, discipline, and idealism made them good organizers. They also knew how to run efficient meetings, and they knew that in order to retain elected office they had to deliver better wages and improved working conditions. Important unions in the 1940s were dominated by members of the Communist Party, including the IWA, the Mine, Mill and Smelter Workers, the Boilermakers and Shipyard Workers, and the Longshoremen. While they were particularly prominent in the BC Federation of Labour industrial unions, they also had a presence in a number of Trades and Labour Congress (TLC) craft unions. The communists were legitimate leaders, having played crucial roles in either organizing the unions or sustaining them. They had gone into plants and camps when no other organizers were either willing or interested. Moreover, unions were elected bodies, and the membership elected the communists. According to Irving Abella, "The British Columbia industrial labour movement was, at least until 1948, almost a personal fiefdom of the Communist Party."[7]

The CPC had many enemies in the late 1940s and these enemies exploited circumstances to their advantage. Employers, who were as anti-union as they were anti-communist, used the image of the foreign, un-Canadian Reds, as the communists were called, to keep unions at bay. Governments distinguished between responsible unions and irresponsible unions, with communist-led unions in the latter camp. The CCF, too, retained its hostility to the CPC, building on years of conflict. The CCF naturally sought the endorsement of provincial unions, seeing unions as important to their eventual political success. Unions could provide money and organizers at elections to help the fortunes of the party. The British Labour Party was the model. In BC, however, the union movement as a whole was not willing to endorse the CCF. Part of the reason for this was the influence of communists in unions. As a result, CCF supporters in the union movement saw the CPC as an enemy.

Communist foreign policy pronouncements, which supported the Soviet Union, also undermined CPC support. In the last half of the 1940s, Canadian communists attacked the Marshall Plan, an American program to rebuild an anti-communist Europe, and the creation of NATO, because it threatened the Soviet Union. They portrayed the United States as a hostile, imperialist, war-mongering nation, arguing that Canada should remove itself from American economic and military influence. In the unions, communists, who had sustained their legitimacy by providing solid leadership and delivering material rewards to members, increasingly began to inject debates about international events into union meetings. The interests of the CPC began to trump bread-and-butter trade union issues, perhaps understandably in the Cold War context. For anti-communists the new environment opened up avenues for attack.

The main communist strongholds were the industrial unions affiliated to the Canadian Congress of Labour, represented provincially in the BC

Federation of Labour. Communists essentially controlled the Federation. The national CCL sent out a special organizer, Bill Mahoney, and he worked with a CCF trade union committee to undermine the influence of the communists. In individual unions, moderates won control of executive positions. In 1948 the anti-communists narrowly secured control of the BC Federation of Labour, capturing five of nine executive positions. The victory was slim; two ballots that the anti-communists won were decided by one vote.[8]

Communists and anti-communists battled for control of the province's largest union, the IWA. Communists had played a crucial role in organizing the woodworkers, and they enjoyed the support of the membership, which was clear in the union elections of 1946. But there was trouble for the Reds. A New Westminster local, known as the White Bloc, spearheaded the opposition, and in 1946 they seized on administrative gaffes to raise doubts about the competency of the Red Bloc executive. In early 1947, the White Bloc took control of the local in elections and began criticizing the provincial leadership. They raised concerns about international communist politics taking precedence over immediate worker needs and claimed that the Reds were not managing union finances appropriately. The international leadership of the IWA in the United States supported the Canadian anti-communist forces, doing what they could to undermine the Reds.

At this point the BC communists made a fateful decision. In October 1948, they set up a new independent Canadian union, the Woodworkers Industrial Union of Canada (WIUC), anticipating that the rank-and-file would follow them and exit the IWA to join the WIUC. It did not go smoothly, and bitter battles ensued in the camps and mills across the province. There was violence and families divided between the two camps, with some brothers supporting the Reds and other brothers supporting the Whites. In the end the IWA prevailed, although in some areas the WIUC remained in operation until the late 1950s. Communists were blacklisted from the union and forced to find jobs in other industries or at non-union sites.[9] Another Red-led union, made up of coastal fishermen, was forced out of the House of Labour in 1953. Nevertheless, communist sympathizers did not totally disappear from BC unions. Those who did not hold direct party affiliation were able to declare that they were not members of the CPC and thus retain union positions.

The upsurge of the CCF in the 1941 provincial election led to a political realignment in BC. After the election there were calls from across the province for the creation of a coalition among the political parties to cope with the war and with fears about the instability of a minority government. Initially the CCF was invited to join, but leader Harold Winch quickly declined, saying that his party was too different from the others, a stance likely anticipated by the Liberals and Conservatives. Premier Duff Pattullo was against any coalition. He was not afraid of the CCF and believed that they would sustain his Liberals in a minority government. For Pattullo, the Tories were worse enemies than the CCF. However, most Liberals thought otherwise, and thus a coalition government made up of Liberals and Conservatives was formed. As a result, Pattullo resigned as premier and leader of the Liberal party. John Hart replaced him. Thus began twelve years of Liberal-dominated Coalition Government rule in British Columbia, a government dedicated to containing the socialist threat.

Partly a response to the rise of the left, reform was prominent in the liberalism of the 1940s, and the government increasingly embraced government action in economic and social life. Reform sentiment also reflected the fact that the war legitimized a greater role for the state. The federal government imposed wage and price controls, rationed goods available to consumers, and coordinated and even dictated production in crucial sectors. Despite glitches and inconveniences, the federal Liberals were given high marks for their management of the war economy. More people were willing to accept a greater role for government in their lives. The new liberalism also drew on the economic thinking of the British economist John Maynard Keynes. His ideas offered an intellectual rationale for an activist government, and for forty years Keynesianism dominated economic thought.

Because the left largely supported the policies and programs put forward by Keynesian liberals, a basic understanding of Keynesian ideas is necessary. The CCF saw these reforms as the beginning of a positive trend: the leftward shift of the political spectrum would ultimately lead to their election and the implementation of their brand of socialism. The momentum was to be encouraged. Keynes' most influential treatise was published in 1936, and in the late 1930s his acolytes took on increasingly influential roles in western governments. Keynes argued that governments could actually play a crucial role in managing the economy. In the 1930s economic orthodoxy stressed that during depressions governments could do little except tighten their belts, control spending, balance budgets if possible, and avoid debt. When governments did spend during economic downturns, it was out of political desperation or to be seen as doing something, rather than as part of a coherent, well-rounded policy.

Keynes argued that during economic downturns governments should increase the money supply, lower interest rates, and initiate government-funded public works. The goal was to stimulate economic activity — prime the pump — with the government seed money flowing through the economy and having a multiplying effect. From this perspective, government make-work projects and even welfare and relief payments to the unemployed were not charity for the needy but instead sound economic policy. These programs put money in the pockets of consumers, who spent the money on goods and services, thus generating jobs and business activities for others. Governments, then, could ameliorate the effects of economic downturns.

On the other hand, when economic indicators suggested inflation and an overheated economy, the government was to intervene, raising interest rates, shrinking the money supply, and increasing taxes, building up a fund to be spent in the next economic downturn. Political pressure for favours, the complexity of the economy, dependence on export markets that could not be controlled, and the difficulty of increasing taxes during a boom made implementation of Keynesianism difficult, but by the end of the war all Canadian jurisdictions at least talked the Keynesian line. In 1945 the federal government's belief in its ability to manage the economy was such that it promised Canadians full employment.

Closely linked to Keynesian economics was increased support for government-run social programs, a long-standing demand from the left. The

model here was again from Britain. The 1942 Beveridge Report laid out
the plans for the British welfare state that were put into practice after the
war. These ideas could not be written off by Canadians as the bleatings
of continental European extremists. These were British ideas through and
through. In 1944 the Canadian federal government brought in a family
allowance program that allowed monthly payments to women for each
of their children. It was at one level a program to improve the health of
Canadian children. At another level it made economic sense because putting money in the hands of women, who would spend it on food, clothing,
and shoes, would stimulate the economy and help avert an anticipated
post-war recession. It was also politically popular. With the Keynesian
welfare state, twentieth-century reform liberalism reached its intellectual
apogee. The benevolent, guiding state would keep the capitalist economy
humming. Unemployment would be temporary, and government programs would help workers move smoothly between jobs. Social programs
would afford all citizens a relatively equal opportunity to succeed in society. Education, welfare services for poor children, and broad health care
would give all a chance at economic success, moderate somewhat the
disparities between rich and poor, and undercut the momentum of more
extreme ideas coming from the left.

   In BC, the Liberal members of the Coalition Government adapted to
the new Keynesian era. In 1941, in anticipation of the eventual successful
conclusion of the war, a post-war rehabilitation council was established.
It was headed by the Liberal Harry Perry and included two CCFers,
Grant MacNeil and Harold Winch. Planning was seen as necessary to
sustain prosperity and to avoid a post-war recession, such as had occurred
after World War I. Spending increased on infrastructure, especially high-
ways, railways, and rural electrification. In 1949 the government put in
place a government-run hospital insurance system, a progressive measure
that was the first of its kind in Canada.

   The CCF agreed with these initiatives, but demanded more, calling for
government control of the production and distribution of electricity, and
the nationalization of the brewing and distilling industries, as well as the
sugar and insurance industries. Members talked about experiments in
collective farming, a government-run forest industry, a more progressive

tax system, and a comprehensive welfare system. The language was getting cocky: in November 1943, BC's CCF leader Harold Winch spoke out in Alberta, stating that "When we become the government, we will institute socialism immediately. . . . If capitalism says 'no', then we know the answer — so did Russia." When asked for clarification, Winch stated, quite sensibly, that force would be used to control those who disobeyed the law.[10] The future for the left in politics seemed bright.

The leftward tracking of BC political culture was paralleled by changes in the social realm in the late 1940s, when blatant anti-Asian racism waned and a human rights discourse gained more traction. For Japanese Canadians, of course, the events of the Second World War were hardly auspicious and, in the early years, the left was of little help. In 1942, responding to the hysteria of British Columbians after Japan attacked Pearl Harbor on 7 December 1941, the federal government launched a program to remove some 22,000 people of Japanese descent, the majority of whom were Canadian citizens, from coastal British Columbia. They were put in internment camps, many in the Kootenays, for the duration of the war. The left did not distinguish itself in speaking out against the mass removal and confiscation of property. Indeed, virtually nobody in white British Columbia spoke out in early 1942; fear, racism, and economic considerations were rampant. But as the war progressed, and especially after the federal government announced a plan in 1944 to encourage all Canadians of Japanese descent to go permanently to Japan, CCFers, including Ernest Winch, Laura Jamieson, Angus MacInnis, and Grace MacInnis, came to the defence of Japanese Canadians.

The race issue also had prominence in unions. By 1941 all the Japanese workers at Pacific Mills in Ocean Falls, about two hundred in all, were organized in the union, while nineteen whites had not yet signed on. Both the pulp and paper union and the IWA hired Chinese organizers and published union material in Chinese and Japanese. By 1944 Chinese and Sikh Canadians had prominent positions in the IWA. In 1943 the District President of the IWA, the communist Harold Pritchett, accompanied the leader of the CCF, Harold Winch, and nine Sikhs when they met with the provincial cabinet demanding democratic rights for East Indians in the province. The United Fishermen and Allied Workers Union, among other unions, also carried on a campaign against racial discrimination in the 1940s and 1950s.[11]

Nevertheless, the issue of race did not disappear. While the pulp and paper union fought for union membership for Asians and no discrimination on the job based on race, the union leaders assumed that quietly over time the company would only hire whites. When the IWA executive put through a measure in 1945 promoting full rights of citizenship for Japanese Canadians, there was grumbling in many locals.[12] But the trend was clear. In 1947 political discrimination against Canadians of Chinese and Indian descent in BC was removed, and Japanese Canadians received the same rights two years later. Dorothy Steeves and Grace MacInnis were particularly vociferous in plumping for the enfranchisement of Asians. The left, particularly those immersed in class analysis, participated in bringing about changes in laws and attitudes regarding race, but it was not solely a project of the left. Asian Canadians, church groups, and reform liberals were also active.

Racial equality was part of a larger program of human rights that increasingly took on a more prominent role in the left agenda. Canadian leftists had long fought for basic civil rights. The Industrial Workers of the World had led public protests in Vancouver in 1909 and 1912, demanding the right of free speech.[13] In the 1920s and 1930s, the Canadian Labour Defense League, founded by communists, fought for the right of workers and unions. Leftists also figured prominently in campaigns protesting heavy-handed campaigns against communists in the post-war era.[14]

Rights talk held a broad appeal in the late 1940s. The United Nations Universal Declaration of Human Rights of 1948 encapsulated the philosophy and aims of the human rights movement. All human beings, in this assertion, were equal, sharing basic rights that they earned by being human, not by being citizens of a certain country, not by belonging to a certain ethnic group, not by being of a particular sex, and not by adhering to a particular religious faith. These were universal rights embodied in individuals, and were seen as being the pinnacle of western progress. These included the right "to life, liberty and security of person," the right

Arrests at Industrial Workers of the World Vancouver free speech demonstration, 28 January 1912. British Columbia Archives D-06368.

of all to be recognized as persons before the law and to be protected by that law, the right to a trial, the right to own property, the right to freedom of opinion and expression, the right to freedom of peaceful assembly and association, the right not to be compelled to belong to an association, the right to equal access to participate in governing, the right to equal pay for equal work, the right of everyone "to form and to join trade unions for the protection of his [sic] interests; the right to periodic holidays with pay, the right to an education," and "the right to a standard of living adequate for the health and well-being of himself and of his [sic] family, including food, clothing, housing and medical care and necessary social services, and the right to security in the event of unemployment, sickness, disability, widowhood, old age or other lack of livelihood in circumstances beyond his [sic] control."[15] The BC left worked to further this agenda in future years.

It was to be a long struggle, and human rights remained a dream for many in the 1940s. First Nations were still marginalized in BC. Life on reserves was difficult, urban Aboriginals faced discrimination, and land claims were ignored. There was one notable leftist Indigenous activist in this era, the Nisga'a chief Frank Calder. He was from northwestern BC, graduated from Anglican Theological College at the University of British Columbia, and spent time as an IWA organizer before being elected to the provincial legislature as a CCF member in 1949, representing the riding of Atlin. In later decades, Calder was at the forefront in seeking recognition for First Nations land claims in the province, but movement on this issue would not come until the 1970s.

Women's rights were another issue that did not advance substantially in the 1940s, though women continued to run for office. In 1941 three CCF women won provincial seats: Dorothy Steeves, Grace MacInnis, and Laura Jamieson. Two other women, one of whom was Helena Gutteridge, ran as CCF candidates but lost. In the 1945 election, two Labour Progressive candidates were women, although their voter support was negligible. All six CCF female candidates were unsuccessful. In 1949 the five female CCF candidates and the one LPP woman lost. In the 1952 provincial contest, Laura Jamieson won in Vancouver Centre although the two other women CCFers lost. In 1953 the results were poorer. Four female CCFers and seven female LPP candidates lost. In terms of candidates, the left was not unique. All parties ran female candidates. Between 1941 and 1952, Nancy Hodges, a Liberal, and Tilly Rolston, a Conservative who changed to Social Credit, won their seats in all four provincial elections.

In male-dominated unions, the Second World War put the gender issue out front. During the war, women moved from domestic life into the paid workforce in great numbers, responding to the opportunity to earn better money than was available in traditional female jobs and the opportunity to do patriotic service and help the war effort. Most notably, increasing numbers of married women were moving into the paid workforce. Serious labour shortages in unionized industries such as shipbuilding, sawmilling, and pulp and paper brought women into these male enclaves. Despite a few exceptions, the male unionist response was to see the change as necessary but temporary, and they remained committed to retain a gender-based hierarchy, celebrating the role of women in the home. The CCF showed more interest in female wage-earners during the war, but the party fully expected that women would return to their domestic role at the war's end. And for activists such as Dorothy Steeves and Grace MacInnis, despite their different perspectives on reform versus radicalism, they agreed that "gender equality was not the first priority." They were "socialists first and feminists second."[16] Many women accepted their subordinate role in the paid workforce, but others chafed, especially when they were either encouraged or forced to leave their non-traditional jobs at the end of the war. Women, however, had shown that they were able to perform a number of jobs that had been largely restricted to men, and this legacy would have an impact in the later women's activism of the 1960s and 1970s.

Despite bumps and omissions, in the late 1940s it seemed to the left, with the notable exception of the communists, that history was moving in a favourable direction. The political question in BC was whether reform liberalism or the left would prevail and operate the levers of power. For the Coalition Government things looked good. The economy was booming, with the government facilitating capital investment and industrial expansion. If this was right-wing Keynesianism, using the state to facilitate economic growth, the government also paid heed to left-wing Keynesianism by enhancing government-spending on social programs, most notably the government-run hospital-insurance scheme. Big government and big business were working together for the economic and physical health of the population. But events moved quickly and in unanticipated directions.

In the early 1950s, the Coalition Government came unglued. Within the Liberal-dominated Coalition, Conservatives chafed because they were unlikely to get access to power or patronage in the present system, and they were unhappy with the reformist agenda of the Liberals. Moreover, after the 1949 election the CCF seemed contained, unlikely to form a government. It was time to terminate the Coalition, and by 1951 there was open warfare between the Liberal and Conservative factions. In early 1952, the Coalition died. To be sure that the CCF did not gain as Liberals and Conservatives fought it out in individual ridings, potentially allowing CCF candidates to win because of the divided "free enterprise" vote, the Election Act was amended in 1951 to allow for the alternative voting system. At election time, voters would not just vote for their preferred candidate. Rather, they would rank the candidates, noting their favourite, then their second favourite, and on and on. Liberals and Conservatives believed that Liberal supporters would vote Conservative as their second choice and that Conservative supporters would vote Liberal on their second choice. After the election, when the ballots were counted, any candidate winning over fifty percent of the vote would be declared a winner, but in ridings where this did not happen, the candidate with the least number of votes would be disqualified, and his or her second choices would be added to the numbers of the remaining candidates. This process of removing the lowest candidate would continue until one candidate secured fifty percent of the vote.

Despite these well-laid plans, the 1952 provincial election results were a shocker. The CCF won eighteen seats in the provincial legislature, the second-highest number. The victorious party won nineteen and formed the government. For the CCF the close defeat was bitter. Remarkably, they lost, as did the Liberals, who won six seats, and Conservatives, who won four seats, to a relatively new party, the British Columbia Social Credit League, known as the Social Credit Party. Social Credit would govern the province from 1952 to 1972 and again from 1975 to 1991. For the left in BC, fighting Social Credit became its main political task for forty years, and because of this, understanding the arrival of Social Credit and its consolidation of power is important.

There was little inkling that the "crackpot" Social Credit movement was a serious threat, even in early 1952. Social Crediters had been around in British Columbia since the 1930s, but they were marginal, rent by internal dissension, and gaining negligible public support, unlike in Alberta, where they formed the government in 1935 and were still in power in the 1950s. A number of factors precipitated the Social Credit victory. In the late 1940s, the various Social Credit factions worked in harmony. There was also a migration of Albertans to BC in the 1940s, and this solidified connections to Alberta Social Credit. In the early 1950s, too, Alberta Social Credit was directly involved in running and funding election campaigns in BC. Further, there was the unseemly bickering of Conservatives and Liberals as they publicly sniped at each other.

Coalition programs were also open to criticism, especially the poorly managed hospitalization scheme, which not only was an administrative nightmare but also raised the spectre of big government forcing the participation of citizens and companies. But most important, perhaps, was the anxiety of many British Columbians over the arrival of full-scale monopoly capitalism and the seemingly exclusive cozy relationship between big government and big business. In the Interior this translated into massive support for Social Credit. The main issue was the Coalition Government's new forest policy, announced in 1947, whereby forest land was to be turned over to large corporations. What would happen to the small family logging and sawmill firms if they could not get access to timber? Would they be reduced to proletarian status? Moreover, workers with dreams of owning their own company and attaining an independent status were also concerned. If it was the forest industry that raised the greatest anxiety, the burgeoning oil, smelting, and mining industries also caused concern to workers, small businessmen, and farmers.[17] Social Credit candidates offered a populist vision of a society made up of small producers and reinforced anti-monopoly sentiment.

Social Credit spoke to the same constituency as the left, making its appeal to the people, ordinary folk who were not part of the business or government elite. Indeed, most second choices of CCF voters, despite the entreaty of CCF leaders to rank no second candidate, were the Social Credit candidates. Social Credit voters also found much that appealed in the CCF discourse, so their second choice tended to be the CCF. But Social Credit and the CCF were different. The CCF championed the state to manage, control, and eventually defeat corporate BC and usher in the socialist society. Social Credit was critical of big government, but while it was wary of big business, it celebrated the capitalist market system, promising to maintain a place for small business in the new order.

Immediately after the 1952 election it was not clear who would form the government. Social Credit had one more seat, and in all ballot counts the CCF had won more of the popular vote. Tom Uphill, the Labour member from Fernie who was anti-CCF, put in writing that he would support Social Credit, and not the CCF. This made it easier for the Lieutenant-Governor to call upon the new leader of Social Credit, W.A.C. Bennett, chosen after the election by the newly elected Social Credit members of the legislature, to form the government. Bennett was a skilled politician. He orchestrated another provincial election in 1953. In this election Social Credit won a majority government with twenty-eight seats. The CCF total dropped to fourteen, the Liberal total to four, and the Conservative total to one. The rising leftist political tide was stemmed; a new era in BC politics had begun.

Nevertheless, by 1952 the accomplishments of the left were clear, and the results reflected the fact that the left was firing on both cylinders, union action and political action. The union movement was entrenched, providing a home for a greater number of workers than before and taking in a greater diversity of workers. Unskilled and semi-skilled workers in factory settings, many of whom were of non-British descent, now enjoyed a sense of dignity at work and an opportunity to meet employers with greater confidence. The left also had a viable political party in the CCF, a party that seriously threatened to become the government of the province. Even without its control of the reins of power, leftist policies were in place. New social programs, such as unemployment insurance, which had been instituted by the federal Liberal government in 1941, and family allowance, were evidence of the greater role of the state in the daily lives of individuals. The state, guided by the interests of the people, was increasingly managing capitalism. Legislation was in place that helped organize and sustain unions. Leftists also contributed to the fight against racism and the struggle to ensure basic human right for citizens. Communists and CCFers stressed the worth and dignity of working people, exposed the inequities of class in liberal capitalist society, and offered unionism and government representing the interests of ordinary people as the key to the good life. There was a sense that history, in its complex way, was heading toward an era when even more leftist dreams would be realized.

CHAPTER 5

Social Credit, New Movements, and NDP Government: 1954–1975

THE BC LEFT WAS energetic in the 1950s, 1960s, and 1970s. Unionism expanded, finally becoming a presence in the public sector, and politically the New Democratic Party (NDP) superseded the CCF in 1961. Just as the left had seemingly perfected its political and union organizational structures, however, new expressions of protest and leftism erupted. A new sensibility, committed to gender and sexual equality, environmental security, and greater democracy, challenged older values and institutions of the left. Despite friction, the new social movements were much more comfortable with the left than the ruling Social Credit Party, contributing to the election of the NDP in 1972. But there were many twists and turns before the left came to enjoy a turn at running the province.

Social Credit, under the leadership of W.A.C. Bennett, was a powerful adversary. British Columbia was prosperous and while Bennett was not solely responsible for the economic expansion — the Coalition

Government set the stage and the post-war ravenous United States market provided a demand for BC resources — the premier took the credit. In British Columbia between 1951 and 1961, the Gross Domestic Product grew 58 percent and by another 73 percent in the 1960s. In per capita terms, this was a 12 percent increase in the 1950s and a 30 percent increase in the 1960s.[1] In Bennett's British Columbia, construction and production jobs abounded.

But Bennett did more than ride the wave of prosperity. He skillfully managed the transition to the era of big capital, big labour, and big government in BC. This was no simple feat. In 1952 corporations were wary of Social Credit because of its rhetorical ambiguity regarding the place of big business in society. However, big business quickly recognized that the Liberals and Conservatives were now unable to stave off the left, and Social Credit became their anti-socialist vehicle. Bennett's strategy was to declare war on the left, and companies spent much money to help Social Credit win this struggle.[2] This kept the Liberal and Conservative parties at bay ensuring, that with the threat of the left, the right-wing vote would continue to congregate in Social Credit.

At the same time that he embraced big business, Bennett undermined the potential growth of the left by playing to two other constituencies, small business and the Interior. Bennett's rhetoric ennobled the men and women who worked hard, produced material goods, and maintained solid families. These townsfolk developed communities and took advantage of the economic opportunities for ordinary people to improve themselves. In Bennett's world, small and big business harmoniously co-existed. The populist rhetoric was not totally hollow. In the forest industry, for example, while the large corporations took control of the timber supply through new forest management licences, the Social Credit government heeded the alarm and concern of small operators, reserving a percentage of logging for smaller, often family-operated logging companies.[3] In the Interior generally, where the efforts of the government were visible in roads, mills, and smelters, the big corporations were accepted as providing the backdrop for the flowering of prosperous small-town life where local people ran the school boards and city councils, sold each other goods and services, and shared in the bounty of the Social Credit good life.

The left vilified Bennett, portraying him as a ruthless, right-wing ogre, but his behaviour as premier was hardly beyond the typical set of activities pursued by liberal governments in the Keynesian era of the welfare state. Social Credit continued, after some adjustment, the BC Hospital Insurance Service, which had been introduced by the Coalition government in 1949. British Columbia was one of the first five participating provinces in the federal cost-sharing hospital insurance program in 1958, and in 1965 the government put in place a Medicare plan to insure all British Columbians. The next year the federal government brought out its own Medicare program, which BC joined in 1968. As the baby boom made its way through the education system, Social Credit built new schools, hired more teachers, and attempted to equalize the quality of service across the province. In 1963 the University of Victoria succeeded Victoria College and expanded, while on the mainland Simon Fraser University became operational in 1965. To service the Interior and to expand access in Vancouver, a college system was inaugurated in 1965. Soon smaller centres such as Castlegar, Kelowna, Prince George, Nanaimo, and Kamloops had colleges offering first- and second-year university courses that were transferable to the major institutions in the Lower Mainland and Victoria. Spending on social welfare programs also increased in the Social Credit years. In health, welfare, and education, the government, of course, had to hire more personnel, and the size of the public-sector workforce grew.

Nor was Social Credit afraid to intervene directly in the economy. In the late 1950s and early 1960s, Social Credit took over two private ferry companies, the Black Ball and Canadian Pacific Railway lines, that ran vessels linking Vancouver Island to the Mainland. The operation was modernized under the aegis of the crown-owned BC Ferry Corporation. To manage the orderly dispersal of power for economic expansion, the provincial government expropriated a long-established private company, BC Electric, with due compensation, in 1962, and a year later, merged it with the BC Power Commission to create the BC Hydro and Power Authority. Both acquisitions generated a furor and debate. Principled right-wingers and anti-government capitalists fumed at the nationalizations, portraying them as attacks on private property. But both ventures strengthened the overall performance of the economy, improved the opportunity for capital accumulation, and served the broader needs of the business community. Businessmen adapted quickly. On the left, some were discombobulated, especially those whose definition of socialism was merely government action. Bennett thus destabilized his opponents and legitimized his government, while at the same time reinforcing the authority of private corporations in exploiting resources and expanding the economy. For the left, Bennett's Social Credit was a difficult target.

Although Social Credit was stridently anti-union, the provincial union movement continued to expand. In 1945, according to the reports of the BC Department of Labour, 110,045 BC workers belonged to unions, represented by 617 organizations. In 1958, 233,972 union members were represented by 952 organizations. In percentage terms, 38.6 percent of workers in the non-agricultural paid workforce in 1945 were organized, and in 1958, the peak year of the 1950s, 53.9 percent were union members. Notably, much of this growth came in the craft union sector, reflecting the construction boom of the 1950s. The left was realizing a major goal, extending unionism in order to decrease economic inequality and protect the rights and interests of workers and their families. In the 1960s, organization tapered off, largely due to the rise of jobs in the service industry, a sector notoriously difficult to organize. In 1972, 41.8 percent of the workforce — 332,091 people — belonged to unions.[4]

Especially important in this era was the establishment of unions in the public sector. For a number of reasons, government workers were deemed different from workers in the private sector and so not deserving of full union rights. First, their employer was the government, and it was feared that strong unions would press for political change to elect sympathetic governments or force weak governments to unduly raise their compensation packages. Second, high wages in the public sector, it was argued, would have a deleterious impact on the private sector, putting an unfair competitive pressure on wage rates. The limitations in union rights and lower wage rates in the public sector were supposedly balanced by greater job security and stable pension schemes. The same arguments are made nowadays, and leftists are forced to defend public-sector unionism against critics.

Despite the difficulties, public-sector unions were organized and they remain cornerstones of the left today. The Hospital Employees' Union, formed on the industrial union model, was established in 1944. In 1968 they won their first province-wide master agreement and were expanding into long-term care facilities. The Registered Nurses Association of BC won their first hospital certification in 1946, and began engaging in province-wide bargaining in 1959. The BC Teachers' Federation (BCTF) had been incorporated as a benevolent society in the heady days of 1919, aiming to improve workers' wages, pensions, job security, and professional interests. A few strikes occurred, notably in Victoria in 1919 and in New Westminster in 1921, but despite teachers seeking full collective bargaining rights under the law, the government imposed a binding arbitration process in 1939. Teachers continued to struggle. In the 1960s the issue of pensions was at the forefront, and teachers chafed under the petty, anti-teacher politicking of the Social Credit government. Teachers played an important role in the defeat of Social Credit in 1972. Still, they had to wait until 1987 for full collective bargaining rights.[5]

Employees working directly for the provincial government were represented by the BC Government Employees' Union (BCGEU), which traced its roots to the formation of an association in 1919. The organization faced the Social Credit government head-on; it was not always pleasant. In the 1960s the government cancelled their right to strike and refused to grant rights enjoyed by other unions.[6] Finally, under new NDP labour laws, the BCGEU was certified with full collective bargaining rights in 1974. Other public service workers in British Columbia were represented by national unions, including the Canadian Union of Public Employees, the Letter Carriers, the Postal Workers, and the Public Service Alliance, and they, too, achieved full legal union status in the 1960s and 1970s.[7]

In the 1950s the union movement in Canada and BC finally resolved the long-festering conflict between industrial and craft unions, facilitating institutional stability and furthering action in the political arena. The Canadian Labour Congress (CLC) was created in 1956, bringing together the Trades and Labour Congress of Canada (TLC), which represented mainly craft unions, and the Canadian Congress of Labour (CCL), which represented industrial unions. In BC, a committee with representatives from the BC Federation of Labour, the body that largely represented industrial unions, and the BC Trade Union Congress, which had been formed in 1952 to represent craft unions, had begun meeting in 1955. The membership of the two bodies was roughly 42,000 and 45,000 respectively. In 1956 a merger was completed; the new provincial body was called the BC Federation of Labour. The creation of the new BC Federation of Labour was a major achievement, but only half of BC unionists were affiliated.[8] Some unions chose not to join the federation, including four railroad running trades and the teachers. Teachers decided that their professional status differentiated them from other workers in the union movement.

Communist-dominated unions were banned, and so in BC the United Fishermen, the Vancouver Outside Civic Workers, and the Mine, Mill and Smelter Workers were denied membership in the BC Federation of Labour.[9] The lack of communist votes in the BC Federation of Labour allowed endorsement of the CCF, and in 1957 the BC Federation of Labour voted 75 percent in favour of endorsing the CCF.[10] With the com-

Meeting of BC Federation of Labour (CLC), Vancouver, November 1956.
British Columbia Archives E-06072.

munists gone and internal bickering under control, the union movement in the late 1950s concentrated more fully on political action.

The political arena was becoming more important to unions in the mid-1950s because of a new threat on the job, automation. In BC the automation debate began in 1955, when the IWA District office circulated reports and press clippings describing the situation in the United States, where technological change was ahead of Canada. Automation was a new stage in the ongoing development of devices to replace human labour in the production process. Whereas previous technological advances had largely mimicked human physical actions — lifting, pushing, and pulling — automation was about using machines to reproduce human character- istics of observation and decision-making. The logic of the trend was to remove human beings completely from production. The future, it seemed, was about to bring greater unemployment, not full employment. It was quickly recognized as a very serious issue.

Unions negotiated with employers, trying to protect workers affected by technological change, as well as attempting to increase the wages of workers that remained in the plants that profited from automation. Sev- erance packages were negotiated when job loss was unavoidable. The collective bargaining process was fine for workers in industries with pow- erful unions, but even leaders of strong unions felt that the social problem was so great that a second strategy, government action, was necessary. A shorter work week, longer paid holidays, earlier retirement with good pensions, a guaranteed annual wage, and richer unemployment insurance benefits were suggested by the Canadian Congress of Labour as a way to spread the remaining work around, to deal with financial difficulties of unemployment, and to ensure that the working class received its share of the benefits of technological change. Automation, then, made political action even more necessary in the mid-1950s.[11]

The CCF was the main political voice of the left in the 1950s and, like labour, it was also changing. In the aftermath of the 1952 election, Harold Winch stepped down as the leader of the provincial CCF, replaced by Arnold Webster, a mild-mannered Vancouver high school principal.

Workers at a Penticton peach cannery, 1950s. Province, Vancouver.
Vancouver Public Library 41821.

Webster presented the face of moderation, emphasizing a balanced economy, increased spending on social programs, and the Christian basis of the CCF, a counter to the overt religious appeal of Social Credit. In the early stages of the 1956 election campaign, Webster was replaced by Robert Strachan, a Nanaimo carpenter. Strachan, too, sought to reassure voters that the CCF represented nothing radical, and that business need not be alarmed.

The BC CCF continued to adjust its image, following in lockstep with the federal party, with which it was closely affiliated. Provincially and nationally the CCF was torn between the siren of power, the urge to open the tent to more moderate voters, and the siren of principle, where the offering of true socialist principles would lead to a transformed society in the future. In 1956 the national party rewrote its manifesto after much debate at a Winnipeg convention. The Winnipeg Declaration replaced the Regina Manifesto, and the shorter, new document lacked the fire and revolutionary tone of the earlier call to arms. Whereas the Regina Manifesto concluded by calling for the eradication of capitalism, the Winnipeg Declaration ended with a less strident rallying cry: "The CCF will not rest content until every person in this land and in all other lands is able to enjoy equality and freedom, a sense of human dignity, and an opportunity to live a rich and meaningful life as a citizen of a free and peaceful world." This reflected a change from the language of revolutionary socialism to the language of social democracy. Such a statement was not out of place in the new liberalism of the day. Private enterprise was not eschewed, though public and cooperative ventures were encouraged, and capitalism was decried as "basically immoral." The growing inequalities of wealth and opportunity were declared unacceptable, and social democrats, building on the many achievements evident around the world, promised to counter the "move toward totalitarian oppression" with a "wider democracy."[12]

In British Columbia, more radical elements in the party were not happy with the trend. After the 1956 provincial CCF convention, Dorothy Steeves criticized the domination of the moderates within the party, writing sarcastically to Colin Cameron, a CCF member of Parliament from BC: "The country . . . is safe against the onslaughts of socialism. A completely rightist Ex[ecutive] is triumphantly enthroned."[13] By 1964 Cameron worried that Canadian social democracy had become indistinguishable from liberalism. The federal Liberal Party had been rejuvenated during its time in opposition from 1957 to 1963, and the party now stressed an aggressive Keynesianism, richer pensions, and a national Medicare scheme, among other things, in many ways echoing the vision of social democracy. For Cameron, capitalism and private ownership remained immoral, inefficient, and against the interests of the majority of Canadians. He asserted, "we must now start devising methods of removing the industrial complex from private hands."[14]

As the 1950s progressed, both the CCF and organized labour faced problems that pushed them closer together. For the CCF, the more moderate stance of the Winnipeg Declaration did not help their political fortunes. At the federal level the party increased its seats in parliament from twenty-three seats in 1953 to only twenty-five seats in 1957. In the 1958 election John Diefenbaker, a Progressive Conservative, won the greatest landslide victory in Canadian history to that time. The CCF presence in the federal parliament dropped to eight seats, three in Ontario, four in British Columbia, and only one in Saskatchewan, a province that had sent ten members to Ottawa in 1957 and eleven in 1953. The strength of the CCF was now in the industrial, unionized regions of Canada. To build on this base, many CCFers wanted to pattern their organizational structure on the British Labour Party, a party that brought together unions and political leftists in a formal alliance. The Labour Party had been successful in Britain, and had overseen the establishment of an extensive welfare state immediately after World War II.

Unionists, for their part, were alarmed by the election of Diefenbaker. It conjured up memories of R.B. Bennett, the last Conservative prime minister. Bennett was notoriously anti-union, a man willing to go to great lengths to crush the left in any of its guises. With regard to the threat of automation, unionists looked to the CCF, which was quick to acknowledge the problem and offer solutions. In the summer of 1955 the BC section of the CCF identified the "new industrial revolution" and bemoaned a future where many workers would be replaced by machines, facing the "dismal prospect of finding other employment." The party proposed increased public works, the encouragement of secondary manufacturing, and complete federal control of unemployment to deal with this national issue.[15]

Unions were also keen to elect left governments in order to secure favourable labour legislation at the provincial level. The Social Credit government in British Columbia was relentless in attacking unions in the 1950s. The Social Credit government passed a new Labour Relations Act in 1954. It restricted the activities of unions during strikes, weakened the power of the Labour Relations Board in favour of the government's minister of labour, and increased financial penalties for unions and union officers breaching the terms of the legislation. The union movement came together, seeing it as an attack on the rights that they had won in the 1940s. A delegation of three hundred union leaders descended on Victoria, demanding amendments to the legislation, but to no avail. Unions were also concerned about the increased use of *ex parte* injunctions, whereby employers could unilaterally obtain the support of one judge, who, if he agreed that a union was acting unfairly in restraint of trade during a strike, could issue an injunction to prohibit picketing.[16] In 1959 the government passed Bill 43, a new Trade Union Act that outlawed sympathy strikes, boycotts and secondary picketing, and made unions liable for legal prosecution. The BC Federation of Labour and the CCF were united in their attack on the legislation.[17]

Unions and the CCF, in BC and in Canada, had problems, and in the late 1950s labour and CCF representatives began talking together about forming a new political party to increase the clout of the left. Although this was a national initiative, the provincial CCF and BC unions, such as the International Woodworkers of America, gave much support to the project. In Ottawa in the summer of 1961, a new party called the New Democratic Party was born and the CCF disappeared. While the CCF had allowed for the affiliation of unions, granting them special voting rights, organized labour actually participated as an equal in the creation of the NDP. Representatives of the CLC played a key role, but once the party was created the CLC did not formally affiliate as a whole, though it still endorsed the NDP. It was left to individual locals to decide whether or not to join the new party.

British Columbia Social Credit responded to the new party in 1961 by passing Bill 42, an amendment to the Labour Relations Act that prohibited unions from contributing funds that came from dues to any political party. The Labour Minister, Leslie Peterson, was honest, stating that Bill 42 was directed at the new NDP-labour alliance. He mounted his defence by arguing that his government was protecting the rights of individual union members, especially those that did not support the NDP.[18] Union democracy was thus again declared illegitimate. There was no equivalent to restrict the rights of employers to give financial support to the Social Credit Party.

Although the CCF/NDP lost six successive provincial elections between 1956 and 1969, they were still the dominant party of the left. The CCF/NDP percentage of the popular vote fluctuated between 27.8 percent and 33.92 percent. In terms of seats, their representation in the provincial legislature ranged from ten to twelve. Other leftists were less successful. Canadian communists suffered a major blow in 1956, when the Communist Party of the Soviet Union acknowledged and made public the litany of crimes, including "assassinations, mass arrests, political executions, torture, false confessions, frame-ups, [and] deportations of whole nations" carried out during the Stalin regime. Many Canadian communists were shocked at the revelations, and party membership declined.[19] According to one account, in some union locals communists burrowed deep into their organizations: "In Local 213 [of the International Brotherhood of Electrical Workers] most of them burrowed so deep as to appear to have abandoned communism."[20]

The Communist Party of Canada, running under the Labour Progressive Party banner in 1956, ran fourteen candidates, almost exclusively in the Lower Mainland and on Vancouver Island. Province-wide they received less than half of 1 percent of the popular vote. In the two-member riding of Delta, CCF dominance was clear: the two CCF candidates received 11,202 and 10,798 votes, respectively, while the two LPP candidates received 355 and 272 votes. Only four communist candidates ran in the 1963 and 1969 provincial elections, while five ran in 1972 and six contested the 1966 election. In 1969 the CPC candidates received 10 percent of 1 percent of the popular vote in the province. In the two-member Vancouver East riding, a left stronghold, the CPC candidates won 159 and 209 votes. The victorious NDP candidates, Alex MacDonald and Bob Williams, won 13,006 and 12,768 votes respectively. Thirteen communist candidates won about one-tenth of one percent of the provincial vote in 1975. Some communists and activists close to the communists became increasingly active in city politics, notably in Vancouver after 1968 where they worked with labour and other leftists in the Coalition of Progressive Electors (COPE) to elect candidates to civic bodies.

Beyond the CPC there was an array of radical Marxists. There were anti-Soviet Maoist groups committed to the Chinese revolutionary way, and Trotskyists who followed the thought of Leon Trotsky. Some leftists were inspired by the Albanian or Yugoslavian versions of communism as the way of the future, and the Socialist Party of Canada still existed.[21] A few groups fielded candidates in the 1970s. There were also people that were not neatly categorized, people who had no official public connection to any leftist group, but who still travelled in the same circles.

Within the left there was ongoing tension among various factions in the post-war era. Communists were denied executive positions and even membership in mainstream unions. In 1955 George Gee was purged from the Vancouver local of the International Brotherhood of Electrical Workers for communist associations.[22] Communists and other non-NDP leftists continued to have small caucuses in unions such as the IWA. In 1973, for example, thirteen woodworkers met in Nanaimo at a conference organized by the CPC to set out their agenda for woods-workers.[23]

The CCF/NDP leadership was also on the outlook for radical leftists in their ranks. In 1949, after the communists had been purged from the BC union movement, the national treasurer of the CCL warned the provincial CCF that if they did not get rid of Reds and fellow travellers in their ranks, no union money would be forthcoming to help the BC CCF at election times.[24] In 1950 a left-wing caucus — The Socialist Fellowship — emerged in the BC CCF. It was mainly a Vancouver group that included Colin Cameron, Wallis Lefeaux, and Rodney Young, but to the party leadership they were too far to the left and thus a threat. The group was forced to disband.[25] In the 1960 provincial election, some CCF candidates had close ties to the radical left.[26] The CCF, and later the NDP, worried about members belonging to two different political organizations, with presumably the more radical connection dominant, and the possibility of radical utterances and relationships sullying the appeal of the party at election time.

While the left continued to fight old battles that dated back decades, new issues and challenges arose. A vigorous Canadian nationalism took on a sense of urgency in the 1960s. The nationalist surge was relevant to both the unionism and politics of the left. In the union movement the new nationalism forcefully raised the question of whether it was beneficial to belong to unions that were headquartered in the United States, unions in which Canadians comprised a minority. In the broader political economy, the new nationalism demanded that the federal government use its powers to control and undermine the influence of American corporations in Canadian economic and cultural life. Nationalists, then, sought to curtail corporate power and to enhance the reach of government to serve the interests of the people, both prominent features of the left.

Already in the late 1940s and 1950s some prominent federal Liberals and Conservatives, such as Vincent Massey, the head of a royal commission that led to the creation of the Canada Council in 1957, Walter Gordon, the head of a royal commission on the Canadian economy, and John Diefenbaker, worried about the negative impact of the United States on Canadian culture and foreign policy, as well as the problems of the high degree of American ownership of corporations active in the Canadian economy.[27] Then, in the mid-1960s, there was growing dismay regarding the direction of American society, where there was blatant, brutal racism and the intensification of the Vietnam War. Whereas often in the past the United States had been seen as a beacon of hope, a model society to be emulated, by the late 1960s in many quarters the United States was considered morally bankrupt, a cruel, racist war machine dedicated to world domination. For many Canadians, the United States had become a failed experiment, a historical project to be rejected.

A sense of optimism based on the ongoing prosperity and a semblance of unity, supported by the propaganda of the centennial celebrations of 1967, created a confident feeling in Canada that it was time to go in a new direction, independent of the United States. In the cultural realm, there was a call for more Canadian movies to reflect the Canadian experience; more Canadian-born professors to explain and discuss Canadian politics, Canadian literature, Canadian history, and Canadian sociology; and more Canadian authors, magazines and publishers to get out Canadian stories. In the economic realm there was a demand for increased control of the Canadian economy by Canadian business. The Canadian economy should be run by Canadians for Canadians. The reach of nationalist sentiment was broad, but the left embraced it with particular gusto.

Nationalism was not new to the left; there had long been a nationalist undercurrent in the Canadian union movement. Most Canadian unionists belonged to American-dominated unions, but a minority fought for independent Canadian organizations. In the 1920s, for example, some BC

All-Canadian Congress of Labour on parade, 1936. Vancouver Public Library 13323.

workers participated in the All-Canadian Congress of Labour (ACCL), formed in Montreal in 1927. The organization sought to bring together Canadian unions and thus challenge the role of international unions in the lives of Canadian workers. These critics of international unionism argued that their dues were going to the United States and that they received little in return. Moreover, they said, decisions made by American leaders at union headquarters in the United States too often did not reflect Canadian concerns. For the majority of union members, though, the larger strike fund, the greater muscle of belonging to a bigger union, and the availability of better services that could be provided by a large organization made international unions desirable. Nevertheless, in Vancouver a group of carpenters and waterfront workers affiliated to the ACCL, and on Vancouver Island coal miners signed up. The ACCL went on to organize labourers, painters, electrical workers, boilermakers and musicians in Vancouver. This nationalist initiative, however, was short-lived; the ACCL merged into the Canadian Congress of Labour in 1940.

Anti-Americanism revived in the union movement in the 1950s, a time when American unions tended to be more conservative than Canadian unions and prone to corruption and undemocratic, dictatorial leadership. Very public investigations by the American government exposed much unsavoury union activity in the late 1950s. In 1963, four coastal BC locals broke away from the international union for pulp and paper workers, the International Brotherhood of Pulp, Sulphite and Paper Mill Workers (IBPSPMW), joining with a new local at a Castlegar facility to form what would become the Pulp and Paper Workers of Canada, an independent Canadian union that waved the Canadian flag and embodied the principles of grassroots, rank-and-file control. The new union continued to poach IBPSPMW locals over the next decade.[28] In the early 1970s, the Canadian Association of Smelter and Allied Workers successfully raided the 1,800-member-strong local that represented Alcan workers at Kitimat, taking them from the United Steelworkers of America.[29]

Leftist concern about foreign ownership in the Canadian economy was an issue before the late 1960s, but it had been a hard sell, as CPC leader Tim Buck found when touring British Columbia during the winter of 1948–49. Workers cared little about the nationality of employers, he noted:

"Their attitude was: What difference does it make to me if the company that exploits me is a Canadian company or an American company? If I've got to be exploited, I don't care who it is. I just want to get the most I can for my labour."[30] Prince Rupert leftist BC union activist Angus Macphee offered his critique of foreign ownership to an American colleague in 1961: "Did you ever stop to realize that Canada to a lesser degree is comparable to Cuba? That American capital dominates our economy? That few secondary industries exist? [T]hat our unemployment figures are higher than yours, and in similar industries (excluding the South . . .) our wages are substantially lower? These facts are related."[31]

In the 1960s and 1970s, leftist analysis offered persuasive support for Canadian nationalism. Montreal economist Kari Levitt published her much-read critique, *Silent Surrender*, in 1970. She argued that Canada was a branch-plant economy, where American firms set up subsidiary operations in Canada. Profits from these facilities largely went back to corporate headquarters in the United States rather than being reinvested in the Canadian economy; business decisions were made from an American perspective; and crucial research-and-development — the creative, high-skilled part of corporate activity that ensured strong future development — was done in the United States. If nothing changed, she argued, the future for Canada was bleak. Stunted economic growth, less-skilled assembly-line jobs, and dependency on the fortunes and decisions of corporate America doomed Canada to a slow slide into total dominance by the United States.[32]

Mel Watkins' analysis of the Canadian predicament was more historical but arrived at similar conclusions. He drew on the writings of an earlier generation of Canadian political economists who argued that Canadian history was built around the development of a series of staples, in Canada's case, natural resources. Fish, furs, wheat, timber, and minerals succeeded each other at the heart of the economy, and their needs drove political, financial, transportation, and technological development. Characteristic of staple industries was a reliance on foreign investment capital and foreign markets, a vulnerable situation in which Canada was dependent on others. Moreover, staple industries required a workforce with little skill. According to Watkins, the Canadian economy was still a staple resource economy in the 1960s. The problem was how to move beyond the staple economy to a fully developed, technologically sophisticated, diverse manufacturing economy. This was not simple, as Canada was locked in a staple trap, unable to progress to the next level.

To escape this situation, a new economy based on equipment manufacturing, consulting services, innovative transportation methods, technologically sophisticated byproducts, and increased local value added to simple products was needed.[33] Business alone was unwilling and unable to do the job; only government, through the increased capture of resource rents and a focused investment and development strategy, could reshape the Canadian economy. The staples analysis became prominent in British Columbia, especially as applied by Patricia Marchak to the provincial forest industry, which was becoming increasingly owned by American firms.[34]

The general thrust of the nationalist economic critique appealed to many, including progressive liberals and some supporters of Canadian conservatism, and they all looked to government to bring about change. It was feared that the greater size of American corporations, with their economies of scale and rich advertising budgets, would in time completely dominate the Canadian film, magazine, and book industries, as well as the Canadian manufacturing and resource sectors; only the state had the power to counteract the pull of American capitalism and keep Canada independent. In the late 1960s, the Canadian state still had cachet. The federal welfare state reached its apogee in the late 1960s. Medicare, the Canada Pension Plan, and the Canada Assistance Program, with the acquiescence and assistance of the provinces, were put in place by the Pearson and Trudeau Liberal governments. Government was still seen as a positive force in Canadian society. In the 1970s, prominent Liberals sang the nationalist song.

In the left there were moderate and radical expressions of nationalism. For the radicals, the nationalist push was seen as a stage on the road to socialism. First, get rid of American capital and then turn the guns on Canadian capital. But the radical voices were drowned out by support for the more moderate social democracy, where the state would manage the economy, provide social services, sustain an independent Canadian culture, and deliver the good life. Indeed, in the public mind, socialism was now largely seen as a strong, democratic government regulating and managing a capitalist economy for the good of society. It was a vision of social democracy, not revolutionary socialism.

The nationalist issue also exposed fundamental fault lines in the federal NDP. In late April 1969, eleven NDP members, including Mel Watkins, met in Toronto. They put forward a manifesto entitled "For an Independent Socialist Canada," also known as the Waffle Manifesto. The unfortunate name came from an early meeting where a member said something to the effect that if we are going to waffle on the issue of public ownership, I would rather waffle to the left than to the right.[35] By the summer of 1969 the Waffle, which wanted to make the NDP "a true socialist party," had ninety-four members, including BC MLAs Dave Barrett, Eileen Dailly, Gordon Dowding, Jim Lorimer, and Alex Mac-Donald.[36]

The Waffle then set about asserting its agenda at NDP conventions. But criticism of American unions, the call for increased public ownership and even worker control of factories did not win over the majority of party members. The Waffle was too nationalist and too socialist. At the 1971 federal NDP convention in Ottawa, Waffle candidate Jim Laxer unsuccessfully challenged David Lewis for the leadership of the party. Lewis' victory was ensured by the overwhelming support of the international unions. By 1972 the Waffle had become an independent group within the NDP, acting publicly on its own account and not adhering to the party line. For this the NDP passed a resolution forcing the Waffle to disband. Many individual Waffle members left the NDP, while others made their peace with the party. Soon after, the Waffle movement disintegrated. A few Wafflers formed the Revolutionary Marxist Group, a Trotskyist organization that ran candidates in the 1975 BC provincial election.[37]

The thread of nationalism was entangled with a number of other threads in the late 1960s, creating the loose knot that was the Sixties in Canada. New social movements called for gender and sexual equality, peace, concern and respect for the natural environment, and student rights. These movements injected fresh ideas and energy into BC political culture,

using tactics similar to those long-employed by the left, including protests, demonstrations, petitions, and marches, and while the analysis may
not have satisfied a Marxist theoretician, there was a general critique of
"the establishment," loosely defined as the ruling elite in business, industry, government and politics, what President Eisenhower had labelled
the "military-industrial complex." The slogan "Power to the People"
captured the alternative. The new movements differed from the established left in that they tended not to form disciplined, hierarchical organizations. Nor did they focus on unionization and working-class issues,
or care about the many doctrinal and personal disputes that had divided
left over the previous eighty years.

Running through the various groups and organizations was the New
Left sensibility. Unlike the nationalist movement, the New Left was not
Canadacentric; indeed, it came from the United States. As the name sug-
gests, the New Left was critical of the Old Left, the union and political
structures developed in the 1930s and 1940s. The New Left emphasized
a coalition of opposition, where unions were just one group among many,
and where the coalition was built from the bottom up, incorporating
grassroots support from a broad spectrum of student, farmer, anti-poverty,
neighbourhood, anti-racist, worker, and women's organizations. There
was a distrust of bureaucracy and entrenched leaderships, and the goal
was a decentralized, democratic, fluid, flexible organizational structure.
The BC section of the Communist Party of Canada offered a perspective
on the provincial New Left in 1967: "This ideology is essentially non-class,
anti-organizational, existentialist, and bourgeois-objective in character,
and has particular appeal to young people. It is significant in that it finds
virtually no reflection in the industrial trade union movement."[38]

Without leaders and a specific organization, it is difficult to locate the
New Left precisely in British Columbia political space. But it did have a
presence. Community protests against freeways through neighbourhoods,
student activism, free speech demonstrations, the peace movement, the
women's movement, and environmental causes all reflected the influence
of New Left thinking.[39] And while class may not have been understood
in the Marxist sense, and theoretical thinking was not rigorous, there was
still radicalism in the New Left, a nebulous class perspective that called

for a new social order, an overthrowing of the establishment, a world beyond capitalism, and a hope for a just society of equals.

And, despite the interpretation of the Communist Party, the New Left impulse could be found in the union movement.[40] In the 1960s, restlessness among the rank-and-file, a restlessness that challenged the control of union leaders as well as employers, expressed itself in wildcat strikes. Wildcats are unauthorized strikes that originate on the shop floor and in camps. A key part of collective agreements was that the union agreed not to strike during the term of the contract. Wildcatters flouted these agreements, putting themselves at odds with the law, employers, and their union. Usually the strikes dealt with local issues such as the demotion of a colleague, the dismissal of a popular foreman, changes in scheduling, or working conditions. A number of factors contributed to wildcat fever. Workers were more educated than previous generations, and they had higher expectations. This was also a time, the Sixties, when young people sought personal satisfaction in their lives and their work, and in the factories most jobs were boring and dreary. High employment levels and richer social welfare programs also gave workers greater security and the confidence to launch "spontaneous" job actions. In British Columbia, wildcats were particularly prominent in the woods in the late 1960s and 1970s, where coastal fallers engaged in years of wildcatting.[41] The decentralized, anti-authoritarian aspect of the wildcats expressed a New Left sensibility as well as an echo of the Wobbly spirit of the early twentieth century.

The New Left sensibility was prominent in student protests. The student movement grew out of a meeting at Port Huron, Michigan, that generated the Port Huron Statement in 1962, and led to the formation of the Students for a Democratic Society. As one of the participants, Tom Hayden, remembered, the goal was to draw together ordinary people, and through active, participatory democracy a new social order would arise. More attuned to the lyrics of Bob Dylan than the texts of Marx and Lenin, student activists hoped to play a key role in this transition.[42] By the late 1960s, student activism was commonplace across North America, championing struggles for peace, racial equality, women's rights, the environment, and a more open democracy.

In British Columbia, Simon Fraser University (SFU), atop Burnaby Mountain, was at the forefront of student protest. Opened in 1965 and committed to a new progressive education, SFU was quickly a hotbed of activism, bringing together radical faculty members and militant students. In the summer of 1966, students launched a series of protests to challenge the presence of a Shell gas station on the campus. Shell's record in Third World countries and a more general grievance against the commercialization of public space were at the core of the student challenge. Activism within the radical Political Science, Sociology and Anthropology Department (PSA) soon superseded the gas station protest. Faculty and students established a democratic organizational structure in the PSA in the 1966–1967 academic year, and after the firing of five graduate students who had supported a high school student's right to free speech, the campus exploded, forcing the university to rescind the firings.

The radicals had momentum in the increasing clashes between activists and the university establishment. By 1968 the governing system of SFU was in chaos. In September 1969, a student occupation of campus facilities led to 114 students being arrested by police. While the activism peaked in 1968, tension continued into the 1970s.[43] The University of British Columbia also felt the new wave of protest, most famously in the occupation of the Faculty Club in October 1968, when American youth activist Jerry Rubin was on campus, offering his vision of anarchist New Leftism.[44] To focus on clashes alone is to miss the broader picture. Students were motivated by real issues, including student participation in university and college government, racism on campus, the influence of corporations in public education, the ability of students from poorer families to get post-secondary education, and Canada's economic participation in the Vietnam War.

Old and New Left activists participated in the revitalized women's movement of the Sixties, a movement that had support from across the political spectrum. The rallying cry of the new movement was equality, a sufficiently elastic term capable of bringing a diversity of women together. Liberal or equal-opportunity feminists, the majority, sought fairness in the established liberal social order — the right for women to participate equally at school and at work — while socialist feminists sought equality through the demolition of capitalist society, and radical feminists focused on dismantling patriarchal structures. By 1969 there were "ongoing, active, youth-based women's liberation movements in Vancouver, Toronto, and Montreal."[45] Key demands uniting women were equal pay in the workforce; accessible daycare, which would allow women to choose whether or not to work outside the home; a fairer division of household labour between men and women; and better abortion legislation.

BC leftists were notable in the 1970 abortion caravan, the first national action of the women's movement in Canada, and it captured some of the exuberance, optimism, and politics of this women's movement.[46] Up until 1969, abortion was illegal in Canada. New federal laws legalized abortion, but only at accredited hospitals after a three-person committee of doctors approved the procedure, confirming that it was necessary for the woman's health. Many women wanted the right to choose to belong to them alone. The idea for the caravan came from seventeen members of the Vancouver Women's Caucus, and they set out on a cross-country journey to Ottawa, arriving on 8 May 1970. Here they were joined by women from other centres across Canada. They demonstrated and chained themselves to chairs in the House of Commons. The importance of the abortion issue was such that it promoted unity: "Most of the traveling Vancouver women were active in the New Left and the anti-war movement. They had some political disagreements among themselves, but they managed to work together well until they hit Toronto, where socialist and radical feminists had just experienced a split."[47] The women's movement was boisterous and internal splits were passionate, but the call for equality that transcended regions, classes, and political differences was very real. In trade unions, many leftist women activists challenged the way things had been done.

A new environmentalism raised questions of a different order. While women and students struggled for social justice, equality, and human rights, principles that were familiar to the left, environmentalists sought to protect the natural world, critiquing the relationship between human beings and nature. This was less familiar to those on the left, most of whom extolled material progress, a rising standard of living, and the rational manipulation of nature. The left was concerned with fairness, democracy, equality, social hierarchy, and unjustifiable power, and these issues focused the debates and set the goals for the future. Environmentalists, however, said that there was a higher plane, nature, that provided the context for economic and social life, and it had to be protected. There was a more important priority, they suggested, than the traditional concerns of the left. Leftists had long complained about pollution and chemicals when they directly affected workers on the job; they had called for better management of resources to preserve jobs; and they had pushed for wage gains for workers in resource industries. But the environment itself was not a high priority.

Drawing on the continental surge in environmental concern that gathered steam after the publication of Rachel Carson's *Silent Spring* in 1962, British Columbians created organizations to change longstanding attitudes and to lobby for new government regulations. The environmental voice often came out of the universities, where students and faculty in the sciences, especially biology, had the training and authority to challenge the science offered by industry and government. It was also influenced by the influx of ideas and activists from the United States. The Society for Pollution and Environmental Control (SPEC) went public in January 1969, holding its first public meeting at Simon Fraser University. Early SPEC causes included strip mining, sound noise at a Surrey planer mill, the BC fisheries, and pollution in the Port Moody area. Within a year, the society had members in Kelowna, Kamloops, West Vancouver, North Vancouver, and Surrey, and it soon boasted a membership of some eight thousand. Initiatives at Simon Fraser University and the University of Victoria in 1969 led to the formation of the Sierra Club of British Columbia, a branch of the century-old organization founded in California. Though focused on forestry practice, parks, and energy policy, the Sierra Club also involved itself in broader issues such as freeway locations and air and water pollution.[48] The new environmental movement was passionate, youthful, and imbued with the spirit of the New Left.

Some BC environmental associations and activists became well-known outside of the province. Greenpeace grew out of the anti-nuclear movement, when a group of activists in Vancouver with close links to the Sierra Club and SPEC organized the Don't Make a Wave Committee in 1970.

In 1972 they took the name Greenpeace and expanded into global environmental causes. By the middle of the 1970s, a number of countries had established their own Greenpeace organizations, leading to the creation of Greenpeace International in 1979. Its headquarters were in Amsterdam.[49] By the early 1970s, too, the Vancouver human rights and environmental activist David Suzuki was reaching a wide audience. Suzuki would become Canada's best known environmentalist.

The new social movements existed in a broader milieu, the Sixties, that challenged the establishment and offered a different view of the good life. The establishment, including much of the traditional left at the time, celebrated science and technology, promoted the mass-production of endless consumer goods and services, accepted the efficacy of regimentation and bureaucracy in delivering the goods, and trumpeted the perfection of the patriarchal nuclear family. The counter-argument was that science and technology brought pollution and nuclear weapons; mass-production factories created boring, tedious jobs; regimentation and bureaucracy stifled freedom and creativity; the focus on material wealth killed spiritual growth; patriarchal families contorted the lives of women and children; and war was unproductive and unnecessary. The counterculture emphasized spirituality, peace, freedom, decentralization, local control, coexistence with nature, gender and racial equality, flexible, fluid living arrangements, and harmony.

The Sixties, however, embodied contradictory impulses. On the one hand, community — reflected in appeals to "brothers and sisters to love one another" and in experiments in communal living — was celebrated. As one insider wrote in the fall of 1969, "Vancouver's hippies in general are not plastic (i.e., kids pretending, generally on week-ends). Complete dropping-out (attempting to live and mold one's life outside the system) is quite widespread. . . ."[50] On the other hand, the Sixties celebrated individualism, the right for people to "do their own thing." And while there was much talk of political alternatives, the ways that goods and services would be produced in the new society of love and equality were little explored. In the days of the late 1960s and early 1970s, when momentum was still on the side of the counterculture, it seemed unnecessary to investigate these tensions.

The Sixties counterculture, broadly conceived, confronted a socially conservative elite in British Columbia that was exemplified by the Social Credit Party. Wary of youth, unconventional dress, long hair on men, the drug culture, rock and roll music, and abortion rights, and committed to a traditional role for women in the family, to religion, and to the rectitude of the existing order and the benefits of rapid resource exploitation, the Social Credit constituency, often older and living in smaller communities, felt besieged. The national wing of the Social Credit party played a leading role in opposing the Trudeau Liberals in 1969 when they amended the Criminal Code to modernize divorce and abortion laws and decriminalize homosexual acts. In BC the Social Credit party was "blatantly homophobic." At an all-candidates meeting during the 1972 election campaign, a Social Crediter responded to a question as follows: "One day society will castrate the whole works of you [gays] to keep you from reproducing your own kind."[51] W.A.C. Bennett, the seventy-one-year-old premier, had little sympathy for or understanding of the rapidly changing social world swirling around him. The NDP provided a more congenial home for the new activists.

In the early 1970s, Social Credit was in political trouble, and in the August 1972 provincial election the left finally came to power in BC. With thirty-eight seats, the NDP had a majority in the legislature, facing ten Social Credit, five Liberal, and two Conservative MLAs. While it was a major achievement for the social democrats, it was not a tipping point in provincial politics. The NDP remained in power for only three years, and in 1975 Social Credit returned to power. Nor was the election the result of a dramatic upsurge of support for the left. The seat count is misleading, for while the NDP won 69 percent of the seats in the legislature, this was based on only 33.9 percent of the popular vote. A majority of voters, then, had voted for the three parties to the right of the NDP.[52]

There is much to the argument that the election was "not so much a victory by the opposition New Democratic Party as it was the break-up of Social Credit."[53] W.A.C. Bennett had been premier since 1952, and his age — he was not "hip" in the Age of Aquarius — as well as his lack of energy and focus undermined the appeal of Social Credit. An ill-advised attack on provincial teachers, cutting funding and rejigging pensions, created a forceful, energetic foe. Bennett's own supporters deserted him in other areas, too, evidenced by the revitalization of the Conservative party: in 1969 the Conservatives won 0.11 percent of the popular vote, electing one MLA, while in 1972 it won 12.67 percent. The Conservatives elected only two MLAs, but their votes across the province came at the expense of Social Credit. The combined Conservative and Social Credit vote in 1972 was very close to the Social Credit total of 1969.

Nevertheless, one cannot ignore the point that the NDP had also positioned itself to nudge more voters into its camp. The NDP had forged connections with the new social movements, which in turn saw the NDP as their great hope for change. Leading lights in the party — including MLAs Bob Williams, Jim Lorimer, Eileen Dailly, Alex MacDonald, and former MLA Norm Levi — flirted with the Waffle Movement[54] and felt comfortable with the youthful social movements. In 1972, 153,816 more people voted (15.7 percent) than had voted in 1969, and many were young people, baby boomers coming of age, who voted NDP.

Leadership was also important. In the late 1960s, two men, representing different factions in the NDP, vied for the leadership. Tom Berger was elected leader of the NDP in April 1969, narrowly defeating Dave Barrett. Berger was close to organized labour, having served as counsel to the BC Federation of Labour. Barrett, a social worker, came from the world of the welfare state, government, and the helping professions. He saw the party as much more than a labour party, much to the chagrin of many labour leaders. After another election loss in 1969, Dave Barrett defeated Tom Berger in a leadership contest.[55]

Barrett's distance from organized labour made him appealing to voters who distrusted unions. At the same time, unionists had nowhere else to go; they wanted to defeat Social Credit. Barrett also had a folksy appeal, taking off his sports jacket and rolling up his sleeves when addressing crowds, deflecting jibes about being a Marxist by invoking Groucho and Harpo, and defusing comments about his earlier connection to the Waffle Movement, by saying that if Bennett called him a Waffle he would call him a pancake. There was also a dollop of left populism in the Barrett NDP, in policy as well as in style. Capitalism and capitalists had to be managed, the economy was to be run to benefit the people and not primarily business, unions were important but would not dominate the government, and local control of government programs would be put in place when possible.

At a personal level, Barrett was not scary and as such attracted Liberal voters. Ideologically, the social democracy of Dave Barrett was close to 1960s liberalism. The Liberal vote dropped slightly, from 19.03 percent of the popular vote to 16.40 percent in the 1972 election, and much of this vote went to the NDP rather than Social Credit. To many Liberals, the NDP was not beyond the pale. State intervention in the economy and society, justified by Keynesian thinking, was acceptable, and British Columbians enjoyed the government-run Medicare system, the Canada Pension Plan, and increased spending in programs such as unemployment insurance that the federal Liberals, under Lester B. Pearson and Pierre Elliott Trudeau, had brought on line.

Moreover, the NDP was seen as more friendly to government workers, a growing constituency. In 1961 there were 10,233 people employed in the British Columbia public service, and that number almost tripled by 1971, when 29,141 people were employed in the government sector.[56] Between 1964 and 1967 alone, under a Social Credit government, the number of provincial employees doubled.[57] The NDP succeeded by broadening its reach by bringing together many disgruntled Liberals, disenchanted government workers, conservative and radical unionists, and moderate and radical activists in the new social movements.

Because the social democrats had never before formed a government, expectations were high and inexperience was rampant. Leftists of all stripes expected that their needs and desires would be addressed. Barrett tried and in a flurry of legislative activity ushered in a wide array of changes. A government-operated automobile insurance system was set up, following what the CCF government in Saskatchewan had successfully done in the 1940s, squeezing the private insurance firms into a secondary role. An agricultural land reserve was created to ensure that sufficient land for agricultural production would remain beyond the grasp of developers. Human rights issues were addressed, prohibiting discrimination in housing and employment and protecting renters from excessive, unwarranted rent increases, to the dismay of many small business people

Dave Barrett (seated) and others at radio station CKNW, 5 October 1972.
Studio: Croton Studio. Courtesy of Croton Studio and Vancouver Public Library 79828.

and landlords. Decentralization and democracy were keywords: control of education and social services were downloaded to local communities.

The government also flirted with the idea of provincial steel and ship-building industries in an attempt to build on BC's natural strength in order to move it beyond a simple resource-based economy to a more stable manufacturing economy with increased value-added taking place in the province. Although these ideas about government directly engaging in heavy manufacturing were shelved, the government took over the pulp and paper concern at Ocean Falls and a poultry operation in the Fraser Valley, but rather than being part of a coherent economic development strategy, they came from a social-worker, humanitarian interest to pre-serve jobs at facilities that capitalists were deserting. Both initiatives failed. The government also sought to take more money from the resource in-dustries and redirect it to education, health, and welfare. A new taxation and royalty structure was imposed on the mining industry, and stumpage fees were raised on timber. The resource companies were not amused.[58]

Hostility from capitalists was to be expected, but the level of animosity from segments of the labour movement was not. The left remained di-vided. When social democratic governments are elected, unions are often dismayed. Having expended money and personnel to get the party elected, they expect that legislation will reflect their interests. However, the new government is faced with having to govern for the whole population, not just labour. In British Columbia, tension between Barrett and union leaders exacerbated the situation. The passage of a new labour code in 1973 brought gains to unions in collective bargaining, but many labour leaders were disappointed because they felt that it did not go far enough, publicly voicing their displeasure.[59] In 1974 and 1975, in a falling market, workers launched a series of strikes in important industries. The Barrett govern-ment responded with back-to-work-legislation, a tactic long-associated with the reactionary Social Credit regime. Many workers and their leaders were angry with the NDP government.

In December 1975, the NDP lost the provincial election. The percent-age of the population that voted NDP in 1975 was virtually the same as had voted NDP in 1972: 39.16 percent and 39.59 percent, respectively. The significant change between 1972 and 1975 was the rebuilding of the right, surprisingly again under the Social Credit label. Bill Bennett, the son of W.A.C. Bennett, became party leader in November 1973. Grace McCarthy, a Social Credit stalwart, rebuilt the party's grassroots support, signing up 32,000 new members in 1974 alone. The business community financed the venture. Through the mining community, Social Credit made links to federal Liberal bagmen, pollsters, and strategists, giving the party a professional, well-financed core. High-profile desertions from the Liberals and Conservatives made Social Credit the only significant alternative to the NDP.[60] In the 1975 election, the Progressive Conservative Party vote disintegrated, dropping from 12.67 percent in 1972 to 3.86 percent in 1975, while the Liberal vote dropped from 16.4 percent to 7.24 percent in the same period. Social Credit won a majority government with thirty-five seats. The NDP won eighteen, and the Conservatives and Liberals one each.

Despite the election loss in 1975, the left in British Columbia was still vibrant. The NDP had sizeable electoral support and it had the ability to scare the business community. Politically it was able to unnerve many Liberals. In its short term in office it had exhibited a leftist edge. It imposed government ownership to help automobile owners and increase efficiency, preserved agricultural land from urban sprawl, experimented with government ownership of manufacturing facilities, improved the lot of society's least fortunate at the expense of the better off, enhanced localism, shifted labour laws to help workers, and improved human rights. While Social Credit had intervened in the economy directly to improve the fortunes of business and begrudgingly enhanced spending on education and health and welfare to legitimize its rule, the NDP sought to redirect society in a way that celebrated fairness and enhanced the rights of working people. The NDP of the mid-1970s had the support of many professionals, such as lawyers, doctors, and academics. They were also supported by government workers, who ranged from skilled teachers, and nurses to truck drivers and clerks, as well as unionists in both the private and public sectors. Not all professionals, government workers, or unionists, of course, supported the NDP, but there were sufficient numbers to form a working bloc.

The NDP had an affinity with the new social movements, but relationships were often complex. General support for women's equality and protection of the environment, the two most prominent movements in the 1970s, was fine, but developing actual policy was difficult. While the NDP was in power there were bitter divisions within the party over feminist issues. Barrett's refusal to create a ministry of women's equality was especially offensive to many, overshadowing positive changes for women initiated by the government.[61] With regard to the environment, were more parks and stricter regulations on pollution sufficient? What if parks and regulations meant the loss of well-paying, union jobs? Should sports fishermen be favoured over First Nations or commercial trawlers? Activists saw the NDP as more pro-environment than Social Credit, but when in power the NDP often did not deliver what environmentalists wanted.[62]

Many unionized workers felt threatened by activists in the new social movements. Unions had long been largely a male world, and even in industries dominated by women workers, men had often served as union leaders. The masculine union culture of late nights, alcohol, and days and weeks away from home on union business was not easily penetrated, making it difficult for women to take on union positions. Moreover, not all union men were sympathetic to the interests of the women's movement. At union work sites, where women took on non-traditional jobs, they often met ridicule and ostracism. In union meetings, issues such as daycare and equal pay for work of equal quality were tabled.

Unions also had tense relations with environmentalists. The creation of parks meant job losses in the short run for loggers. Environmentalists, often unfamiliar with the way union democracy worked, made unrealistic demands on union leaders. In 1969 the IWA was stunned when a prominent leader of SPEC argued that workers were just as responsible for forest devastation as employers and that workers should forgo wage increases because they led to increased consumption of goods that were produced in non-environmentally sensitive ways.[63] There was also a cultural divide that pitted educated middle-class university personnel in the environmental movement against much less educated, often older, sawmill and factory workers.

Overall, though, for many in the mid-1970s the future still looked positive. The 1975 election was merely a setback: leftists were prominent in Vancouver city politics; the union movement seemed healthy, recharged by the influx of government workers into its ranks (the percentage of workers organized was still about 44 percent of paid workers[64]); and the economic downturn of the 1970s appeared to be a typical recession. However, such optimism was misguided. The new social movements that had shaken the traditional left in the 1960s and 1970s would continue to be a challenge in future years, but now a new, revitalized right was emerging to confront the left head-on. A historical shift was taking place, and the left-leaning ideological and institutional regime that had reigned since the 1940s was being replaced by a new order, the order that continues to shape the world today. In BC, the turbulent 1980s gave birth to this new world.

CHAPTER 6

A New Reality:
1976–1990

THE NDP CONTINUED to do well in the late 1970s. In the 1979 provincial election, the party increased its seat count to twenty-six from the eighteen it had won in 1975. This was only five fewer seats than Social Credit won. In the 1979 popular vote, the NDP garnered 46 percent and Social Credit 48 percent. The NDP percentage of the popular vote remained stable in 1983, when it won 44.9 percent of the vote and twenty-two seats. The more radical left, punch-drunk from exhausting internal squabbles, as well as more fearful of the possibilities of a full realization of a right-wing agenda, were either silent or involved in the NDP. Stan Persky wrote in 1983: "As for what used to be known a decade ago as the 'revolutionary left,' its organization has diminished to a few grouplets or has self-destructed entirely."[1] In 1979 the Communist Party of Canada ran seven candidates, and the Communist Party of Canada (Marxist-Leninist) ran two; together they attracted 1,394 votes, about 0.10 percent of the total provincial vote.

But if the NDP was staying alive, the other key element of the left, unions, entered a period of distress in a failing economy. An economic downturn was already evident during the Barrett years. Export markets for mineral and wood products were down. The unemployment rate rose from 7.6 percent to 8.5 percent between 1972 and 1975.[2] In 1978 unemployment was at 8.2 percent, bankruptcies were running at double the yearly rate over the early 1970s, and inflation had dropped only from 10.5 percent to about 9 percent in the years from 1975 to 1978.[3] There was worse to come. In the depression of the early 1980s, the unemployment rate was over 14 percent, inflation was rampant, interest rates approached 20 percent, and many people lost homes when mortgage rates skyrocketed. Working people were anxious and fought back as best they could. The number of strikes dropped to 67 in 1977 but climbed to 160 in 1981. In 1977 some 448,000 worker-days were lost to strikes; in 1981 the total was over 3,232,000.[4]

Their collective strength gave unionized workers advantages over non-union workers, but to many non-union workers, unionists seemed to be struggling for their own interests, not for the long-term betterment of workers in general. Trade union opposition to federal wage-and-price controls, imposed by the Canadian government between 1975 and 1978 to fight rampant inflation, reinforced a sense that unions were largely self-interested. The controls were a form of state socialism supported by provincial NDP governments and parties. But in the union argument, free collective bargaining trumped state economic management. The big unions had the power to defend their interests. Non-unionized workers, and indeed workers in weaker unions, were left to fend for themselves.

In the public sector, the Barrett government had instituted full-scale, free collective bargaining, but Social Credit whittled away these gains: in 1977 the right to strike by public employees was restricted by Essential Services legislation.[5] Still, public service unions retained greater job security, ostensibly in return for lower wages in comparison to the private sector. And because of the large contingent of women workers in the public service, issues such as pay equity, daycare, and abortion rights had a higher profile, and women were more prominent in positions of leadership. Nevertheless, in the economic context of the late 1970s and early 1980s there was anxiety in the public sector, too.

The economic malaise of the 1970s and early 1980s was not just another downturn in the business cycle; it was a reflection of deeper global structural and ideological changes. The full recovery of the European and Japanese economies after the devastation of World War II made international capitalism much more competitive, shrinking corporate profits in North America. American involvement in Vietnam proved costly, destabilizing the United States economy, fueling inflation, and increasing the national debt. The United States was no longer a reliable manager of global economic affairs. At a more immediate level, the shock of rapidly increasing oil prices in 1973 and 1974, due to the success of mid-eastern oil producers in controlling production, created a frenzy and increased production costs.

The intellectual underpinning of progressive liberalism and much leftist thought since the 1940s, Keynesianism, was now questioned. Keynesian economic strategies seemed impotent in the 1970s. Keynesianism posited that high inflation could be countered by using fiscal measures to slow economic growth. This would lead to slightly higher unemployment levels, but it would presage economic recovery. However, inflation, slow growth, and rising unemployment all coexisted in the mid-1970s, leading to the invention of a new term to describe the situation: stagflation.

For governments, the new situation was difficult indeed. As the economy weakened, revenues fell and unemployment rose. The demand for social services increased, meaning more government spending. In dealing with this fiscal crisis, governments ran deficits and drove up their debts. The business response, though uneven, was summed up in the term "flexibility," which meant contracting-out parts of the production process, changing union contracts to undermine job security, and lowering wage rates and benefit packages. Business also attacked government debt, social programs, and tax policies, measures that supposedly constricted their ability to prosper.

The corporate agenda was closely aligned with a rising right. The 1979 election of Margaret Thatcher in Britain and the 1980 election of Ronald Reagan in the United States signalled the rise of the New Right, whose economic program was labelled neo-liberalism. This manifestation of liberalism stressed the primacy of the individual, while supporting the sacred nature of private property and the power of the market to generate wealth and economic fairness. It also attacked the supposedly demoralizing trap of social welfare programs that sapped personal initiative and criticized most government-led equity schemes. Not only did the New Right meet corporate goals, it resonated with struggling working-class families who saw, they believed, too much of their paychecks being redirected by the state to welfare recipients who were allegedly uninterested in pulling their weight in the economy. This version of individual action and responsibility also attracted people from the 1960s who adhered to the ideological strain that promoted the libertarian "do-your-own-thing" philosophy.

In British Columbia, the Fraser Institute spread the anti-government, pro-market doctrine. Formed in 1974, the think tank, sponsored and well-funded by corporate British Columbia, promoted market economics. In its many pamphlets and books, experts at the institute attacked government intervention in the economy in such areas as rent control, affirmative action for women and minorities, minimum wage laws, the agricultural land reserve, and government-run automobile insurance. For the Social Credit government of the 1970s and 1980s, the Fraser Institute was important in the broad war of position against government socialism, legitimizing a pro-corporate, free market orientation.[6]

Shortly after taking office in 1975, the Social Credit government under Bill Bennett started planning the sell-off of a number of businesses, notably in the forest industry, businesses that had been taken over and run by the government during the Barrett years. In August 1979, the government lumped together the nationalized companies in the British Columbia Resources Investment Corporation (BCRIC, which was referred to as "brick"). As well as privatizing these government assets, the Social Credit government used the opportunity to educate the population about the wonders of capitalism, turning over a portion of the shares to each citizen in the province. It was hoped that this move would both legitimize the privatization of the government's plan and help teach British Columbians how to take care of themselves by managing their money in the stock market. It was ultimately unsuccessful because the shares became worthless.[7] The BC left initially did well in this growing hostile climate, playing a pivotal role in staving off the full brunt of neo-liberal policies. As such, the Social Credit government, ideologically sympathetic to the stance of the Fraser Institute, did not totally dismantle the social welfare infrastructure.

In 1983 the strength and weakness of the left in BC were exposed in a dramatic confrontation with neo-liberalism. In the summer and fall of that year, British Columbians took to the streets as part of the Solidarity movement to protest the actions of the Social Credit government of Bill Bennett. The premier had inaugurated a Restraint Program on 18 February 1982 in a television address to the province.[8] Government spending was to be reined in, public-sector wage increases limited, and a wage freeze implemented for seven hundred senior public-sector managers.[9] The wage guidelines were made even more severe in July 1982. Still, collective bargaining was pursued and government workers secured a new agreement in the fall of 1982. Overall, the first Bennett restraint program antagonized government workers, but more broadly was not seen as draconian.

On 5 May 1983, Social Credit won a provincial election, winning thirty-five seats with 49.76 percent of the popular vote. On 7 July 1983 the new government brought in its budget. This was the restraint program in earnest. Twenty-six bills were introduced. Little in the measures curbed overall government spending. The thrust was to weaken the public sector and its unions by reducing the number of government workers, deeming certain areas such as scheduling and assignment of duties non-negotiable, and giving the government the power to fire workers more easily at the end of a collective agreement. On the day after the budget, 400 of the 1,600 workers who were to be terminated by 31 October 1983 were given their pink slips. Public-sector workers, then, were to be the first sacrificed in the interest of restraint and as part of the broader move to weaken social programs, government services, and unions generally.

But the government went beyond attacking government workers and focusing on major money matters. The Rentalsman's Office, which supervised rent control in the province, was abolished, much to the pleasure of landowners and investors. The Human Rights Commission, a watchdog organization, was done away with, and a new Human Rights Act, which was less stringent in rooting out discrimination, was brought in. Education was centralized, removing taxing authority from local school boards and locating it in provincial government hands. Another measure, Bill 24, allowed doctors to opt out of Medicare, thus opening the door for increased privatized medicine in the province. The restraint program, then, ostensibly about fiscal management, reached out to attack popular values, including local participation in educating children, the right to reasonable rent, and the positive role of government in protecting women and minorities from discriminatory practices.

The union movement, anticipating a tough budget, though not as devastating as the one that came, was somewhat prepared. The Vancouver and District Labour Council's Unemployment Action Centre, steered by more leftist union activists, converted its 11 July 1983 demonstration against unemployment to a meeting to plan mobilization against the budget. Representatives from fifty organizations, including unions, advocacy groups, and political bodies attended, and they set up a coalition. Other meetings followed in the next few days. On 12 July, hundreds of demonstrators in Vancouver protested the dismantling of the Human Rights Commission, and the next day Women Against the Budget was formed. "All these initial gatherings took advantage of existing networks and organizations in mobilizing hundreds of trade unionists, community activists and others."[10] The largest labour central organization in the province, the British Columbia Federation of Labour, led by President Art Kube, acted, and by 15 July Operation Solidarity was set up. Notably, non-BC Fed unions, including the Pulp and Paper Workers of Canada and the Hospital Employees' Union, participated. "Representatives of more than 500,000 organized workers (37 percent of the entire workforce) were now committed to opposing the budget. Within three weeks more than $1,500,000 had been raised, all but $200,000 generated in British Columbia."[11]

There were now two extra-parliamentary opposition groups in BC, the Lower Mainland Budget Coalition, dominated by community groups, and Operation Solidarity, the vehicle of the trade unions. The strength of these organizations was evident when twenty thousand protested in

Art Kube, BC Federation of Labour president, surrounded by
reporters, addressing Solidarity crowd at BC Legislature, Victoria, 1983.
Photographer: Sean Griffin, *Pacific Tribune* Archive.

Vancouver on 23 July and 25,000 in Victoria on 27 July. Outside Victoria on Vancouver Island and in the Interior, Solidarity centres were organized. On 3 August the Lower Mainland Budget Coalition and Operation Solidarity united, and the Solidarity Coalition was born. Sociologist William K. Carroll summed up the nature of the new organization:

> The Solidarity Coalition was to be non-partisan in its opposition to government austerity, welcoming support from all quarters of the community. Its member groups, while uniting around a common programme of action, would retain the right to act independently in opposition to particular aspects of government policy. Community group members of the Coalition would participate in it directly, while trade union members would participate through Operation Solidarity, which retained its executive along with its mission to unify the provincial labour movement. An interim advisory committee made up of Art Kube, Roman Catholic priest Father Jim Roberts and former Human Rights Commissioner Renate Shearer was mandated to assemble a Coalition steering committee representing 27 distinct areas of interests, ranging from injured workers, the unemployed, women and youth to professionals, environmentalists, small businesses and consumers.[12]

This broad left bloc challenged the right-wing agenda of a government that represented corporate interests and free market economics. At a massive rally on 10 August at Empire Stadium in Vancouver, some forty thousand protesters demanded that the government withdraw its offensive legislation. Smaller centres, such as Kelowna, Nanaimo, and Prince George also experienced demonstrations.

The government stood fast, dismissing the protests as the grievances of a minority. But the government did little to pass its controversial agenda. At this time the NDP, led by Dave Barrett, was a non-entity; the protest was under the control of the unions and community groups. Then, on 19 September the government began to steer its bills through the legislature. The NDP challenged and filibustered — Dave Barrett was physically ejected from the House and banned for the rest of the session — but Social Credit had a majority and used the procedure of closure to end debate. Extra-parliamentary protest continued, and on 14 October sixty thousand people marched past the Vancouver hotel where Social Credit

Solidarity rally at Empire Stadium, Vancouver, 10 August 1983.
Photographer: Dan Keeton. *Pacific Tribune* Archive.

was holding its convention. On 20 October the government adjourned
the legislature. The key bills, most notably those that dealt with government workers, had been passed. They received Royal assent the next day.

The next ten days were tense. On 31 October the collective agreement
of the BC Government Employees' Union was due to expire. Sixteen
hundred workers in the thirty-five-thousand-member union were then
up for dismissal. Moreover, the measures recently passed in the legislature
would essentially gut the union as a meaningful organization. Government workers, then, were angry and prepared for job action. If the
behaviour of these public-sector employers was clear, the actions of others
were not. Would nurses and teachers, who were not engaged directly,
support the BCGEU? What about the private-sector unions? No government legislation threatened their existence. Moreover, anti-government-
worker attitudes were shared by many private-sector workers, many of
whom believed that public service workers were pampered with privi-

leged job security. And how deep was the solidarity of the unions with the broader community groups?

For community groups the future was uncertain. With the focus now on the BCGEU and their contract problems, could they count on the unions for support on their issues? Jack Munro, the BC leader of the powerful and influential private-sector union, the International Wood-workers of America, did not believe that his members would support a strike during the worst recession since the 1930s, especially, he later noted sarcastically and revealingly, if it was merely going "to make sure that sexual preference is written into the human rights code."[13] Within the Solidarity Coalition there were calls for a general strike, recognition of the anger and frustration, as well as the many pockets of militancy and radicalism, but what would such a strike be aimed at? Were the majority of the demonstrators prepared to overthrow the government? Why not wait until the next election to turf the scoundrels out?

Despite the size of Solidarity, it did not fully represent the broader population. Public opinion, especially difficult to gauge in a fluid situation, was uncomfortable with the behaviour of the Social Credit government, but while a poll by the *Vancouver Sun* on 24 September showed that 75 percent of respondents thought that the government was overbearing in its actions, the majority still supported the idea of fiscal restraint. There was little support for killing the Human Rights Commission and cutting social welfare programs.[14] To many, the government had overplayed its hand by including unnecessary issues in the restraint agenda, especially the non-monetary measures and those not directly rationalizing the public service. But how were these excesses to be resolved? Social Credit was the recently elected, legitimate government, and the legislature was the established forum for sorting out political disputes. If one was opposed to the legislative program there was an alternative in the NDP. The events of 1983 had not shattered these fundamental values.

On 14 October the Solidarity Coalition had publicly presented a statement of its principles, entitled "A Declaration of the Rights of the People of British Columbia."[15] The statement endorsed parliamentary democracy, declaring a fundamental right "to open and democratic government, scrutiny of government actions, due process of law, full parliamentary debate and consultation with affected groups on all legislative proposals, and express submission of fundamental changes in law or rights to the electors."[16] Further assertions included support for minority rights, freedom of expression, Medicare, an equal role for women and men in society, protection from arbitrary, unjustified rent increases, and free collective bargaining for all workers. Social Credit had transgressed fundamental values in a modern liberal society — curtailing the citizenship rights of public-sector workers, undermining commitments to gender and racial equality, and failing to ensure affordable accommodation — but the transgression was not sufficient to raise questions about the legitimacy of established state and democratic institutions.

In early November, the stand-off came to a head. On 1 November the BCGEU went on strike. One week later education workers, including twenty-eight thousand teachers, went out in sympathy. The solidarity of the teachers had been an unknown, and so the walkout invigorated the government workers. Most teachers across the province defied court injunctions and possible decertification. The BCGEU action was a legal strike; the teachers' action was in the more nebulous legal area of a political protest. The stakes had been raised. As events unfolded, the escalation of job action was seemingly the only strategy. Civic and transportation workers were primed to go out next. Soon the private-sector unions would be called upon to go out. Eventually the strike would be general. The union movement was now running the show, and there were concerns. Striking to win collective bargaining positions was one thing, but a massive political protest with no clear final objective was another. Moreover, it was a real question as to whether the private-sector unions would go out, or, if they did, whether they would stay out. The government was well aware of the split between private- and public-sector unions.[17]

Two settlements brought the issue to an end. On 13 November the BCGEU reached a settlement with the government. Collective bargaining rights, the main concern of the unions, were preserved. Later in the day, Jack Munro, representing the BC Fed, flew to Kelowna to meet with Premier Bill Bennett at his home. The meeting resulted in the Kelowna Accord, which entailed vague commitments from the government to maintain human and tenant rights, labour consultation on the new labour code, and use of the money saved while teachers were on strike to forestall layoffs. These would later largely be ignored. The announcement of the truce was made at midnight on Sunday, just in time to ensure that the next stage in the job action scheduled for Monday morning would not go ahead. Operation Solidarity and the Solidarity Coalition were spent forces.

Solidarity was an impressive mobilization by the left. But despite the achievement, the constituent groups could not celebrate. Community groups won nothing and felt betrayed by the trade unions that had pursued their collective bargaining interests at the expense of the advocates for human rights, tenant rights, and local control. Nor would the NDP remember its participation with warm nostalgia. The NDP had played a marginal role. The leadership of the broad protest was made up of unionists and community activists, not the social democrats. NDPers were wary of the unruly, extra-parliamentary actions, concerned about illegalities tainting their image and electoral possibilities, and embarrassed by their bystander status in a struggle against their true foe, Social Credit. The union movement was tarnished by its marginalization of community groups. Radical leftists both within and outside the labour movement loudly accused the BC Fed leadership of being conservative and selling out the interests of the people by not taking the protest further. But while the hard-left activists could talk stridently, it was also evident that they lacked broad support and that their language of revolt and confrontation was not sufficient to guide the unfolding of events. The Solidarity critique was restricted to one government, Social Credit, and not the broader institutions of capitalism. Corporations were on the sidelines, unscathed, as Social Credit fought their battles. The result of the fluid, rollicking events of 1983 was disappointment. The crisis created by the government allowed a broadly based opposition bloc to coalesce, but the moment was short-lived.[18]

During the turbulent 1980s, the unions operated within the context of industrial relations law and the NDP in the world of parliamentary democracy, but in 1982 a small group emerged that was willing to use violence. A few activists with anarchist leanings came together in Vancouver,

convinced that direct action could jolt people into more widespread revolt. Members of the core group set up two organizations: Direct Action
and the Wimmin's Fire Brigade. Linking environmentalism, feminism,
and revolutionary visions, the group, later dubbed by the press as the
Squamish Five, first vandalized the property of a mining company that
had been granted exemption from environmental laws by the provincial
government. They then began accumulating weapons, supporting themselves by various forms of fraud and theft. In May 1982, three of the
activists exploded a large bomb at a BC Hydro substation on Vancouver
Island, destroying four transformers. The action was symbolic, an attempt
to criticize the anti-environmental behaviour of the public power company. In the fall of 1982, the group, now made up of five people, drove a
stolen pick-up truck filled with 250 kilograms of dynamite from Vancouver to Toronto. The destination was the corporate headquarters of
Litton Industries, a company that produced guidance systems for American cruise missiles. There was intent to injure property, not people.
Indeed, the group took much action to ensure that the exploding truck
parked in full view of company security would not injure any human
beings, including telephoning the security desk to warn them of the explosion. The people at the desk, however, suspected a hoax and reacted
slowly. The evacuation process was still on when the bomb exploded,
minutes ahead of schedule, injuring ten people. The facilities sustained
no serious damage. Now in hiding from the law, the bombers returned
to Vancouver.

On 22 November 1982, a few of the militant anarchists reemerged as
the Wimmin's Fire Brigade, firebombing three franchises of Red Hot
Video, a chain store that sold pornographic films. On 20 January 1983, all
five were captured just south of Squamish by an RCMP tactical unit dis-
guised as a highway construction road crew. The five received jail sentences ranging from six years to life. One of the defendants, Ann Hansen,
upon hearing her life sentence, threw a tomato at the judge.[19] Despite the
agreed worthiness of the causes — most leftists were uncomfortable about
Red Hot Video, cruise missiles, and the destruction of forests by BC Hydro
— there was little support for the Squamish Five. The violence against
humans was decried, but so was the attack on private, corporate property.

Dissent was only legitimate in certain frameworks, namely parliamentary action, legal union activity, non-violent marches, letters to the editor, and consumer choices. In British Columbia, even among the vast majority of leftists, the acceptance of the legal and political systems themselves, cornerstones of liberal capitalism, was overwhelming. The Squamish Five were beyond the pale.

After 1983 the left was largely in retreat, winning some battles but losing the larger struggle. The IWA won a four-and-a-half-month strike in 1986 against companies demanding concessions and the right to contract out current union jobs to non-union subcontractors, but the forest industry was changing.[20] Sophisticated technology in the woods allowed fewer workers to do the logging. Similarly in the conversion plants more automated machinery cut payrolls. The IWA lost members.

The construction industry unions suffered setbacks. In the early 1980s, the Social Credit government began planning for a world exposition to be held in Vancouver in 1986. This was Expo 86. Jimmy Pattison, BC's most prominent businessman, was recruited to manage the preparations, and he recommended using union labour for all construction in return for a no-strike pledge from the unions. Traditionally in BC, industrial construction was done by union firms while non-union contractors dominated in the house-building sector. The Social Credit government had different ideas and a big Expo contract was given to a non-union firm. In 1984 there was confrontation and conflict on the Expo site. Pattison even suggested that the fair be cancelled if labour peace could not be secured. In the end, the non-union workers remained. According to Pattison, overall, 70 percent of the fair was built by union labour, but the non-union firms had slipped into the commercial and industrial sector, and within ten years, according to former civil servant Bob Plecas, 90 percent of commercial and industrial construction was done on open-shop sites where union and non-union worked by side, a clear defeat for the unions.[21]

Social Credit's attack on the left continued when they turned their attention to public-sector unions. In 1987 the government sought to undermine the teachers union, the British Columbia Teachers' Federation, by creating a Teachers College to oversee the professional aspects of teaching. The government also wanted to eliminate compulsory union membership. At this time, teachers did not have full collective bargaining rights; they could only negotiate salaries. As part of this package, the government offered teachers a choice: they could either adopt a "union model" with full collective bargaining rights and the right to strike, or an "association model" with no right to strike and limited collective bargaining rights. The government assumed that teachers would see themselves as professionals and thus choose the "association model." Teachers rallied, beginning protests and study sessions in late April. On 1 June, a one-day general strike, which included the wider union movement, was held, and teachers demonstrated their commitment to the BCTF and the principles of unionism. After the legislation was passed, all seventy-six provincial locals chose the union option.[22] It was a labour victory in a difficult time.

Social movements were also experiencing change. During the 1980s the anti-nuclear movement had a strong presence in British Columbia, especially in Vancouver. Anti-militarism generally was part of a long tradition in the provincial left, and at times some had hoped that opposition to militarism would rally the people and create a unity to overthrow the power bloc. In the radical leftist critique, militarism and capitalism were inextricably intertwined. Members of the Communist Party had played a prominent role in the diverse organizations dedicated to the achievement of world peace, but others were also involved, and the movement represented a broad spectrum.[23] Protests were notable during the Vietnam War, and during the 1980s, on many spring days, over fifty thousand people would take to the streets of Vancouver in peaceful marches to voice opposition to the arms race and the Cold War conflict between the United States and the Soviet Union. However, the end of the Vietnam War, the dismantling of the Berlin Wall in 1989, and the collapse of the Soviet Union in 1991 sapped the sense of urgency.

The women's movement, which included almost all leftist women, was divided, unable to mobilize for specific actions, and ignored by political powers. Part of this was due to success. Opportunities for women at work

Peace march, Vancouver, 1980. Photographer: Sean Griffin. *Pacific Tribune* Archive.

and in the education system had been enhanced: abortion rights and access were stronger, especially after 1988, when the Supreme Court of Canada struck down the existing abortion law, leaving Canada with no criminal provisions against abortion; and young women increasingly sensed that their ambitions could be realized. To be sure, a gender-equal society had not come into existence — poverty rates, income levels, safety in public places, job mobility options, household labour, and child care responsibility, among other things, remained gender biased — but for middle-class women there was access to the capitalist good life.

The sagging of the women's movement was also due to a resurgence of a counterattack. In the late 1970s the North American religious right, those with biblically based traditional views of the family and women's social roles, successfully organized to challenge the women's movement. In Canada an organization called REAL Women was especially effective in presenting the case for traditional views. In 1989, International Women's Day in Vancouver could still muster 2,500 marchers. This mobilization was, however, largely a negative response to the actions of Social Credit leader Bill Vander Zalm, a conservative Christian who led an anti-abortion crusade from the premier's office between 1986 and 1991.[24] Overall, Second Wave feminism had crested. The National Action Committee on the Status of Women, the main group that represented the diverse interests of Second Wave Canadian feminism, and a good barometer of the movement's fortunes, disintegrated and disappeared from public view over the course of the 1990s. Whether a third or even fourth wave of feminism has emerged remains debatable.

Like the women's movement, the lesbian and gay movements also faced a right-wing backlash beginning in the late 1970s, a backlash that spread from the United States into Canada. The modern struggle for gay and lesbian rights, which challenged the left to respond as it did the broader society, was evident in 1964 when Canada's first gay organization, the Association for Social Knowledge, was founded in Vancouver, modelled on a San Francisco group. In 1969, at a New York gay and lesbian bar called Stonewall on a June night, patrons stood up and challenged a police raid, thus beginning a much more public and aggressive movement for gay and lesbian liberation and basic human rights. The Vancouver Gay Liberation Front and the Vancouver branch of the Gay Alliance Toward Equality were both formed in the spring of 1971. Vancouver's first gay pride celebration was held in 1973 and the first lesbian caucus in the province, the British Columbia Federation of Women, was formed in 1974. Feisty and provocative, the public struggle for basic gay and lesbian rights had begun.[25]

The left and progressives generally took up the lesbian, gay, bisexual and transgender (LGBT) struggle over time, but segments of the right remained hostile. Police harassment remained a problem, and then the scourge of AIDS arrived in full force. Acquired Immune Deficiency Syndrome was talked about in the Canadian media in 1981, but the first Canadian death came a few years earlier, although it was not diagnosed as AIDS. Dealing with the complexities of AIDS became the focus of many in the gay community. AIDS Vancouver, Canada's first community-based

AIDS group was formed in early 1983.[26] Hostility and misunderstanding remained: according to Gary Mason and Keith Baldrey, journalists who wrote about the government of the era, Premier Bill Vander Zalm in the late 1980s "figured the best way to combat AIDS was really quite simple: stop having sex. Of course, that attitude was more in keeping with the 1950s, not the 1980s."[27] Moreover, during the Vander Zalm years, activists largely gave up on amending the provincial Human Rights Code to include sexual orientation. This was only achieved in June 1992, after the election of an NDP government.[28]

Canadian nationalism, which the left had largely embraced, reached a turning point in 1988. In 1979 nationalist sentiment was such that even the Social Credit premier came to the defence of provincial industry when MacMillan Bloedel, the BC-based forest industry giant, experienced a hostile takeover attempt from CP Investments, a central Canadian firm, suggesting that his government would make life difficult for the interlopers should they succeed, declaring that "BC is not for sale." This was a defence against central Canadian business, but it served notice to American capital as well. Federally, the 1988 election was in essence a referendum on free trade with the United States. The governing Progressive Conservative Party, which was already moving Canada closer to the United States in foreign policy and general attitude, favoured the deal while the Liberals and NDP opposed it. The argument against closer economic ties to the United States was highly emotional, based on fears of losing control over culture, economic policy, social welfare programs, and the provision of public services.

In this hotly contested federal election, British Columbia elected nineteen New Democrats, one Liberal, and only twelve Conservatives. The federal Conservatives, however, won the election and the free trade agreement was implemented in the following year. The federal Liberals had attacked free trade in 1988, but soon changed sides. By the time they returned to power in 1993 the Liberals supported the continental trade deal. In 1999, to illustrate the overall waning of nationalist sentiment, the US corporation Weyerhaeuser took over MacMillan Bloedel with the support of the provincial NDP government and barely a whimper from the general population.[29]

Canadian nationalism had been a powerful force, and many on the left had hoped that it would be at the forefront in bringing about fundamental change. After all, it effectively defined the problem as being the type of society developing in the United States. The United States, it was argued, undermined global peace, the success of Canadian culture, the survival of the welfare state, the ability of governments to serve their citizens, and the development of the Canadian economy beyond a resource base. The United States was also the home of militant, traditional, moral-funda-mentalist movements. Unions, women's groups, anti-poverty groups, and even segments of the business community that were negatively affected by US competition rallied under nationalist colours.

However, this nationalist version was unable to carry the weight. First, the economic malaise of the post-1975 period accentuated a perceived need for American investment and American markets. Economic fears, effectively cultivated by the business community, made nationalism ap-pear a luxury. Second, the free trade agreement did not destroy the Ca-nadian economy or immediately undermine social programs.

Third, nationalism had less appeal to the younger generation. In the 1990s, the aging activists of the 1960s complained about the apathy of youth in general and their lack of interest in the nationalist issue, but as Robert Wright notes, the context for youth had changed. Young people coming of age in the late 1980s and beyond lived in a world of poorly paid part-time jobs, high unemployment rates, heavy student debt loads, weak career possibilities, a shrinking civil service, lengthier times living at home with their parents, and a general intolerance of deviant youth behaviour. While the Sixties generation benefited from the growing state, which supplied unionized government jobs, as well as unemployment insurance and pension programs, the next generation had no such opportunities, and indeed believed that they would have to pay for the entitlements of the older generations. More conservative attitudes coupled with more tolerant social attitudes and a greater comfort with American culture became the order of the day. According to Wright, "Left-nationalism is graying, in short, and there is little evidence to suggest that progressive youth can be mobilized around an ideology that seems so anachronistic."[30] And finally, while nationalists declared war on an external force, the

United States, the most direct threat to the left came from within Canada in the form of a new political party.

The Reform Party, established in 1987, was a forceful expression of the New Right in Canada. It was a federal party that did not run in provincial elections, and although it is often associated with Alberta, it was also powerful in BC.[31] In the 1990s, the BC provincial vote went NDP, while the federal vote went Reform. The Reform Party had financial backing, media support, skilled organizers, and a thoughtful leader in Preston Manning. The new party was not prepared for the 1988 federal election and so did poorly. Moreover, the election was a referendum on free trade, and important business interests in the West were committed to free trade, and so the Reform Party showing was tentative, winning only 4.9 percent of all votes in BC.[32] They won no seats. However, in the next federal election in 1993, Reform won fifty-two seats nationally, supplanting the Progressive Conservatives on the right of the political spectrum. In British Columbia, Reform won 36.4 percent of the popular vote in this election, sending twenty-four members to the federal parliament. The NDP won two and the Liberals six. In the 1997 federal election, Reform won twenty-five BC seats with 43.1 percent of the popular vote, while the Liberals won six seats (28.8 percent) and the NDP three (18.2 percent).[33]

As Trevor Harrison has noted, both populism and neo-liberalism coalesced in the Reform Party.[34] The populist edge focused on external threats to the people in BC. Central Canadian political influence in federal government institutions was seen as notably evil. The political clout of Quebec in cultural and language issues also raised concerns. In Reform rhetoric, the federal government, driven by the interests of central Canada, willfully undercut economic development in the West and stymied the legitimate aspirations of westerners to be equal partners in Confederation. This drew on a long tradition of western grievance and protest.

Significantly, Reform did not criticize large corporations or the inequities of the marketplace. Reform populism blamed government for social and economic ills, demonizing the state and not capitalism. Governments were inefficient, they had become too big, they supported people who did not deserve to be supported with welfare programs, they favoured an educated inside clique of bureaucrats, and they stunted the initiatives of hard-working, decent citizens. Reform advocated a greater role for private enterprise in health care and education, favoured individuals planning for their own pensions by being active in the private financial sector rather than relying on government, and demanded the reduction of the federal debt.

There was also a cultural conservative element to Reform, one that was exploited by other parties to brand them as racist, homophobic, anti-immigrant, anti-First Nation, anti-feminist, and rural and unsophisticated. To be sure, traditionalist religious and women's organizations were represented within Reform, and the party advocated restrictions on immigration, championed heterosexual marriage, and saw no need to have the government fund women's programs so extensively, but, as Trevor Harrison notes in his study of Reformers in the early 1990s, "The degree of support for traditional conservative values is not as pronounced as the support for economic liberalism and demands for less government."[35]

The British Columbia academic and professional left was flummoxed by the rise of the Reform right. Many in the provincial working class endorsed the New Right. Citizens were voting NDP at the provincial level and Reform at the federal level. Could you be both left and right? Explanations were diverse, and culprits included the influence of a capitalist media, which overwhelmingly supported shrinking the size of government,[36] as well as the relentless barrage of market celebration provided by the business elite and their think tanks, especially the Fraser Institute. Also cited was the general trend of the global swing to the right after 1980, the anemic response of the NDP, which was tracking right and ineffectively defending leftist positions, confusion over the economic response to rapidly growing government debts, and the fear of economic collapse.

Less mentioned, on the left at least, was the fact that big government was legitimately open to criticism. If big business thwarted equality, social justice, and the development of human potential, that is, people participating fully in their own lives, then so too did politicians and bureaucrats. From the lunchroom of a unionized brewery, from behind the till in a women's clothing store, from behind the wheel of a five-ton truck taking fruit from the Okanagan to Vancouver, or from above the handle of a mop cleaning a detox centre on Vancouver Island, the welfare and Keynesian state was often seen as the preserve of a well-paid, educated elite, and a hardcore underclass. The elite raised taxes on ordinary working people to subsidize business ventures, pay the high salaries of bureaucrats and professors, and run social programs that benefitted undeserving people at the margins. At the same time, though, it should be emphasized, people were largely grateful for welfare services during times of need, desired quality education for their children, and respected the political and legal systems. Many hoped that their children would enter that upper echelon. Working-class political identities in a liberal capitalist society are indeed complex.

The Reform Party was one important force that would shape the future, but so, too, would the environmental movement and the new activism coming from the Indigenous world. In the 1970s and 1980s preserving forests and creating parks brought together a large swath of the population, including leftists. The movement was becoming increasingly adept at using publicity, political alliances, and political pressure. Beginning in 1974, for example, a small number of people on Haida Gwaii began organizing to preserve the forests of the South Moresby area, including Lyell Island, from logging. The Haida people were prominent and were initially joined by a few former Americans and a number of homegrown British Columbians, but the issue moved beyond the shores of Haida Gwaii to become an international cause, attracting many environmental groups, including the Audubon Society and the Sierra Club; environmentalists such as David Suzuki; Canadian celebrities including musician Bruce Cockburn, historian and journalist Pierre Berton, writer Farley Mowat, painters Robert Bateman, Toni Onley and Jack Shadbolt, and author Margaret Atwood; and international names such as Pete Seeger.

The British Columbia Social Credit government, the provincial logging industry, and the International Woodworkers of America wanted to log the area. The forest industry companies argued that the growing number of parks decreased their timber supply and thus the viability of their businesses. The IWA worried about jobs.[37] But members of the New Democratic Party and the federal Liberal party endorsed the plan of the environmentalists, and after 1984 the prime minister, Brian Mulroney, his environment minister Tom MacMillan, and most of the caucus were also supporters. From 1986 to 1988, Elizabeth May, a well-connected environmental activist and future leader of the federal Green Party, served as a special advisor to Minister MacMillan. The British Columbia Social Credit government, which also contained a few sympathetic voices, was forced to cave.[38] In July 1987, an agreement was reached between the BC government and the Progressive Conservative federal government to make the area a national park.[39]

First Nations successfully pushed for greater inclusion in public debates in this era. The issues were many, including racism and the legacy of residential schools, as well as poverty and unemployment, high incarceration rates, and low educational levels in the Aboriginal community. To bring change, Indigenous peoples and organizations were active on a number of fronts, seeking self-government, the maintenance of languages and cultural traditions, improved social and economic conditions, the honouring of existing treaty obligations, and, where there had been no treaties, settlements or full recognition of inherent rights. All of these goals were interrelated in the search for a better way of life and a just relationship with the non-Indigenous society.

In BC, the land question reemerged as a public issue in the early 1970s. Since the late 1800s, the BC government, as well as the federal government, had largely refused to recognize that the settler society had any treaty obligations with regard to the provincial land that they had appropriated from First Nations. There had been a few treaties concluded in the middle of the nineteenth century, covering tiny areas on Vancouver Island. Areas east of the Rockies were also included in treaties at the end of the century, but the vast majority of provincial land was not covered by treaties. Then, in a 1973 Supreme Court of Canada case, which was brought forward by long-time Nisga'a activist Frank Calder to support the land claims of the Nisga'a and which was lost on a technicality, a majority of the justices said that Aboriginal title could exist, though they were divided on whether or not these rights had been extinguished. It now seemed that First Nations had more rights than had been previously accepted. This led to willingness by the federal government to negotiate treaties. The BC government was less enthusiastic, but the extent of its authority over provincial land was now called into question. Companies interested in mining or forestry projects began to wonder whether their investments would be secure. By the late 1980s, pressure from First Nations, the courts, and investors undermined the stonewalling strategy of the government. For moral, legal and economic reasons, it was becoming clear that something had to be done.

By the end of the 1980s a new order was taking shape. Environmentalists were increasingly active in a wide range of issues. Beyond concerns about forests, wildlife, and water, climate change, an international problem, threatened the world in a most fundamental way. The right continued to reshape Canadian political culture, and while the federal Reform Party, with its brand of neo-liberal, right-wing populism, did not participate in provincial politics, a revived BC Liberal Party would draw on its ideals and personnel. First Nations, for their part, demanded action on social and economic issues, initiated protests against logging in their territorial lands, and had support from the courts in their search for recognition of land rights and the fulfillment of government obligations. As the century drew to a close, the left was operating in a new reality.

CHAPTER 7

The Left after 1991

THE HISTORICAL SHIFT of the 1970s and 1980s that ensconced right-wing ideals and institutions in the western world continued to set the boundaries of political debate in Canada after 1991. The left in BC was forced to respond defensively, and in this difficult context maintaining integrity and a sense of direction was no easy feat. The besieged union movement lacked the heft to counter the momentum of the right, as did the more radical left. Marxism was seemingly passé in this era of the right, a historical encumbrance that lingered in some university departments and union backrooms, the analysis of political parties at the fringe, the discussions of well-read activists, articles in small left-wing magazines, and the conversations of some NDP members. In provincial politics the face of the left was the NDP, and the party dressed itself in the garb of moderation to retain influence.

The NDP formed the government between 1991 and 2001.[1] The party took power largely because Social Credit, the vehicle of the right, im-

ploded and lost credibility under the shaky stewardship of Premier Bill
Vander Zalm. The NDP offered a restrained, social democratic leftism,
trying to create a positive business climate and control government spending, while at the same time defending a role for the state and the merits
of social programs, as well as basic equality and union rights.[2] The line
between the moderate left and the progressive section of Canadian liberalism was at times difficult to find. Mike Harcourt, a congenial lawyer
and former mayor of Vancouver, who would have been at home in the
federal Liberal Party, was the NDP premier from 1991 to 1996.[3] Harcourt
was replaced by Glen Clark, who was closer to the union movement and
more biting in his attacks on the power bloc, and he managed to eke out
a win in the 1996 provincial election. Clark resigned in 1999 and a new
leader, Ujjal Dosanjh, led the party in the defeat of 2001. Dosanjh moved
to the federal Liberal Party in 2004, becoming a high profile cabinet minister.[4]

The relatively moderate posture of the NDP in the 1990s did not mean
that there were no controversies or issues of long-term importance for
the left. Especially stormy and significant was the relationship between
the left and environmental organizations. In opposition the NDP had
offered a green platform that included doubling the amount of protected
wilderness areas in the province from 6 percent to 12 percent, and in the
1991 election the NDP won the support of many greens who were eager
for change. Once in power, the NDP was keen to satisfy environmentalists within and outside its ranks, but this was easier to say than to do, for
the NDP also wanted to satisfy workers and unions concerned about jobs
and financial security in a difficult economic time. The left had long focused on social justice and workers' rights, and as such, environmental
issues were seen through this lens. The new government was in a tricky
position, attempting to reconcile the interests of workers and their families
with the interests of environmentalists.[5] Solutions were elusive.

   The confrontation to save the old-growth forests of Clayoquot Sound
on the west coast of Vancouver Island, the most high-profile battle of the
"War in the Woods" of the 1990s, began in earnest in 1984, when First

Nations were joined by the Friends of Clayoquot to save one area of the sound, Meares Island. In 1992, Premier Harcourt, who, according to one prominent environmentalist was "arguably one of the greenest premiers Canada has ever had," used his persuasive managerial style to establish the Commission on Resources and Environment that allowed local communities, First Nations, and environmental groups to participate in decisions about future land and resource use.[6] The commitment to shared decision making did not produce harmony.[7] On 5 July 1993 environmentalists began a peaceful blockade of a bridge in order to stop the clear-cutting of nearby old-growth timber stands, logging that had been permitted by the provincial NDP government. The five First Nation bands in the region, about three thousand people, were engaged in pursuing land claims in the area. As well as First Nations, the local Friends of Clayoquot Sound had the support of many larger outside environmental organizations, including Greenpeace, the Sierra Club of Western Canada, and the Western Canada Wilderness Committee (WCWC).

The struggle went international, attracting celebrities such as Robert Kennedy Jr, who put in an appearance on 29 July. Thousands of people made the trek to the protest camp, and over the course of the summer some 856 protestors were arrested and charged with criminal contempt of court for violating a BC Supreme Court injunction that gave the logging company, MacMillan Bloedel, the right to use a road unimpeded. The activist camp was eventually dismantled. Many of those arrested were given tough jail sentences.[8] Logging continued.[9] The social democratic left had antagonized environmentalists.

The NDP clashed with environmentalists on another front. In August 1993, environmentalists adopted a new strategy, targeting companies in the United States and Europe that used wood products made from old-growth trees in British Columbia, eventually winning over Home Depot and Victoria's Secret, as well as a number of European firms. The campaign infuriated the lumber companies and others. Premier Harcourt toured Europe with Nuu-chah-nulth Chief George Watts to persuade corporate buyers that BC logs were harvested according to the highest environmental standards. Throughout the trip, Greenpeace activists organized a parallel tour, criticizing the Harcourt argument.[10] The campaign also raised the ire of Premier Glen Clark, who alienated many in the environmental community in 1997 when he declared Greenpeace an enemy of BC because of their international campaign to get consumers to boycott BC wood products.[11]

The other mainstay of the left, the union movement, also confronted environmentalists. In part, this was driven by insecurity and the waning clout of unions, especially the International Woodworkers of America (IWA), the major union in the forest industry. The number of workers in forestry was declining due to technological change, employer attacks on unions, and the increased use of non-union subcontractors. IWA membership shrank from some 42,000 members in 1982 to about 28,000 by the late 1990s.[12] There was a fear of job loss in a tough economy, and many unionists focused their anger on environmental activists. The IWA allied with the corporations against the environmentalists at Clayoquot Sound, persuaded that the creation of parks, not new technologies and industrial forestry, created unemployment. In the spring of 1994, twenty thousand workers from many Vancouver Island communities demonstrated against a government proposal to increase park space and preserve forest areas.[13]

In 1997, the IWA harassed two Greenpeace ships entering Vancouver harbour by setting up a blockade. The IWA said that it was frustrated by Greenpeace activists terrorizing their logging sites and costing them union jobs.[14] The leader of the provincial IWA, Jack Munro, had earlier called Greenpeace activist Tzeporah Berman "a menace to society."[15] In 1999 some one hundred employees of International Forest Products attacked protestors affiliated with the Western Canada Wilderness Committee, Forest Action Network, Friends of Elaho, Elaho Earth First, and People against Threatened Habitat who were working to protect old-growth forests in the Elaho Valley, near Squamish, from being logged.[16]

The distance between the left and environmentalists existed not only because leftists sometimes lacked sympathy and understanding with regard to particular environmental issues, but also because the environmental movement at this time often had little sympathy for the concerns of unions or workers and their families. One commentator noted in 1999, "The depth of working-class hatred towards environmentalists is hard to overestimate, especially in rural communities." But he goes on to note that the environmental movement, especially Greenpeace, had been crucial in deepening this divide: "That most environmentalists see this [working-class hatred] as a fact to be expected, rather than a terrible deficiency to be counteracted, points to the single greatest weakness of the environmental movement — the stubborn refusal to incorporate people's social needs into ecological concerns."[17] Michael M'Gonigle, a University of Victoria professor and co-founder of Greenpeace International, made a similar point, also in the 1990s: "Environmentalists talk to each other, but rarely to First Nations leaders, and even less to progressive labour leaders."[18]

The strategy of environmentalists was to focus on specific issues. Militant activists stood firm to protect particular rivers, animal species and forests, at times bravely exposing themselves to danger and legal repercussions. They felt that the immediacy of the threats to the environment demanded fast action; how issues were resolved was less important. Government regulation could be appropriate in one circumstance, while new technologies developed by capitalists seeking profits might be appropriate in another situation. It mattered little if the company was union or non-union. In this expedient approach, notions of left and right were old-fashioned, and more pejoratively, ideological and irrelevant. Indeed, persuading capitalists to change the way that they logged or to make profits in ventures that were more ecological was often the best way to bring about rapid change.

From a short-term tactical position, this approach to environmental issues made sense. Adopting leftist social and economic positions would alienate many people, perhaps splitting the movement along left-right lines, undermining the ability to mobilize across the political spectrum in order to get swift responses to pressing environmental threats. After all, many on the right liked parks and animals, too. While the left over the last century had built up an understanding of the world that wove together the social, moral, economic, political and environmental, the new environmental movement often focused on single, albeit crucial, issues. The structural inequities of capitalism and the interests of working-class families were of secondary importance, and to many in the movement, not concerns at all.

There was a push in the 1990s to move the BC Green Party to the left. The party had been founded in 1983 by, among others, Paul George and Adriane Carr, a husband-and-wife team that had also founded the Western Canada Wilderness Committee. In the provincial elections of the 1980s, the party had been unable to get even one percent of the popular vote. After 1993, under the leadership of twenty-one-year-old Stuart Parker, the BC Green Party attempted to broaden its appeal, attracting more youth, anti-poverty activists, and First Nation militants. In the 1996 provincial election, the party secured 1.99 percent of the vote. But Parker was closely linked to the NDP, and sought closer relations with the party and organized labour.

The founders were uneasy, and Carr, George, and Colleen McCrory, who were former supporters of the NDP, became increasingly disgruntled by the behaviour of the NDP government on environmental questions and worried that Parker had strayed too far from a focus on important environmental issues. In March 2000 the old guard, which included the Valhalla Society, the Sierra Legal Defence Fund, the Western Canada Wilderness Committee, and the David Suzuki Foundation, orchestrated a coup, bringing the party more firmly back into the environmental camp.[19] According to two academic researchers, the Green Party served a different constituency. The NDP's preoccupation with wealth redistribution, class interests, and social justice did not resonate with environmental activists who were more committed to the post-materialist values of democracy, personal autonomy, and identity.[20] In the May 2001 provincial election, the BC Green Party ran seventy-two candidates and amassed a significant 12.39 percent of the popular vote. Parker supported the NDP. The left and the Greens remained aloof from each other.

When the NDP came to power in 1991, First Nations issues were prominent, and the new government offered some hope for a more positive relationship. Building on actions by the previous Social Credit government, Premier Mike Harcourt established the BC Treaty Commission in 1992, and this put in place a process to help facilitate treaty settlements.

Parallel to the Commission, the NDP government negotiated the Nisga'a Treaty, covering a large area in northwestern BC that came into effect in 2000. NDP treaty initiatives were attacked by the provincial Liberals, who whipped up anti-First Nations sentiment, claiming that the social democrats were giving up too much at the expense of non-Indigenous British Columbians. But despite the actions of the NDP, overall progress was painfully slow.

In 2001 the left suffered a blow when the NDP was devastated at the polls in a provincial election. The alienation of the environmental movement and concomitant success of the BC Green Party chipped away somewhat at NDP support, as did the rightward tracking of the province's political culture. But an accumulation of scandals over the decade also played a significant role. Mike Harcourt had resigned as premier in February 1996 over a high-profile scandal of previous years that involved the misuse of money by the NDP, a scandal in which Harcourt had no responsibility. In August 1999, Glen Clark also stepped down because of a scandal. There was a perceived conflict of interest involving the government granting of a casino licence and $10,000 worth of renovations on Premier Clark's house by the person who received the casino licence. However, no criminal breach of the law was found.

There was more, and it was exploited to the hilt by the mainstream press, which was not supportive of the NDP. After the 1996 election, much was made of the fact that, prior to the election, the Clark government had chosen sympathetic and generous assessments of the performance of the provincial economy in order to proclaim a budget surplus. The press and the Liberal Party made much of the so-called fudge-it-budget in ensuing years. The other scandal was the fast ferry fiasco. The Clark government inaugurated a program to build a fleet of new ferries in British Columbia, a defensible project, but the program was poorly managed and led to major cost overruns, reinforcing the view of the NDP as poor economic managers, a perspective constantly reinforced by the Liberal opposition and the press.

Also significant in the defeat of the NDP was the reinvention of the right. The Social Credit Party disappeared after 1991 and a new anti-leftist political front emerged in the guise of the provincial Liberal Party, led, after 1993, by Gordon Campbell. The party was more socially progressive than Social Credit, and morally conservative elements were marginalized. Women's equality and lesbian and gay rights were recognized in the new version of BC liberalism. More urbane, projecting itself as the party of economic management and development, and reflecting the economic values of neo-liberalism, the Liberal Party won an amazing 77 seats with 57.62 percent of the popular vote in 2001. The NDP won only two seats and secured a measly 21.56 percent of the popular vote.

After the election, workers and unions soon felt the impact of aggressive liberalism. The focus was on government workers, reflecting the fact that in the private sector the decline in union membership density and worker militancy had been underway for decades. In the private sector there were fewer jobs in industry, a long-term trend, while the number of workers in the service sector, which constituted 78 percent of the work force by the end of the century, increased.[21] Throughout the industrial sector, union membership numbers were falling, and unions, such as the International Woodworkers of America, tried to compensate by organizing in the service sector. By 1999 about one-third of IWA membership was outside forestry. Locals included three video rental outlets, an airport car-rental operation, a few car dealerships, a Value Village location, and a group of cab drivers.[22] Other established unions organized employees at some White Spot, Starbucks, and Kentucky Fried Chicken locations, but overall the results were meagre.[23] The service industry in the private sector, which relied on younger, temporary workers and had low margins, was notoriously hard to organize.

Overall, the size of the workforce and the number of unionized workers was growing, but the proportion of the workforce in unions was falling. Approximately 46 percent of provincial workers were organized in 1984, a number that decreased to just over 30 percent in the new century.[24] Union militancy had also declined. There were fewer strikes in the 1990s than there had been in the 1980s, and BC was below the Canadian average in the proportion of workers in the work force engaged in a job action during any given week.[25]

The new Liberal government targeted workers in the public sector, where union density was highest: about 75 percent of public-sector workers were organized but only 18 percent of private-sector employees.[26] Public-sector unions, too, were closely associated with the NDP, a situation that rankled Liberal supporters. Labour relations between the government and its employees had at times been difficult during the NDP years — public-sector workers had been ordered back to work and had settlements imposed on more than one occasion[27] — but the Liberal action was of a different magnitude. The day after taking office Premier Gordon Campbell reduced income taxes for all British Columbians, a regressive though popular measure, and reduced corporate income taxes. Thereafter he pleaded that BC was in tough economic times and needed sacrifices from government workers. Teachers, whose contract expired on 30 June 2001, were declared to be providing an essential service and lost the right to strike in August. In October the British Columbia Teachers' Federation (BCTF) secured a membership strike vote of over 90 percent, and in early January 2002 began a "work-to-rule" campaign, refusing to work outside school hours or perform volunteer activities. On 17 January 2002, the government brought down a budget. Funding cuts averaged 25 percent over all ministries, and some 11,700 jobs were to be cut from the public service, about one-third of the public service workforce. As in the restraint program of 1983, this offensive launched by the right was more than just an assault on unionism. Legal Aid funding was cut, post-secondary tuition freezes were eliminated, and welfare payouts, already constrained in the NDP years, were reduced and made more difficult to secure. Funding was also removed from women's centres, the fisheries renewal program, and the BC Festival of the Arts. Environmental standards were lowered.

On January 27, Black Sunday, closure was invoked to bring in three bills to tame government workers. Teachers were ordered back to work, and the government gave itself the power to reopen signed agreements with government workers and to impose contracts on them. Bill 29 reopened the nurses' collective agreement imposed by the government a year earlier and rolled back the wages of approximately one hundred thousand workers in the health sector. The government also opened the door to increased privatization, especially in long-term health care. In May the Human Rights Commission's authority was circumscribed and employment standards were weakened.[28] Overall, the onslaught of 2001 and 2002 was much more draconian than the restraint program of the Bill Bennett Social Credit government in 1983.

The left fought back. The first protest was held on 23 February 2002, when some twenty thousand people descended on Victoria, and smaller groups met in communities across the province. On 25 May some thirty to forty thousand people rallied in Vancouver. However, the momentum of 1983 was not achieved; the Liberal government had much legitimacy, having recently won a staggering majority government; the NDP was in

Supporters of the 2005 teachers' strike. Photographer: Elaine Brière.
Pacific Northwest Labor History Association Collection.

tatters; and there was a lack of solidarity between private-sector and public-sector unions, against whom the anti-union attack was levelled. Especially hard hit were hospital and care facility employees, most of whom were women and many of whom were recent immigrants.[29] The weakness of the left was exposed.

Of course, militancy was not completely dead, especially in the public sector. In October 2005, for example, some thirty-eight thousand BC teachers went on strike over wages, class sizes, and the bargaining framework. The strike was deemed illegal by the Labour Relations Board and the BC Supreme Court. Despite the illegality of the strike, the teachers had much public support; they represented themselves successfully as defenders of education and the broad public interest. However, notwithstanding the militancy, solidarity, and support, the teachers won little, and after an arbitrated settlement they returned to work.[30] In the private sector, the once pattern-setting forest industry unions continued in decline. In 2006, the International Woodworkers of America merged into the United Steelworkers of America in an attempt to increase its influence, and in 2007 some seven thousand coastal forest workers struck. A notable aspect of the 2007 strike was the fact that its impact was so small. Whereas in the 1980s a coastal strike was major news, in 2007 the strike received far less interest. Moreover, as one union activist noted, once government workers had sought parity with forest industry workers in their contracts, but the reverse was now true.[31]

A 2009 strike by 450 Lower Mainland HandyDart drivers revealed much about the state of labour and the left in the province. HandyDart drivers provide a service, transporting disabled people who are unable to use the bus system to and from social centres, doctors' appointments, and clinics. The drivers had worked for a number of service providers across greater Vancouver, but in January 2009 a private US-based corporation won the contract to deliver all HandyDart service in the Lower Mainland. The American for-profit company, with little understanding of provincial labour culture and regulations, sought to gut the workers' pension scheme, cap health benefits, stop benefits for part-time workers, remove the guaranteed hours per day for full-time drivers, and contract out office and maintenance work. On 23 October 2009, the workers, members of the

HandyDart strikers, 2009. Courtesy of photographer, Michael Atkinson.

Amalgamated Transit Union, voted 97 percent in favour of a strike, which began on October 26. After a ten-week strike, an arbitrated settlement, largely maintaining the pre-strike status quo, ended the dispute. In this instance, holding on to what one had was a victory, and union solidarity won out against globalization, privatization, reduced government funding of social services, neo-liberalism, and North American anti-union pressures.[32]

The NDP remained the party of the left in the electoral arena, and after 2001 began rebuilding. Carole James became leader of the provincial NDP on November 23, 2003. While James brought the party back to a level of respectability in 2005, she could not win. In the 2005 provincial election, the NDP won 33 seats with 41.52 percent of popular vote, and in

2009 the party won 35 seats and 42.06 percent of the popular vote. Over-all, though, the Liberals remained in power during the decade, winning 46 seats and 45.8 percent of the vote in 2005 and 49 seats and 46.02 per-cent in 2009.[33] James, who was more aligned with the social service rather than the union wing of the party, sought to take the party even closer to the centre by reaching out to the BC business community and loosening its ties with organized labour in an attempt to win over more moderate voters. Little, however, changed.[34]

Then, shortly after the 2009 provincial election, politics in BC became frenetic, creating opportunities for the left. Premier Gordon Campbell announced that his government was going to enter into an agreement with the federal government to combine the provincial sales tax and the federal tax into a new harmonized sales tax (HST). The far right and the left combined to attack the Liberal policy. This spawned a popular revolt that forced a referendum on the issue, started recall campaigns against Liberal members of the legislature, and led to the resignation of the pre-mier. For the far right, the policy was seen as a tax grab, especially odious because it was introduced by a government that had just won an election without mentioning the new policy. The left criticized the illegitimate timing of the tax and argued that it shifted the tax burden from business to ordinary British Columbians. There was, then, a populist irruption, in which both the left and the far right sought to harness it to serve their own ends. They successfully drove down Liberal support. To staunch an impending political defeat, Premier Gordon Campbell resigned on 3 November 2010 to clear the air and make way for a new leader, Christy Clark.

Campbell was not the only political casualty of the political upheaval. Within the NDP, which sensed victory in the fall of 2009, a group of thirteen members of the legislature came to the conclusion that Carole James would be unlikely to win against a new Liberal leader. In a revolt that was based on a critique of leadership, not ideology, they spoke out openly, and James, fearing party disunity, officially stepped down as leader of the BC NDP on 20 January 2011.[35] She was replaced by Adrian Dix three months later, but he did not exploit the weakness of the Liberals. Anticipating an easy election victory, the Dix NDP offered no populist passion against the powers that be, and the party's pragmatic, understated program did not win over sufficient numbers of workers concerned about their economic future. To the surprise of many, Christy Clark won a Liberal majority government on 14 May 2013.[36]

Leftists and environmentalists continued to mix it up in the new century. Oil and gas production, pipeline construction, oil tanker traffic on the coast, forest and wildlife preservation, urban development, transportation infrastructure, hydro-electric development, and the health of rivers, among other things, were all interconnected, and both understanding the problems and developing solutions were extremely complex, creating political difficulties for the left and the right.

Environmental problems were also increasingly recognized as global, as well as local and national, and the threats to human survival stimulated a sense of urgency among activists. The 1987 report from the United Nations World Commission on Environment and Development called *Our Common Future*, also known as the Bruntland Report, emphasized the global nature of environmental problems and solutions. The goal was sustainable development, a new catchphrase that linked economic and environmental development in a supposedly coherent vision of the future. This was followed by the Earth Summit meeting at Rio de Janeiro in 1992, an international conference that produced twenty-seven principles in the Rio Declaration on Environment and Development, a guide for the twenty-first century. Climate change or global warming also became common currency. The Kyoto Protocol of 1997 came into effect in 2005. It called for international cooperation in reducing greenhouse gas emissions into the atmosphere. Canada was one of the signatory countries.

But if recognition of the threat of climate change and the danger of oil-based economies was spreading, there was also strong resistance on the right of the political spectrum. In 2012, BC's Rex Weyler, a long-time ecological writer, director of Greenpeace between 1974 and 1982, and a co-founder of Greenpeace International, noted that despite the hoopla surrounding big environmental issues, fifty years after the emergence of the international environmental movement in the early 1960s, "the most troubling trends — Earth's temperature, species diversity, soil health, toxic dumps, shrinking forest, expanding deserts — appear worse. The testimony of our collective failure blows around us like a chilling polar wind."[37] Canada, under Conservative Prime Minister Stephen Harper, largely ignored the concerns of environmentalists, dismantling regulations and reneging on commitments. In December 2012, Canada became the first country to withdraw from the Kyoto Protocol.[38]

In politics, the left, including the NDP, contained a strong environmental contingent, but not all environmentalists were on the left. Green Parties at the federal and provincial levels, which put forward environmentally focused programs, catered to a diverse constituency. There were supporters from the left, but many, if not most, were not. Some wanted to draw on the power of capital and markets, to work hand in hand with businessmen, to find practical technological solution to environmental problems, while others wanted to halt economic expansion and stifle global trade. In some instances environmentalists looked favourably on the behaviour of corporations and political leaders on the right, including Gordon Campbell in British Columbia and Arnold Schwarzenegger in California, in that they promoted environmentally friendly policies at times. The Green Parties attracted committed environmentalists, as well as people who had general worries about the environment and thought that the NDP was too far to the left and the BC Liberals too far to the right. Liberals, social democrats, people disgusted with traditional party politics, and even Conservatives found a home in the Green Parties. As well, some environmentalists and environmental organizations floated among the Liberals, Greens, or New Democrats, depending on party stances on particular issues.

In the 2004 federal election, the national Green Party was led by a former Progressive Conservative, Jim Harris, offering a platform that supported military interventions, tax cuts, and "fiscally conservative" policies.[39] Greens, though, were not predominantly conservative and balked at the anti-environmentalism of the federal Conservative party led by Prime Minister Stephen Harper. Further, Greens tended to look favourably on government regulation to solve problems, a position often at odds with business perspectives.[40] In BC, the Greens held much appeal and after the 2008 federal election, the leader of the federal Green Party, Elizabeth May, moved to BC, winning a seat in the Saanich-Gulf Islands riding in the 2011 federal election, a first for the Green Party in Canada.[41] May appealed to many former Liberal voters, middle-class voters, and environmentalists wary of the NDP, as well as social democrats who voted strategically to oust a Conservative incumbent.

Green-NDP-Liberal relations were also extremely complicated and fluid in provincial politics. In 2008 Premier Gordon Campbell announced a new Climate Action Plan that included a tax on carbon. The extra cost for carbon fuel, it was argued, would lessen the use of carbon fuel and speed the search for alternatives. Many environmentalists were pleased. Jane Sterk, the leader of the provincial Green Party, criticized some of the details, but supported the initiative, as did the David Suzuki Foundation, ForestEthics, and the Pembina Institute. The NDP spearheaded the populist attack on the unpopular tax that would be added at the gas pumps beginning on July 1, 2008, using the slogan "Axe the Gas Tax." The NDP strategy played to the Interior, where long driving distances suggested that residents were enduring an undue burden. The NDP also argued that the tax would especially hurt the poor, despite the targeted credits for lower income groups. The NDP party proposed capping emissions from large industrial sources, harmonizing those efforts with a North America cap-and-trade system, and enhancing public transit, but details were sparse and to many environmentalists the plan was insufficient.[42]

The tax was unpopular and the NDP's attack on it arguably improved the fortunes of the party in the 2009 election, but it alienated many environmentalists both within and outside the NDP. It smacked of political opportunism, a calculated appeal to the populist right that was at times hostile to environmental initiatives. Both David Suzuki and Tzeporah Berman, high profile environmental crusaders, endorsed the Liberal tax and criticized the NDP position. Nevertheless, environmentalists were divided. While those who decried the NDP tactic argued that the tax was a step in the right direction, other prominent environmentalists, such as Alexandra Morton, a wild salmon advocate, and Michael M'Gonigle, argued that the Liberal proposal was an ineffective smokescreen that failed to address deeper issues, a program, moreover, that was hypocritical when seen in conjunction with other Liberal actions, such as the development of oil and gas in the province, that were anti-environment.[43]

In 2013 the Green Party won its first seat in the provincial legislature. Andrew Weaver, a climate scientist, won the middle-to-upper-middle-class riding of Oak Bay in Victoria, on the strength of many votes coming from former Liberals. Other renowned environmentalists supported the NDP: when NDP leader Adrian Dix announced during the election campaign that he would change his mind and oppose the Kinder Morgan plan to twin its pipeline that took bitumen from northern Alberta to Burnaby, because it would increase coastal tanker traffic, some environmentalists, including Tzeporah Berman, who had come out strongly against the NDP in 2009, publicly endorsed the party.[44] However, Dix's stance also alienated others, including workers, who thought that his stance was rash, suggesting that the NDP was against all economic development. For the left, environmental politics were fraught with difficulties.

Beyond electoral politics, however, there were signs of increasing co-operation between the left and segments of the environmental movement. In 2002 the David Suzuki Foundation, the Pulp and Paper Workers of Canada (PPWC), a union that had already supported environmentalists during the 1993 "War in the Woods," and the Communications, Energy and Paperworkers of Canada worked with the Sierra Legal Defence Fund to challenge the log export policy of the BC government.[45] In 2003 the BC Coalition for Sustainable Forest Solutions, which included a number of First Nations, the BC Carpenters Union, the Hospital Employees' Union, the PPWC, the International Longshore and Warehouse Union Local 400, and the BCGEU, as well as many environmental groups, including the West Coast Environmental Law and the Dogwood Initiative, produced a program for sustainable communities and greater local control in forest management.[46] In 2004, when the Haida people moved to take more control of the forest resources in their traditional area, a coalition of more than thirty unions and environmental groups, including the BC Government Employees Union, the PPWC, the Hospital Employees' Union, the Sierra Club, and the David Suzuki Foundation, supported the First Nation against the policies of the provincial government.[47]

During the strike by coastal forest workers in 2007, the Western

Canada Wilderness Committee (WCWC) and the Sierra Club of Canada supported the workers. According to Ken Wu of the WCWC, "The fact is, in order to establish sustainable forestry on Vancouver Island, it's also important that the thousands of workers in the industry are also treated justly and fairly. That's what a compassionate society would ensure, in order to minimize conflict and maintain a decent life for people while we work to sustain nature."[48] The WCWC action was significant. As unions have increasingly over time rallied to support environmental causes and groups, environmental organizations have not always followed suit by visibly supporting left issues such as better wages and working conditions, union rights, and greater income equality. Increased reciprocity offers the promise of a broader left-green alliance.

Collaboration between leftists and environmentalists is an important step, but it is not straightforward. For example, Green Jobs BC, an organization formed in 2011, brings labour and environmental groups together to advance policy initiatives that result in green, community-sustaining jobs and to increase cooperation among sympathetic groups in society. In 2013 the steering community included representatives from unions, Vancity Credit Union, the Sierra Club, and the David Suzuki Foundation. But despite the promise, there is reason for caution. Jim Sinclair, president of the BC Federation of Labour, noted at a September 2012 Green Jobs BC conference: "We can find our differences in about 30 seconds. The question is to find common ground."[49]

In 2012 many people from the left, the environmental movement, First Nations, and even segments of the centre and right came together to challenge the plans of a Calgary-based corporation, Enbridge Inc. The company, with the support of the Alberta and federal governments, proposed to build a pipeline to transport bitumen from the tar sands of northern Alberta to Kitimat, on the west coast of British Columbia. From this coastal port the bitumen was to be transported by tankers, largely to China. The potential environmental threats of such a proposal to First Nations territories in the Interior and to the coast are immense. Adrian Dix, the NDP leader, was firm in his opposition to the project, as he would be later to the Kinder Morgan proposal. The provincial Liberal party, under Christy Clark, was willing to consider the project only if certain

Environmental rally against Northern Gateway Pipeline, Victoria, 22 October 2012.
Courtesy of the *Vancouver Sun*.

environmental and First Nation concerns were met and if the financial
return to the province was more significant. Although a few construction
unions and First Nations seeking economic benefits were supportive publicly, there was much unity among progressives and leftists against the
project, and the measure seemed doomed. Since the 2013 election victory,
however, the Christy Clark Liberals, keen to secure economic development, have been entertaining pipeline proposals more openly. The pipeline issue, like other environmental questions, has the potential to be
divisive on the left.

For all political parties, integrating environmental, economic, and social dimensions in a persuasive vision that captures public enthusiasm is
an ongoing priority, requiring thinking beyond the election cycle, as well
as beyond the simple binaries of environment versus jobs or environment
versus a buoyant economy, to grasp the long-term implications of environmental degradation. On the left, of course, environmental problems must
be analyzed from a left perspective, pointing out the role of corporate
activities and the dynamics of capitalist market economics in creating
environmental problems. Solutions must reflect left goals, including economically and environmentally sound jobs, as well as resources managed
to benefit the long-term interests of the people, socially, economically, and

environmentally. This is no simple task. Whether the future delivers a predominantly right-wing or left-wing environmental movement is of great consequence. The right is not idle. Preston Manning, speaking at a gathering of right-wing thinkers in March 2013, offered a strategy to conservatives that put first, taking "the high moral ground on environmental issues."[50]

Like the environmental movement, the Indigenous community is internally complicated and diverse, trying to working out a future in a context being shaped by outside forces on the right and on the left. The provincial Liberals continued to disparage the treaty process and First Nations demands after forming the government in 2001, but then, in 2005, Premier Gordon Campbell reversed his position: his government would now seek a positive, new relationship with the province's First Nations. While treaty settlement was slow, there were initiatives to encourage partnerships between companies, government, and First Nations to pursue economic development in traditional First Nations territories. This was appealing to some First Nations leaders and bands who were already moving into business, choosing entrepreneurship and engagement with the economy to improve the lot of their people. Others looked to a more cooperative, community-based approach to development, an approach drawing on Aboriginal community traditions. Positions are diverse, of course, but there is a sense of emerging left-right sensibilities in the Indigenous world, with the political right in Canada encouraging the adoption of private property on reserves, accelerated resource exploitation, the establishment of Aboriginal businesses, a greater sense of individualism, and engagement with competitive markets.

There is much sympathy on the left for Indigenous struggles for a better standard of living, access to education, and basic human rights. Nevertheless, there are also points of conflict. Treaty claims which, if successful, would include Aboriginal control of fish, timber, and minerals, as well as territorial land, could have serious implications for workers and their communities. What would be the fate of non-Indigenous loggers and miners, as well as their families, in areas where First Nations demands were met? Would they have no work? Workers and their unions are concerned.[51] Moreover, as many First Nations bands go into businesses such as logging in order to improve the economic condition of their people, left environmentalists are faced with balancing their support for Indigenous social and economic gains against their perceptions of possible environmental harm when considering First Nations ventures.[52]

For leftists, too, Indigenous aspirations force reflection on the ideal of equality, a fundamental, if difficult, tenet of the left. First Nations and their supporters argue persuasively that Indigenous peoples deserve "special treatment" because they have lived in British Columbia for generations before the arrival of the new settlers and experienced the debilitating effects of colonialism, a process that included losing their land. On the left, a nuanced understanding of equality is necessary in order to accommodate First Nations and to counter the idea contained in the stark populist slogan, "Equal rights for all, special privileges for none," a slogan that embodies a deep-seated sentiment that has been used by those on the right to mobilize non-Indigenous British Columbians against Aboriginal aspirations. In the 2013 provincial election campaign, the NDP committed to further the treaty process and to improve the everyday lives of Indigenous people, but just how this would have worked out if they had formed the government is unclear.

The history of the left in recent years has not only involved the union movement and electoral politics. A new left-oriented research centre adroitly countered the interpretation of the world presented by the mainstream media. The Canadian Centre for Policy Alternatives (CCPA) was established in 1980 by a group of academics at Carleton University. In 1997 it opened a BC office with Seth Klein as director. Funded by unions and individual donors, the CCPA publishes academically sound, rigorous analysis of economic and environmental policies. The quality of the work is such that the established media publishes many of their findings and suggestions. The voice of the right, which comes often from think-tanks such as the Fraser Institute, now faces a strong challenge. The internet and social media have also opened up opportunities for alternative views, connecting British Columbians to national and global issues. While small left-wing magazines have long been a staple of communication for leftists, more easily accessible, polished, online sources deliver news and opinions more quickly and more broadly. Notable for BC news coverage is *The Tyee*, an online magazine that was established in November 2003 by David Beers to provide an alternative to corporate media. The magazine offers stories and analysis that provide critical perspectives on provincial politics, environmental issues, and economic policies.

A new generation of leftists, evoking the ideas and tactics of the Wobblies of the early twentieth century and the New Left of the 1960s, and wrapping them up in a modern anarchist vision, is another important component of the recent left. This movement, invigorated by youth, took aim at international corporations and global organizations. Toronto-based journalist and activist Naomi Klein offers a window into the anti-globalization and anti-corporation world. Klein, who was born in 1970, remembers growing up in Ontario as a mall rat, enthusiastically embracing consumer culture. She was, however, aware of the identity issues of race, gender, and sexuality that mobilized many of her peers. In the mid-1990s she became conscious of a change in some student activism, "a broadening out to include corporate power, labor rights, and a fairly developed analysis of the global economy."[53] In 2000 she published a best-selling book, *No Logo*, which analyzed global capitalism in the 1990s, suggested possibilities for action, and summed up the aspirations of an international movement. Klein focused on major corporations with distinct logos that produced consumer goods, criticizing the clout of the buying power of big companies, the part-time, insecure sales jobs in North America, the sweat shops in developing countries that produced the goods for the western world, and the intrusion of corporate logos into public space.

Klein also saw hope, arguing that "it is in the ranks of the millions of temp workers that the true breeding grounds of the anti-corporate backlash will most likely be found."[54] She also discussed pockets of resistance, such as culture jammers who counter, contort, and undermine the messages of corporations on billboards and online.[55] Prominent in the international culture jamming scene is *Adbusters*, published by Vancouver-based Media Foundation. The magazine was founded in 1989 by Kalle Lasn and Bill Schmalz to counter a campaign by BC forest industry companies against the environmental movement. *Adbusters* also spawned Buy Nothing Day in Vancouver in 1992. This campaign in November to protest excessive consumerism has grown and is celebrated in more than sixty countries. Other resisters included European activists who mobilized to reclaim the streets for the people from corporate hands and organizations that challenged the excesses of corporate behaviour in the courts. Klein concluded that "ethical shareholders, culture jammers, street reclaimers, human rights hacktivists, school-log fighters and Internet corporate watchdogs are at the early stages of demanding a citizen-centred alternative to the international rule of the brands."[56]

In dramatic street actions at international meetings, protestors challenged major corporate and political interests. The forty-thousand-strong protest in Seattle on 30 November 1999 at the meeting of the World Trade Organization, which came into being in 1995 as the successor to the 1947 General Agreement on Tariffs and Trade, gave notice of the momentum of the emerging sensibility. The cooperation of many environmental, human rights, union, and feminist groups with new activists offered hope for a more cohesive left. The size and strength of the protest surprised authorities. Some of the younger militants also engaged in direct action, smashing windows and challenging authorities. Over six hundred people were arrested.

If Seattle was the coming of age of the new movement, events two years earlier in Vancouver served notice that something new was in the air. The November 1997 meeting of the heads of the Asia-Pacific Economic Co-operation (APEC) economies attracted thousands of protestors at the University of British Columbia campus where the meeting was held. Among the protesters, diversity was the order of the day: "The protest brought together a large array of groups and individuals holding divergent, even contradictory positions. Some were protesting the suppression of traditional civil rights in APEC countries; others took issue with a broader range of rights violations; others focused on states' colonialist ambitions — China in Tibet, Indonesia in East Timor; and still others expressed more general concerns about world exploitation and oppression, and the growing power of transnational corporations." The common theme, though, was hostility to neo-liberalism.[57] The heavy-handed way that the Liberal federal government managed the APEC affair, including restricting free speech and arresting and pepper spraying peaceful protestors, also alarmed thoughtful Canadians.

Naomi Klein offered insights into the political sensibility of the anti-corporate crusaders, especially the hostility to the state, centralized power, and political parties. As she wrote in December 2000, "I've never joined a political party, never been to a political convention. Last election, after being dragged by the hair to the ballot box, I was overcome by stomach pains more acute than those suffered by my friends who simply ingested their ballots."[58] In the same article she notes: "Listen to the most economically and socially excluded Canadians and you hear an idea entirely absent from the mainstream left: a deep distrust of the state. This distrust is based on lived experience: police harassment of dissenters and immigrants, punitive welfare offices, ineffective job training programs, patronage and corruption, and scandalous management of natural resources."[59] This anarchist tinge, celebrating localism and direct democracy, did not fit well with the hierarchical, electorally focused NDP that was dedicated to using the state as the vehicle for social change. Despite this, some NDPers recognized the spirit of the new movement, and in June 2001, a few members of the federal NDP began to seek ways to welcome radical activists, including the anti-corporatists.[60] Two British Columbia members of parliament, Svend Robinson and Libby Davies, were prominent supporters of this New Politics Initiative. However, no concrete organizational structure was put forward to find a suitable place for the social movements in the NDP.

The 2010 Winter Olympics in Vancouver was another venue for protest. Vancouver won the bid to host the games in 2003, supported by both the provincial and federal Liberals as well as the NDP. Prosperity, jobs, and economic growth, as well as fun and excitement won over the majority of British Columbians. Many, however, disagreed with the expenditure when there were so many social and economic problems in the province. Anti-corporate and anti-globalization activists began protesting before the games, hoping to leverage government funding for housing for the homeless, better health care, and better treatment of the poor. In February 2007, the Anti-Poverty Committee engaged in militant protest, including the ransacking of the premier's office. Other protest groups included the Impact on Communities Coalition and the Olympic Resistance Network (ORN), formed in early 2008. By the time the Olympics rolled around the ORN had hundreds of members and about forty core organizers. Their list of grievances was broad, including environmental destruction, native subjugation, billions of dollars in public debt, and police-state repression. Olympic Games sponsors were targeted for their environmental policies. The militants, often younger and boisterous, attracted like-minded folks from across North America.[61]

The BC Civil Liberties Association was also active, championing the right of free speech. On Friday, February 12, 2010, some 1,500 peaceful protesters marched through Vancouver. The next day, however, a militant group of protesters committed violence against property, earning a hard response from the police and major news coverage.[62] Anti-Olympics sentiment was hardly restricted to the often-masked protesters engaging in militant acts on the streets of Vancouver, but while NDPers, other leftists and members of the anti-globalization forces had similar enemies and often attended the same rallies and supported the same causes, the extra-parliamentary focus and at times illegal occupation of public space ensured division.

In the fall of 2011, British Columbians participated in the worldwide Occupy protests. The economic collapse of 2008 framed the uprising. The economic downturn, precipitated by a deregulated, chaotic, uncontrolled financial system in the United States, spread around the world. Governments responded with financial assistance for big corporations, owners and shareholders. The wealthy carried on and indeed increased their wealth while the rest of the population suffered. Unemployment, bankruptcies, postponed retirements, and lost houses became the order of the day. If the extreme was not as evident in Canada, there were still tough economic times, and in Canada, too, it was recognized that there was a growing disparity between rich and ordinary Canadians.[63] The Vancouver-based *Adbusters* is credited with beginning a movement by putting out a Twitter hashtag: #OccupyWallStreet. The taking over of public space began in New York City on 17 September 2011. Thereafter it spread, accelerated by social media.[64] On 15 October, activists occupied sites in the centre of Vancouver and Victoria, as well as other BC cities including Nanaimo, Prince George and Kamloops.

With much public sympathy, occupiers set up tent cities, which were governed based on the principle of consensus. The issues raised were many. As one Nanaimo protester said: We "want banking reform, market reform, corporate reform, and transparency of government."[65] Homelessness, First Nations claims, and environmental issues were also part of the BC discussion. The most captivating slogan, though, was the analysis of the economy as divided between the 1 percent who controlled and benefitted from the current economic climate and the 99 percent, the rest of the population that endured. By the end of November the highly publicized occupations had largely ended. More broadly based than the anti-Olympics protest and more successful in putting economic inequality front and centre, the malaise and discontent exposed by the Occupy movement did not translate into concrete organizations and clear political goals, in the short run at least.

More recently, in late 2012 and early 2013, a national protest movement, Idle No More, irrupted within the First Nations community. Beginning in Saskatoon, it spread across Canada, including into British Columbia, and it gained supporters around the world. There was a youthful edge to the movement that executed flash mob demonstrations in shopping malls and used social media to mobilize activists. The goals were to raise awareness regarding native issues such as treaty rights and social and environmental sustainability. The movement actively sought supporters outside of the Indigenous community, and had an affinity with the leftist Occupy and anti-globalization movements.

The rise of Idle No More was a reflection of frustration in the Indigenous community. The Liberal government of Paul Martin had begun to embark on a process of reconciliation with First Nations, but after he was defeated in 2006, the Stephen Harper Conservatives took a harder, less conciliatory line. The policies that the Harper government imposed on First Nations, as well as the dismay of some First Nations activists with their own leaders in not sufficiently opposing these policies, spawned Idle No More. Indigenous people, the left, and progressives found much common ground in battling the Harper Conservatives on these issues.

A new generation at Occupy Nanaimo, October 2011.
Courtesy of Roy Ostling Photography.

For leftists, incorporating Aboriginal people and their particular interests into a vision that is shaped by a search for social and economic justice,
as well as environmental health and sustainability, is an important part of
the project to develop an alternative society. Having said this, of course,
the difficulties of the task must be acknowledged, that identifying issues
and the need for new thinking is easy when compared to the hard, long-
term work of actually formulating practical policies and programs.[66]

CONCLUSION

Looking Forward

THE LEFT IN BC HAS had a dynamic, multi-faceted history that goes back to the late nineteenth century. Speaking in front of an enthusiastic gathering in Northfield, on Vancouver Island, in 1892, Mattie A. Bridge anticipated a time "when the doctrine of equal rights for master and employe[e] shall become the social law of the land," and when the political millennium, "bringing a balm for the wounded of spirit and a panacea for all . . . shall be at hand."[1] She dreamed of a society that operated to benefit the people, a society made up of relative equals, where ordinary people had a decent standard of living. Her range of thought was rich, broad, and textured, and she offered practical proposals to achieve these ends. Over the next 120 years, leftists would continue this struggle for a new society.

British Columbians mobilized on many fronts. Male, skilled workers established unions to protect their interests and further their vision of the good society. Unskilled workers, women, people of all ethnicities, and government workers also became union members, believing that unions could provide justice at the workplace, a secure financial base, a better standard of living, and dignity. As Bridge understood, the workplace and the economy created inequalities on and off the job and, as such, unions were integral to meaningful social change.

Bridge also saw political action as necessary, and leftists developed a rich political tradition over the years. Associations rallied for the Single Tax and greater representation for working people in the legislature. Marxist-based parties called for wholesale economic, political, and social change, and in the 1960s the New Left challenged both the existing left and the established order. Later, anti-corporate, anti-globalization movements added their energy and ideals to the mix. The left was ever changing: revolutionary radicalism rose and fell, as did Canadian nationalism; human rights came to the fore; racism was largely marginalized; gender and women's equality incorporated; and environmental and First Nations issues addressed more prominently. In electoral politics, the Co-operative Commonwealth Federation and the New Democratic Party proved the most resilient and influential.[2]

Optimism was stronger in some periods than in others. The left emerged as a force in the late 1880s, surged from 1916 to 1920, made concrete gains in the 1940s, and challenged the establishment in the 1960s, 1970s, and early 1980s. But there were stagnant periods, too, notably the 1890s and the 1920s. In the long period since the 1980s, the left has been on the defensive.

The modern left, within BC and beyond, continues to further social justice and environmental causes and, while criticizing the actions of corporations, it supports unionism and works to improve the operation of the economy to benefit the larger society. However, what the left has not been able to do, is offer a significant, substantial economic alternative to the current order, an alternative that is both credible and capable of winning supporters. Capitalism reigns triumphant. The command economies of the Soviet Union and twentieth-century Communist China hold little appeal, and there is no clamour for government ownership and management of key industries, as was advocated by the socialist Co-operative Commonwealth Federation of the 1930s. Radical workplace alternatives, such as worker control of production in democratic coop-eratives, do not come up in public debate. Environmental issues have prompted new ways of thinking, such as proposals for no-growth or stable-state economies, coming from critics who see capitalism as inher-ently expansionary and thus by its nature harmful to the environment, but their impact has been minimal. Social democracy, the dominant po-litical expression of the left, does have supporters; it promotes moderate change, however, and social democratic parties promise to manage the capitalist economy better than parties to the right, rather than to restruc-ture it dramatically or replace it.

Social democracy is at the core of today's left, and because of this, its limitations and current predicament deserve further comment. The goal of modern social democracy, the position of the BC NDP, is to control capitalism as much as possible to benefit the people as a whole. In this perspective, strong governments and unions counter blatant economic, social, and environmental injustices, but business interests and private corporations largely control the generation of wealth. The social demo-cratic government captures and redistributes some of this wealth to pro-vide welfare programs, education, Medicare, and a decent standard of living for all. A healthy welfare state, then, depends on the success of the capitalist system, a system that must be maintained and, in times of dif-ficulty, propped up. Managing the economy for the good of the people while at the same time relying on a prosperous, accommodating corporate class, is not easy, as the dramatic shift of wealth and political power to the business class and corporations in recent decades shows. Big business, with its control of production, access to large financial resources for political action, and influence in the media, has great clout, and is able to push the social democratic agenda to the right or bring about governments that better serve its own needs.

There are other voices on the left beyond the social democrats that have a high public profile. A web of activists, for whom periodic elections and the circumscribed world of labour relations are less relevant, intermit-tently prod and challenge the social democratic world view. Armed with a wide-ranging critique of modern times and expressing frustration, these activists are committed to direct action on the streets, as well as a deep sense of democracy. They raise many important questions about corporations and neo-liberalism, but as is the case on the left in general, a view of what a society beyond capitalism might look like has not been clearly articulated.

At the same time that the left has been unable to imagine a bold, engaging alternative to the present order, it has also been out of touch politically and culturally with many workers and lower-middle-class people who are attracted to the rhetoric of the right, people who should be in the left constituency. That is, if the left truly speaks for the interests of the majority whose lives, according to leftist analysis, are stunted because of the actions of an elite minority. Right-wing populism feeds on economic and social anxiety, directing it against unionism and activist governments. In this world view, the NDP is seen as largely speaking for government workers, teachers, and nurses, a sentiment reinforced and encouraged by newspaper columnists such as Black Press's Tom Fletcher, who speaks disparagingly of the NDP as the "champion of public sector union members whose pay and benefits make them the new upper class."[3]

There is some truth to this statement in that, due to the decline of union density in the private sector, the NDP is linked more closely with workers belonging to government unions. In right populism, however, the attainments of unionized public-sector unions (which, it must be noted, are often portrayed in misleading ways) are not seen as goals to be achieved by all workers whenever possible. Rather, they are criticized as unfair rewards that undermine the operation of the market economy and work to the detriment of other workers. The model of public-sector workers has not stimulated union drives in the private sector, but instead has been effectively used to divide workers and as an argument against unionism in general. The NDP is condemned by the right as the party of the public-sector employees, high taxes, and big government.

In the long-term, if the goal is to construct a society based on leftist principles and ideals, and not merely to elect an NDP government, the battle for the hearts and minds of working and lower-middle-class-right populists will be important. To be successful, the left will have to acknowledge the insecurities, hopes and interests of these right populists. It will have to go beyond particular policy issues about tax rates, union laws, or a specific resource development, for example, to reflect deeper interests — such as economic security, opportunities for children, meaningful work, peace, and environmental health. The left will have to develop solutions that are more persuasive than those coming from the right.

As always, there is hope and, for the left, much will depend on its wherewithal to build a left-based cultural and social movement that speaks to and shapes deeper values and aspirations and that recognizes the interconnection of the cultural, social, intellectual and political spheres. The NDP, a political party with the chance of forming a government, is preoccupied with the daily grind of securing advantage in the legislature and winning elections. Thus, the left, beyond the NDP, remains important in generating ideas, movements, critiques, organizations, protests, arguments and philosophies that will win converts, push the political spectrum, including the NDP, to the left, and facilitate social and economic change in the future.

In building the left, class remains important. Class, defined here in terms of the collection of human interconnections that flow from workplace relations between employers and employees, remains relevant as both a lived experience and as a way to create solidarities. The modern tendency is to deny the existence of a working class and the importance of class divisions. The mainstream press labels such talk divisive and counter-productive, and talking in terms of class has come to be seen as old-fashioned and even quaint. However, the working class, the makeup of which has changed over time to include more women, government employees, and service industry workers, continues to shape identity and prompt action. Divisions in the working class, of course, remain, as teachers, nurses, sales clerks, factory workers, construction workers, chambermaids, truck drivers, and secretaries, to name a few, work out places in society independently. Nevertheless, the shared experience of working for employers still has the potential to unite people and effect change.

Moreover, as "middle class" jobs in medicine, business, law, and high-tech are increasingly deskilled by new technologies or outsourced to cheap labour countries, and as employers squeeze their employees in a competitive international market, more and more people may begin to understand the centuries-long struggles of the working class. In this situation the relevance of unions is obvious, and although the state of the union movement, especially in the private sector, remains problematic for the left, increased stresses on the job, the enthusiasm of youthful and ethnically diverse organizers, attention to the needs of the unemployed, and a focus on community issues and not only the interests of members, suggest the possibility of a reinvigorated labour movement.[4]

Because parties, both socialist and social democratic, along with the union movement, are historically at the core of the left, they will remain significant, but there is the possibility of other organizations or movements stepping up to provide leadership. In the 1950s and 1960s many looked to the peace movement to galvanize the left.[5] In the 1960s and 1970s Canadian nationalism brought together a variety of people and organizations. In the near future, alarm about the state of the environment has perhaps the most potential to create a broad left constituency, either through environmental organizations that work backwards from purely environmental issues to embrace a leftist political economy and a commitment to social justice, or a left that works forward from its traditional orientations to incorporate a deeper environmental agenda.

A political and union movement that integrates the left and environmentalism or an environmental movement that critically engages capitalist institutions and ideals, that links environmental problems with social and economic problems, could serve as a catalyst: weaving together a coherent understanding of the shared concerns of the majority of the people and pushing society in a direction that reflects leftist ideals. According to Naomi Klein, the climate-change crisis actually offers opportunities. She wonders whether "some countervailing popular movement will step up to provide a viable alternative to this grim future. That means not just an alternative set of policy proposals, but also an alternative worldview to rival the one at the heart of the ecological crisis — this time, embedded in interdependence rather than hyper-individualism, reciprocity rather than dominance, and cooperation rather than hierarchy."[6]

The future, as always, is uncertain and predictions risky. There are many possibilities. Authoritarianism, new forms of racism and sexism, environmental degradation, and a brutal, no-holds-barred international scramble for resources may emerge, driving the left underground. Or, capitalist chaos might ignite a radical, revolutionary left. In a less cataclysmic vein, leftists, along with progressive voices, could continue to advance particular policies, and even create a climate more hospitable to leftist ideals. Perhaps, too, the left in some guise might take the tiller and steer history in the direction of greater justice in economic and social relations, toward a society where environmental health is a guiding principle. In the unfolding of any scenario, the left, anchored by a critique of capitalism, will continue to organize workers on the job, mobilize politically, and put forward a vision of a society that celebrates equality, human dignity, community, environmental security, and cooperation.

Glossary of Political
and Union Terms

This glossary offers a brief, rough guide to terms used in this book. These terms are explained with a particular eye on the BC context. It is also important to note that the meaning of some words changed over time. For a helpful international perspective, see Andrew Levine, *Political Keywords: A Guide for Students, Activists, and Everyone Else* (Oxford: Blackwell Publishing, 2007).

▶ **American Federation of Labor**
The American Federation of Labor (AFL), founded in 1886, was an umbrella organization that represented unions that were largely committed to *craft unionism*. It was in many ways a counterpart to the *Trades and Labour Congress of Canada* (TLC). Canadian workers in international unions often were tied to both the AFL, through their international union, and to the TLC. In 1955 the AFL merged with the *Congress of Industrial Organizations* to form the *American Federation of Labor-Congress of Industrial Organizations* (AFL-CIO).

▶ **American Federation of Labor and Congress of Industrial Organizations**
The AFL-CIO was formed by a merger of the *American Federation of Labor* and the *Congress of Industrial Organizations* in 1955.

▶ **anarchism**
Anarchism as a political philosophy is anti-statist, anti-hierarchical, and anti-bureaucratic. In this view, human beings are disposed to cooperate, and so constraining political institutions are unnecessary and negative. In British Columbia, anarchist tendencies are associated with the Industrial Workers of the World, the New Left, and the more recent anti-corporate, anti-globalization, and Occupy movements. Violence is at times, though not necessarily, associated with anarchism.

▶ **Canadian Congress of Labour**
The Canadian Congress of Labour (CCL) was formed in 1940 as an umbrella organization to represent largely *industrial unions* in Canada. Most of these unions also belonged to the American *Congress of Industrial Organizations*. The CCL was not a union. It did not call strikes. This authority remained with the unions that belonged to it. It was largely a research and lobbying group that was at times capable of coordinating the actions of constituent unions. In 1956 the CCL joined the *Trades and Labour Congress of Canada* to form the *Canadian Labour Congress*.

▶ **Canadian Labour Congress**
The Canadian Labour Congress (CLC) was formed in 1956 by a merger between the *Canadian Congress of Labour* and the *Trades and Labour Congress of Canada*. It is Canada's largest labour body, representing many unions in Canada.

▶ **capitalism**
Capitalism is an economic system noted for the private ownership of productive facilities and organizations, market exchanges of goods and services, and the powerful influence of capitalists, the people who own and direct companies.

▶ **Christian socialism**
This version of *socialism*, popular in the late nineteenth and early twentieth century, takes its cue from the teachings and behaviour of Jesus

Christ. With Christ as a socialist, cooperation, forgiveness, peace, and harmony are ruling ideals.

▶ communism

In this text, communism largely represents the ideas of left activists who were members of the Communist Party of Canada (CPC) and followed the policy set out by the international communist movement headquartered in Moscow, as well as those who adhered to the philosophies set out by other existing communist countries, especially China. Canadian communism was *Marxist*. The CPC was dedicated to an eventual revolution, but in the shorter term to maintaining the survival of the Soviet Union, the base and model for worldwide revolution. Under the communist rubric we also find *Stalinism, Leninism*, and *Maoism*.

▶ Congress of Industrial Organizations

This is an organization that began in the United States in 1935 to represent unions disenchanted with the *American Federation of Labor*. Committed to *industrial unionism*, the CIO represented Canadian industrial unions as well. It was the American counterpart to the *Canadian Congress of Labour*. Canadian workers, through membership in their international, industrial unions, were often affiliated to both the CIO and the Canadian Congress of Labour. In 1955 the CIO merged with the AFL to form the *American Federation of Labor and Congress of Industrial Organizations* (AFL-CIO).

▶ craft unionism

Craft unionism refers to a form of union organization in which workers in a particular trade form a union to look after their affairs. These are skilled workers with training. In the nineteenth and much of the twentieth centuries they were often white males of British descent. Thus, in the craft union structure, painters would form a painters union, decorators would organize an association for decorators, and millwrights would organize their own union. The alternative to craft unionism is *industrial unionism*.

▶ international unionism

In Canada many union members belong to unions that have headquarters in the United States. Consequently, Canadian carpenters or electricians are in the same unions as workers in the United States. These Canadian workers believe that the larger North American union will benefit them in terms of larger strike funds and greater access to research resources. They will also be more able to stabilize wages and costs across the border by acting in concert. International unions also reflect a belief in the importance of the continental economy and the solidarity of workers beyond the confines of a particular nation. International unionism is at times in competition with *national unionism*.

▶ **impossibilism**

Impossibilism is a version of *revolutionary socialism* associated with the British Columbia branch of the Socialist Party of Canada around 1900. Impossibilism posits that reforms such as better wages or better working conditions are an impossible way to bring about wholesale, radical, necessary changes to the economic and social order. In fact, piecemeal reforms undermine the revolutionary ardour of the working class by making member of this class believe that slow gradual change to a better world is possible.

▶ **industrial unionism**

Industrial unionism is a union structure in which all workers in a particular industry belong to the same union. In the forest industry, for example, when the painters, carpenters, production workers, millwrights, and electricians in sawmills all belong to the same union, they are in an industrial union. The alternative to industrial unionism is *craft unionism*, whereby each group of workers in a mill, such as painters or electricians, would have their own union. Industrial unions have also tended to be more hospitable to unskilled workers, those who were often not of British descent.

▶ **Keynesianism**

Keynesianism refers to the ideas associated with the British economist John Maynard Keynes (1883–1946). For our purposes, most important are the basic ideas that Keynes articulated in the 1930s. He argued that governments had a strong role to play in managing the economy. His thinking was indeed radical. Up to this time orthodox economics postulated that in times of an economic downturn the role of the government was to avoid debt and weather the storm. Keynes, on the other hand, argued that in downturns investment froze, and that it was the role of the state to spend money in such times to stimulate economic activity, to prime the economic pump. In boom times, governments should increase taxes and raise interest rates to slow investment and to build up a fund to allow for spending in the next downward business cycle. Thus, fiscal policies could be used to stabilize economies over time, getting rid of the wide swings between good times and bad times. In the western world, governments, economists, and bureaucrats increasingly talked the language of Keynes after 1940, and his ideas, though never implemented to the letter — governments, for example, had a hard time using measures to slow economic growth because of the political implications — were in vogue until the 1970s. In the 1970s Keynesianism came increasingly under attack, and in economic and political circles it was largely jettisoned in the 1980s. The circumstances of the 1970s were seemingly not amenable to Keynesian solutions. In the 1970s there was both inflation and high unemployment. Keynesians had postulated that an increase in inflation should bring down unemployment and visa versa. However, in the 1970s both high inflation rates and high employment rates persisted in what was dubbed stagflation.

Keynesian fiscal policy also went hand-in-hand with government-funded and government-operated social welfare programs. As well as being seen as morally good, such programs also made economic sense. In tough times, welfare or unemployment payments to individuals served an economic good, as the people receiving these payments would spend the money they received and thus stimulate broader economic activity.

Keynesian ideas were at the core of Canadian liberalism from the 1940s into the 1980s. *Social democracy*, too, subscribed to Keynesianism.

▶ **left liberalism** (see welfare liberalism)

▶ **Leninism**
Vladimir Ilyich Lenin (1870–1924) led the Bolsheviks who completed the Russian Revolution of 1917 and founded the Soviet state. Lenin led the Union of Soviet Socialist Republics until his death in 1924. Lenin offered a rich interpretative account of *Marxism*, but most important for us,

his *communism* stated that a disciplined, dedicated vanguard of activists that included peasants, class-conscious workers, and professional revolutionaries could lead the working class in a successful revolution.

▶ **liberal capitalism**

This text uses liberal *capitalism* and *liberalism* interchangeably. The use of liberal capitalism emphasizes the sometimes forgotten economic component of modern liberalism.

▶ **liberalism**

Like *socialism*, liberalism is a complex, slippery term with different meanings at different times and in different countries. In this text, liberalism is a set of ideas and practices built around individualism, personal self-fulfillment, the powers of reason, and the merits of private property. As noted in the "liberal capitalism" entry, this book uses liberalism and *liberal capitalism* interchangeably. Nineteenth-century liberalism is associated with the rise of Enlightenment ideas and the business-oriented middle classes who wanted to be freed from the restrictions of a traditional society and government dominated by the land-owning aristocracy. In this liberalism, government should be used to open the powers of capitalist enterprise and allow market transactions to be as unfettered as possible in order to secure the general good of all. There was also a strain of liberalism, radical liberalism, that celebrated a society of independent, small, relatively-equal producers. This was a version of *populism*. By the late nineteenth and early twentieth century, it was clear that liberal capitalism did not serve all well, and socialist groups were mobilizing against the degradation of cities and people. The new liberalism or *welfare liberalism* moved increasingly to use the reformist state to ameliorate the excesses of the new order. By the middle of the twentieth century, the dominant liberalism supported the welfare state and regulation of the economy by bureaucrats. The older liberal tradition, however, did not die. Indeed, it revived in the 1970s as *neo-liberalism*, a version of liberalism dedicated to taming the excesses of government regulation and the welfare state. Throughout these changes, liberalism remained, in its various ways, committed to the merits of private property and private enterprise, market economics, individualism, and the goals of personal self-fulfillment. While socialism sought a degree of equality of condition, whereby all members of society had roughly the same standard of living, liberalism supported equality of opportunity, whereby individuals were given the opportunity to succeed in society. How high they rose was based on their energy, intelligence and merit. Classes and variations in living standards were thus acceptable, although there were and are debates within liberalism about the range.

▶ Maoism

Maoism is variation of *Marxism* associated with Mao Zedong (often written Mao-Tse-tung) (1893–1976), who led the revolution that established the People's Republic of China in 1949. Maoism is distinguished from other types of *communism* by its emphasis on the peasant class and a broader coalition of subordinate groups, rather than the working class, in bringing about revolution. In the late 1950s, foreign policy disputes further distinguished the Soviet Union from the People's Republic of China. In British Columbia, hostility to the rigid Stalinist and CPC party line led to the creation of pockets of Maoist activists.

▶ Marxism

Marxism describes a set of ideas associated with the ideas of Karl Marx (1818–1883). At its root, Marxism is a critique or analysis of capitalism, stressing the negative aspects of private property, inequality, and class dominance. Workers are exploited by owners, the search for profit dominates productive activity, and the owners of the means of production have undue, if not complete, control over government and the state. Solutions to the problem are many, ranging from a belief in the collapse of capitalism due to its "inherent contradictions," the education of the population and largely peaceful succession to a new social order based on socialist principles, to the necessity for capitalism to be destroyed by a working class led by dedicated revolutionaries.

▶ national unionism

National unionism refers to the commitment of some Canadian workers to maintain unions that have no connections to unions that are also active in the United States. Those in favour of national unions argue that they have more control over their own affairs, that they are not bound by more conservative American workers, and that they do not lose financially when their dues go to the United States and they get little in return. National unions also often trumpet a broader commitment to Canada as an independent country. In Canada, national unionism and *international unionism* have at times been in competition.

▸ **neo-liberalism**

Neo-liberalism in the post-1980s era celebrated a particular strain of nineteenth-century *liberalism* that stressed unfettered markets, small governments, and full respect for the rights of capital. Government economic intervention and government social programs were seen as economically debilitating and responsible for undermining both freedom and the creation of a vibrant social order. Individual failures in the marketplace were to be accepted as necessary costs.

▸ **New Left**

The New Left is associated with youth and the radicalism of the 1960s and 1970s. It was an attack on the established left of the 1940s, 1950s and 1960s that was made up of unions, communist organizations and the CCF/NDP. According to New Left critics, this Old Left tended to be doctrinaire, rigid, old-fashioned, and uncreative. Career bureaucrats stifled thought and discussion in the Old Left and failed to appreciate the revolutionary potential of students, environmental activists, and the women's rights movement. The New Left was still vaguely Marxist, seeing a basic conflict between the people and the establishment. There was however, no New Left party. Rather, New Left ideas flowed through a number of organizations and causes, including the student movement, the environmental movement, the women's movement, the nationalist movement, and even the NDP. Adherents of *Trotskyism* and *Maoism* were comfortable with the New Left and its commitment to grassroots democracy and the organization of a broad swath of people, not just the male working class.

▸ **new liberalism** (see welfare liberalism)

▶ New Right

The New Right, which for Canada was largely an American import, can be traced back to the 1950s and even the 1940s as a counter to *welfare liberalism* and *Keynesianism* but it came into its own in the 1980s with the election of Ronald Reagan. In Britain, Margaret Thatcher offered similar nostrums, but in North America there was a more religious edge. The North American New Right wedded economic *neo-liberalism* and a conservative social and moral orientation associated with some fundamentalist and evangelical Protestant churches. Patriotism and militarism were also part of the program. The New Right attacked big government at the same time that it defended "family values" and the decency of ordinary working people and their families. Despite the religious tinge, the connections to big business, and the celebration of the rights of capital, the New Right tapped into the legacy of *radical liberalism*, appealing to working class and ordinary families. *Populism* was an important aspect of the movement. In Canada, the Reform Party was the main exponent of the New Right. In BC the Campbell Liberal Party adhered to the economic policies of the New Right.

▶ open shop

An open shop is a production facility or other workplace where there is no recognized union. Usually, there is no union presence, although in some cases workers can belong to a union as individuals but the company refuses to deal with them as union members.

▶ populism

Populism, a notoriously difficult term to nail down with precision, refers to a political uprising in particular circumstances, known as a populist moment. Populism is usually associated with middling and lower class people and their fears and aspirations. In a populist moment, a large swath of society defines itself as the people. Moreover, the group has a vision of the good life where people of relatively equal standing — farmers, skilled workers, teachers, nurses, and small business people — share basic assumptions and values and work together in harmony to create the good society. A populist uprising occurs when there is a perceived threat to the interests of the people. In right populism, the enemy is big government. In left populism, the enemy is big business, which manipulates the politicians, thwarts the economic ambitions of the people, and sucks money out of the pockets of hard-working folks. Populist movements can also identify outside interests as the enemy. For western Canadians both the government in Ottawa and the big corporations of central Canada have served as the entities that have, in populist rhetoric, stunted the aspirations of the people.

▶ **progressive**
In this text, to be a progressive is not necessarily to be a leftist. Progressive is a larger category that includes much of the left, but is also home to a variety of liberals and greens. In modern Canada, being progressive, in general, is to be against conservative social positions and most environmental, military, and business policies of the Stephen Harper government. In recent years there has been much talk at the federal level of forming a broad progressive alliance that would bring together Liberals, Greens, and New Democrats to defeat the Conservatives.

▶ **revolutionary socialism**
In British Columbia, revolutionary *socialism* embodies a Marxist understanding of the social and economic order and the necessity for a fundamental overthrow of that order. Reform is not an option. The term is used especially to describe the philosophies of radical socialists who were around before the creation of the Communist Party of Canada in 1921 and who later did not belong to the CPC or other *communist* parties that were in power across the globe.

▶ **social democracy**
Social democracy is a complex, important perspective in British Columbia that became particularly notable in the middle of the twentieth century. Social democracy is a moderate version of *socialism* and not easily distinguishable from *welfare liberalism*. Democracy and respect for slow, gradual change through accepted processes are key. Control of government is seen as crucial in regulating and moderating capitalism. The redistribution of wealth, greater equality between rich and poor, social justice, equal rights for all races, religions, and genders, respect for unions, and

environmental health are all part of the social democratic vision. Ultimately, whether social democracy will eventually lead to a classless, socialist society or whether an acceptance of a controlled capitalism is the only realistic option depends on the social democrat speaking. In BC, arguably, the socialist Co-operative Commonwealth Federation of the 1930s became the more moderate social democratic New Democratic Party of the 1970s, although within both organizations there was a range of positions from independent liberals to independent Marxists. On the whole, Marxists and liberals tend to denigrate social democrats, the Marxists seeing them as non-revolutionary reformers; the liberals seeing them as somewhat impractical and trying to rush the reformist liberal program. Social Democrats respond that revolutionary socialists and Marxists are woolly-headed dreamers who do not understand the political and cultural values of most British Columbians, and that welfare liberals are too much bound by a reliance on capitalism and business.

▸ Social Gospel

The Social Gospel was a social and religious movement that emerged in Protestant churches. It was dedicated to creating a "Heaven on Earth." Christians were expected to care as much about improving the material circumstances of their fellow human beings in this world as they were to care about saving their souls for the next. The heyday of the Social Gospel in Canada was from the 1880s through the 1920s, and the movement provided a respected and respectable Christian strain in Canadian *socialism*. Both J.S. Woodsworth and Tommy Douglas, prominent federal socialists, came out of the Social Gospel tradition.

▸ socialism

The term "socialism" has been beaten, battered, and misused by critics over the past one hundred years to the extent that even people on the left have largely conceded that in modern times the word is almost meaningless. Their preference for "the left" or "progressive" reflects the destruction of the term. In its late nineteenth-century connotation it was a broad term that embraced a variety of criticisms of the emerging industrial capitalist order. Socialism stressed cooperation rather than conflict, acting for the good of the community or the commonwealth rather than the good of the most ambitious or ruthless individuals, greater equality in access to the resources of a society rather that an unequal distribution of wealth, production for the benefit of all and not profits for a few, and the sense that there was more to life than the production of goods to buy and sell. *Marxism*, *social democracy*, and *Christian socialism* all fit within this large tent. As the twentieth century progressed, socialism came increasingly to be seen as the use of the power of the state to achieve a more cooperative, equal, fair, and just society.

▸ **Stalinism**

Joseph Stalin (1879–1953) was the leader of the Soviet Union from the late 1920s to 1953, and thus head of worldwide communist activities. While the cruelty of his rule was much publicized after his death, in the 1930s and 1940s, British Columbia members of the Communist Party of Canada, unaware of many of the details of life in the Soviet Union, saw him in a positive light. Stalinism, a term that came into use through his Trotskyist opponents, refers to a version of *communism*, which included the ruthless crushing of dissent, including other Marxist ideas, rigid bureaucracy, and the emphasis on a worldwide communist policy to ensure the survival and growth of the Soviet Union, known as "socialism in one country." The Communist Party of Canada was Stalinist in the years after the late 1920s.

▸ **syndicalism**

Syndicalism in the British Columbia context is used to describe the position of the Industrial Workers of the World in the first decades of the twentieth century. Rooted in *Marxism*, syndicalism argues that political action by the working class is no way to achieve a socialist revolution. Parliaments, legislatures and even socialist political parties serve no good. In capitalism all democracy is a sham. The goal should be to organize workers into one big union. This class-conscious, organized working class will call a general strike and bring capitalism and the capitalist class to its knees. This will allow for the beginnings of a new socialist society. With its aversion to governments, syndicalism shares an affinity with anarchism. Syndicalists, too, tend to be wary of bureaucracy in unions and demand that ordinary workers, not business agents or a union bureaucracy, control and run unions.

▶ Trades and Labour Congress of Canada

The Trades and Labour Congress of Canada (TLC) was formed in 1883. It was an organization that represented constituent unions and lobbied governments, pushing for social change, providing research, and coordinating union activities. Workers belonged to the TLC through their union, which sent money to the TLC. The constituent unions also sent delegates to yearly conventions to debate issues of common concern. After 1902 most TLC unions were committed to *craft unionism* and *international unionism*.

▶ Trotskyism

Leon Trotsky (1879–1940) was a revolutionary, Marxist communist who played a crucial role in the establishment of the Soviet state in 1917. After Lenin's death, however, he lost to Stalin in the battle to head the Communist Party. Trotsky went into exile and was assassinated by Stalin's forces in Mexico in 1940. Trotskyism is a form of *Marxism* that is critical of *Stalinism*. It has come to be a perspective that encourages intellectual debate within Marxism, that stresses the need to guard against the emergence of bureaucratic interests in communist states, and that recognizes the inadequacy of building socialism in only one country. In Trotskyism there is also a call for "permanent revolution," a somewhat ambiguous notion. In British Columbia, Trotskyism appealed to many leftists who found the Stalinism of the CPC unsavoury, and to many young people in the 1960s and 1970s.

▶ union recognition

Before the 1940s, governments in Canada did little to force companies to deal or negotiate with elected unions that represented workers in their operations, and, as a result, companies refused to recognize unions. The only way workers could force negotiations in these circumstances was to go on strike to force union recognition.

▶ **utopian socialism**

Utopian socialism, much maligned by Marxists and many other leftists, bothers little with careful analysis of capitalism as an historical system. It tries to build a better world by drawing on conceptions of the possibilities for a more perfect society. To critics this is merely dreaming.

▶ **welfare liberalism** (also left or new liberalism)

While nineteenth-century *liberalism* in Britain and Canada emphasized letting market forces operate freely without state interference, it became increasingly evident that unfettered capitalism created social problems, including extreme poverty, unsafe working conditions, and increasing class differences between rich and poor. Class conflict between the haves and have-nots also became more obvious. *Liberalism* began to embrace government provision of regulations to manage the excesses of the industrial capitalist order. Minimum wage laws, hours-of-work regulations, public education for the working classes, insurance against unemployment and sickness, and state support for unions were all touted as necessary and beneficial. The goal was to moderate the inequality in society and allow everybody an equal opportunity to succeed in the capitalist, market economy. In Canada, the federal Liberals moved in this direction in 1919, adopting policies that anticipated a new agenda for *liberalism*. In the 1940s, *Keynesianism* was added. In the 1980s and 1990s, Canadian liberalism became less committed to this policy perspective, increasingly embracing *neo-liberalism*.

Notes

INTRODUCTION (pp. 1–8)

1 This line of thinking draws on the work of Ronald Inglehart. For an introduction, see *The Silent Revolution: Changing Values and Political Styles Among
Western Publics* (Princeton: Princeton University Press, 1977). For British
Columbia, see Donald E. Blake, "Value Conflicts in Lotusland: British Columbia Political Culture," in R.K. Carty, ed., *Politics, Policy, and Government
in British Columbia* (Vancouver: UBC Press, 1996), 11–16; Kathryn Harrison,
"Environmental Protection in British Columbia: Postmaterial Values, Organized Interests, and Party Politics," in Carty, 290–309.

2 For some, the left is understood in terms of the Marxist-informed socialist
ideals, policies, individuals, and organizations that were especially prominent in the years roughly from 1900 to the 1960s. From this perspective the
left of the late nineteenth century as well as the modern left are suspect,
dismissed as too centrist and conciliatory, too closely intertwined with liberalism, and maybe not leftist at all. But as well as seeing continued relevance

in a modern left, this text locates a leftist presence or discourse in the nineteenth century, one that is evident in the critiques of the developing capitalist order, the concerns about equality, the attacks on monopolies in resource industries, and the worries about the lack of worker representation in the legislature. Moreover, in the 1880s and 1890s unions were established and workers put down their tools for better conditions and reduced working hours. This leftist impulse was intertwined with a version of liberalism, but the moderate left of later years also overlapped with forms of liberalism. The era when Marxist-influenced socialism had some clout was just one period in the history of the left in BC.

3 This book sees the left as a discourse. Discourse has been defined in many ways, but can be usefully defined as an identifiable convergence — "system" seems too strong, "pattern" seems too outwardly imposed — of ideas, texts, and practices. Importantly, discourse, as conceived here, is not only language but also practices, which include institutions, legislation, and a range of behaviour.

CHAPTER 1 (pp. 9–34)

1 *Nanaimo Free Press*, 22 June 1892; *Vancouver Daily World*, 12 October 1892. Mattie A. Bridge was born into a wealthy family in Milwaukee in 1834. Her father was a doctor. She married Samuel Ingersoll Bridge, a prominent educator and Oddfellow, in 1853. Samuel died in 1876, leaving Mattie almost impoverished due to some bad business deals. She went to work as a journalist in Boston and New York and then began lecturing. Her topics included a history of the Oddfellows and human freedom, as well as the labour problem. Increasingly she spent time on the west coast of the United States, speaking in places such as Eugene, Salinas, and Sacramento. In September 1884 she spoke in Victoria. Her lectures drew large crowds. In Los Angeles in late January 1883, according to a newspaper report, she "fairly electrified the immense audience who listened to her." The paper ranked her lectures with the best of Henry Ward Beecher and Theodore Tilton. *Daily Globe*, St. Paul, Minn., 16 November 1880; *The Eugene City Guard*, 20 January 1885; *Los Angeles Daily Herald*, 30 January 1883; *British Colonist*, 21 September 1884; William Frederick Bridge, *An Account of the Descendants of John Bridge, Cambridge, 1632* (Boston: J.S. Cushing, 1884), 28.

2 Census data in Jean Barman, *The West beyond the West: A History of British Columbia* (Toronto: University of Toronto Press, 1991), 441.

3 Paul Phillips, *No Power Greater: A Century of Labour in British Columbia* (Vancouver: BC Federation of Labour/Boag Foundation, 1967), 7–9; Eugene Forsey, *Trade Unions in Canada, 1812–1902* (Toronto: University of Toronto Press, 1982), 30, 89; Rennie Warburton, "The Workingmen's Protection Association, Victoria, BC, 1878: Racism, Gender Sectionality and Status Politics," *Labour/Le Travail*, 43 (Spring 1999), 105–120.

4 Phillips, 13.

5 A short-lived, province-wide labour congress, representing the unions of Vancouver, New Westminster, Nanaimo, and Victoria, was organized in 1890. It was essentially unnecessary as informal links between the four centres worked well enough. The real power remained with constituent unions, and political lobbying was effectively done by city trades and labour councils, or in the case of Nanaimo, the Miners' and Mine Labourers' Protective Association (*Victoria Daily Colonist*, 5 September 1890; 25 September 1890; 4 November 1890; *Nanaimo Free Press*, 4 November 1890; *The Truth*, 6 November 1890). There were extra-territorial links. In 1892 the American Federation of Labor appointed a general organizer for Washington State and British Columbia (*Victoria Daily Times*, 19 August 1892). Nanaimo miners were affiliated with the San Francisco Federated Labor Council, due to the importance of the San Francisco market for Nanaimo coal (*Nanaimo Free Press*, 29 September 1891). Vancouver and Victoria unionists often met with unionists from Washington State (*Victoria Daily Times*, 23 April 1892). Beginning in 1890, British Columbia also began sending delegates to the Canadian Trades and Labour Congress. This was important both to further the anti-Chinese cause at the federal level and to keep central Canadian workers, potential migrants, apprised of labour market conditions in BC (*Victoria Daily Times*, 11 September 1890). For a history of the early Vancouver Trades and Labour Council, see Mark Leier, *Red Flags & Red Tape: The Making of a Labour Bureaucracy* (Toronto: University of Toronto Press, 1995). For more on labour in this period, see Carlos A. Schwantes, *Radical Heritage: Labor, Socialism, and Reform in Washington and British Columbia, 1885–1917* (Vancouver: Douglas & McIntyre, 1979).

6 See Daryl Ashby, *John Muir: West Coast Pioneer* (Vancouver: Ronsdale Press, 2005).

7 *Vancouver Daily World*, 15 April 1889.

8 *Victoria Daily Colonist*, 7 May 1890; *Nanaimo Free Press*, 20 June 1890.

9 *Nanaimo Free Press*, 25 July 1890.

10 *Morning Ledger*, New Westminster, 3 July 1891; 19 July 1891; 21 July 1891.

11 *Vancouver Daily World*, 30 April 1891; 8 May 1891; 14 May 1891; 15 May 1891.

12 *Victoria Daily Times*, 12 September 1891; 6 October 1891.

13 *Nanaimo Free Press*, 19 April 1892.

14 *Victoria Daily Colonist*, 12 July 1890.

15 Sermons were printed in local newspapers: Bishop Lemmens, St Andrew's Cathedral (*Victoria Daily Colonist*, 22 July 1890); Rev. Percival Jenns and Rev. P. Macleod, St Andrew's Presbyterian (*Victoria Daily Colonist*, 29 July 1890); Rev. Dr. Reid, Reformed Episcopal Church (*Victoria Daily Colonist*, 30 July 1890); Rev. Bishop Cridge, Reformed Episcopal Church (*Victoria Daily Colonist*, 5 August 1890); Rev. Rugg (*Victoria Daily Colonist*, 19 August 1890); Rev W.W. Baer, Wallace Street Methodist Church, Nanaimo (*Nanaimo Free Press*, 28 July 1890, 9 September 1890); Rev. Jas. A. Banton, First Baptist Church, Nanaimo (*Nanaimo Free Press*, 19 August 1890). See too, Rev. W. Pudley's sermon on "Labor Organizations, Their Uses and Abuse," at the Vancouver Congregational Church (*Vancouver Daily World*, 29 September 1890).

16 *Victoria Daily Times*, 26 July 1890. Emphasis in original. In 1894 the federal government established Labour Day. See Craig Heron and Steve Penfold, *The Workers' Festival: A History of Labour Day in Canada* (Toronto: University of Toronto Press, 2005).

17 See Jeremy Mouat, "The Politics of Coal: A Study of the Wellington Miners' Strike of 1890–91," *BC Studies*, 77 (Spring 1988), 3–29; Allen Seager and Adele Perry, "Mining the Connections: Class, Ethnicity, and Gender in Nanaimo, British Columbia, 1891," *Histoire sociale/Social History*, 30/59 (May 1997), 55–76.

18 *Nanaimo Free Press*, 1 February 1890; *Victoria Daily Times*, 19 May 1890; 20 May 1890.

19 *Victoria Daily Colonist*, 26 August 1890.

20 *Victoria Daily Times*, 8 August 1891.

21 *Victoria Daily Times*, 16 November 1891; 23 February 1892.

22 *Victoria Daily Colonist*, 16 February 1889.

23 *Vancouver Daily World*, 17 March 1891; *Victoria Daily Times*, 15 April 1891.

24 *Daily Columbian*, 18 June 1892; *Vancouver Daily World*, 18 June 1892. For disputes in Nanaimo and New Westminster that were resolved without strikes, see *Daily British Columbian*, New Westminster, 8 February 1890; 26 March 1890; *Vancouver Daily World*, 26 March 1890; *Nanaimo Free Press*, 9 September 1890; 9 December 1890.

25 *Victoria Daily Times*, 5 September 1891.

26 *Nanaimo Free Press*, 14 March 1892.

27 *Victoria Daily Times*, 2 November 1892; 2 August 1893; 4 August 1893; 7 November 1893; 9 November 1893.

28 *Victoria Daily Times*, 4 August 1893.

29 *Victoria Daily Colonist*, 13 July 1890; *Nanaimo Free Press*, 24 June 1890; 26 June 1891.

30 *Vancouver Daily World*, 24 April 1893.

31 *Daily Colonist*, 6 March 1884.

32 *Victoria Daily Times*, 20 February 1890.

33 *Victoria Daily Times*, 8 September 1893.

34 *Vancouver Daily World*, 23 September 1893.

35 *Victoria Daily Times*, 12 January 1891. Cooperatives were commonly seen as a solution for worker problems in this period. See Gregory S. Kealey, *Toronto Workers Respond to Industrial Capitalism, 1867–1892* (Toronto: University of Toronto Press, 1980), 78–81.

36 *Victoria Daily Times*, 16 May 1892.

37 *Vancouver Daily World*, 6 June 1892.

38 *Daily British Colonist*, 28 May 1886.

39 *Daily British Colonist*, 17 June 1886.

40 *Vancouver News*, 28 November 1886. For a close study of politics in Vancouver, see Robert A.J. McDonald, *Making Vancouver: Class, Status, and Social Boundaries, 1863–1913* (Vancouver: UBC Press, 1996), especially Chapters 3 and 4.

41 *Victoria Daily Times*, 6 March 1892.

42 *Daily World*, 5 December 1889. City politics are given short shrift in this book. For interesting insights into the left in Vancouver city politics, see Andrea B. Smith, "The CCF, NPA, and Civic Change: Provincial Forces behind Vancouver Politics, 1930–1940," *BC Studies*, 53 (Spring 1982), 45–65;

Paul Tennant, "Vancouver Civic Politics, 1929–1980," *BC Studies*, 46 (Summer 1980), 3–27; Donna Vogel, *Changing Politics: COPE, Electoral Politics and Social Movements* (Halifax: Fernwood Publishing, 2003).

43 *Victoria Daily Times*, 19 May 1890.

44 *Vancouver Daily World*, 19 May 1890.

45 *Victoria Daily Times*, 27 May 1890. In October 1885, D. Cronin, a Seattle Knights of Labor organizer, spoke in Victoria, as part of an organizing drive. He noted that "the chief aims of the society are to make industrial and moral worth, not wealth, the true standard of individual and national greatness, and to secure to workers the full enjoyment of the wealth they create, sufficient leisure in which to develop their intellectual, moral and social faculties; all of the benefits, recreation and pleasures of association; in a word to enable them to share in the gains and honors of advancing civilization." *Daily British Colonist*, 4 October 1885. The Vancouver platform contained the following phrases: "the principle of representative government aims at the greatest good for the greatest number," and "the moral, intellectual and physical progress of the people should be the first aim of a government of the people." *Vancouver Daily Herald*, 19 May 1890.

46 *Victoria Daily Colonist*, 17 June 1890. The paper judged that provincially the Government won 20 seats, the Opposition 6, and Independents 7. All unreferenced data regarding provincial election results are from the following government publications: Elections British Columbia, *Electoral History of British Columbia, 1871–1986* (Victoria: Legislative Library, 1988) and Elections British Columbia, *Electoral History of British Columbia Supplement, 1987–2001* (Victoria: Legislative Library, 2002), both of which are accessible online.

47 For a concise summary of George's ideas, see Louis Wasserman, "The Essential Henry George," in *Critics of Henry George: A Centenary Appraisal of Their Strictures on Progress and Poverty*, ed. Robert V. Andelson (Cranberry, NJ: Associated University Press, 1979), 29–43. George, by the way, spent a season in Victoria during the Fraser River Gold Rush.

48 Ramsay Cook, "Henry George and the Poverty of Canadian Progress," Canadian Historical Association, *Historical Papers*, 12/1 (1977), 153.

49 *Daily British Colonist*, 30 December 1886. For an account of the influence of Henry George in Ontario during the 1880s, see Ramsay Cook, *The Regenerators: Social Criticism in Late Victorian English Canada* (Toronto: University of Toronto Press, 1985), 105–122.

50 *Victoria Daily Colonist*, 12 December 1888.

51 *Nanaimo Free Press*, 21 January 1889.

52 *Nanaimo Free Press*, 27 May 1889.

53 *Nanaimo Free Press*, 8 October 1889.

54 *Nanaimo Free Press*, 27 June 1890.

55 Gordon Hak, *Turning Trees into Dollars: The British Columbia Coastal Lumber Industry, 1858–1913* (Toronto: University of Toronto Press, 2000), 80–94.

56 *Victoria Daily Times*, 6 May 1889.

57 *Daily British Columbian*, 21 June 1890.

58 *Victoria Daily Times*, 2 February 1892.

59 *Daily News-Advertiser*, Vancouver, 26 September 1889.

60 *The Truth*, New Westminster, 22 October 1890; *Vancouver Daily World*, 11 December 1891.

61 *Daily News-Advertiser*, 6 December 1891; *Vancouver Daily World*, 11 January 1892; 12 January 1892.

62 *Daily News-Advertiser*, 20 January 1892.

63 *Victoria Daily Times*, 28 November 1892.

64 *Victoria Daily Times*, 31 May 1890.

65 *Victoria Daily Times*, 12 July 1890.

66 *Victoria Daily Times*, 20 February 1892; 15 June 1892; 27 June 1892; 22 October 1892.

67 *Victoria Daily Times*, 16 December 1892.

68 The two camps were not completely distinct, of course. Dr. J.T. Carroll was a Single Taxer and a Conservative; Arthur Dutton was an anti-Single Tax union leader.

69 Daniel Francis, *L.D.: Mayor Louis Taylor and the Rise of Vancouver* (Vancouver: Arsenal Pulp Press, 2004), 82–83. For Williams, see Geoff Meggs and Rod Mickleburgh, *The Art of the Impossible: Dave Barrett and the NDP in Power, 1972–1975* (Madeira Park, BC: Harbour Publishing, 2012), 179.

70 John Douglas Belshaw, *Colonization and Community: The Vancouver Island Coalfield and the Making of the British Columbian Working Class* (Montreal-Kingston: McGill-Queen's University Press, 2002), 119.

71 Barman, 364.

72 See Patricia E. Roy, *A White Man's Province: British Columbia Politicians and Chinese and Japanese Immigrants, 1858–1914* (Vancouver: UBC Press, 1989), 37–150; David Goutor, *Guarding the Gates: The Canadian Labour Movement and Immigration, 1872–1934* (Vancouver: UBC Press, 2007), 35–84.

73 Charles A. Price, *The Great White Walls are Built: Restrictive Immigration to North America and Australasia, 1836–1888* (Canberra: Australian Institute of International Affairs with Australian National University Press, 1974), 244. For more on contract labour in an international context, see Hugh Tinker, *A New System of Slavery: The Export of Indian Labour Overseas, 1830–1920* (London: Oxford University Press, 1974); David Northrup, *Indentured Labor in the Age of Imperialism* (Cambridge: Cambridge University Press, 1995).

74 *Daily British Colonist*, 20 April 1886; 2 September 1885.

75 *Victoria Daily Times*, 1 April 1890; 22 April 1890; *Victoria Daily Colonist*, 19 December 1889; 2 April 1890.

76 *Daily British Colonist*, 22 May 1885.

77 *Vancouver News*, 28 November 1886.

78 *Daily British Colonist*, 27 June 1885.

79 *Vancouver News*, 17 November 1886; 26 November 1886.

80 *Daily Columbian*, 11 January 1887.

81 *Daily British Colonist*, 26 February 1887; 27 February 1887; *Vancouver News*, 25 February 1887; 27 February 1887; Patricia E. Roy, "The Preservation of the Peace in Vancouver: The Aftermath of the Anti-Chinese Riot of 1887," *BC Studies*, 31 (Autumn 1976), 44–59.

82 *Vancouver Daily World*, 28 January 1892; 4 February 1892.

83 *Daily Columbian*, 5 February 1892.

84 *Victoria Daily Times*, 9 April 1892.

85 *Victoria Daily Times*, 5 September 1892.

86 Tabulated by Barman, 363.

87 See John Sutton Lutz, *Makúk: A New History of Aboriginal-White Relations* (Vancouver: UBC Press, 2008); Rolf Knight, *Indians at Work*, 2nd ed. (Vancouver: New Star Books, 1996); John Lutz, "After the Fur Trade: The Aboriginal Labouring Class of British Columbia, 1849–1890," *Journal of the Canadian Historical Association* (1992), 69–94; Andrew Parnaby, "'The best men that ever worked lumber': Aboriginal Longshoremen on Burrard Inlet, BC, 1863–1939," *Canadian Historical Review*, 87 (March 2006), 53–78; James

K. Burrows, "'A Much-Needed Class of Labour': The Economy and Income of the Southern Interior Plateau Indians, 1897–1910," *BC Studies*, 71 (Autumn 1986), 27–46; Michael Kew, "Making Indians," in *Workers, Capital, and the State in British Columbia: Selected Papers* (Vancouver: UBC Press, 1988), 24–34; Cole Harris, *Making Native Space: Colonialism, Resistance, and Reserves in British Columbia* (Vancouver: UBC Press, 2002).

88 *Daily Columbian*, 4 January 1893; 11 January 1893. Letters from clergymen were necessary to show that the applicants were deserving of work.

89 *Victoria Daily Times*, 14 March 1893.

90 *Victoria Daily Times*, 21 August 1893. See, also, Leier, *Red Flags & Red Tape*, 63.

91 *Vancouver Daily World*, 20 September 1892. For a discussion of unemployment in this period that includes Vancouver and Victoria in its analysis, see Peter Baskerville and Eric W. Sager, *Unwilling Idlers: The Urban Unemployed and Their Families in Late Victorian Canada* (Toronto: University of Toronto Press, 1998).

92 *Vancouver Daily World*, 19 December 1893; 7 February 1894.

93 *Victoria Daily Times*, 9 June 1894. Victoria Single Taxers worked together with the city Trades and Labour Council, each running a candidate in the 1894 provincial election. *Victoria Daily Times*, 3 May 1894; 8 June 1894. In Vancouver the Single Tax movement created a new political party in the spring of 1894, the Nationalist Party. The name was inspired by the American writer Edward Bellamy, author of *Looking Backward*. Bellamy did not like the word socialism linked to his utopian vision of a new order, preferring nationalism. *Vancouver Daily World*, 24 March 1894; 7 April 1894; 16 April 1894; 11 August 1894; 4 April 1895; 20 April 1895.

94 *Vancouver Daily World*, 28 February 1893; *Victoria Daily Times*, 23 May 1893; 28 August 1893.

95 *Victoria Daily Times*, 10 February 1892; *Vancouver Daily World*, 7 September 1893; 20 September 1893; 22 September 1893; 14 October 1893; 27 February 1894; *Daily Columbian*, 23 February 1894.

96 *Vancouver Daily World*, 4 February 1893; 11 February 1893; 29 November 1893; 2 December 1893; 4 December 1893; 7 December 1893; 18 January 1894; 31 January 1894; 12 April 1894; *Daily Columbian*, 10 February 1893; 30 October 1893; 30 November 1893; 5 December 1893; *Victoria Daily Times*, 8 February 1893; 14 October 1893; 26 October 1893; 28 October 1893; 2 December 1893; 6 December 1893; 17 January 1894.

97 *Victoria Daily Times*, 2 December 1893.

98 *Victoria Daily Times*, 16 August 1890.

99 *Victoria Daily Colonist*, 12 August 1890; 16 August 1890; 19 August 1890; 30 September 1890; 1 October 1890; 2 October 1890; 11 November 1890; *Victoria Daily Times*, 16 August 1890; 18 August 1890; 19 August 1890; 29 September 1890; 30 September 1890; 1 October 1890; 11 November 1890; 15 November 1890; 10 March 1891; 16 March 1891; *Nanaimo Free Press*, 16 March 1891.

100 *Vancouver Daily World*, 7 November 1890; 22 January 1891; 30 January 1891; 18 February 1891; 18 August 1891; 19 August 1891; 20 August 1891; Mark Leier, *Red Flags & Red Tape*, 73–74.

101 *Nanaimo Free Press*, 23 March 1891. For an interesting take on the courts, labour and property rights in the 1890s, see Alan Grove and Ross Lambertson, "Pawns of the Powerful: The Politics of Litigation in the Union Colliery Case," *BC Studies*, 103 (Autumn 1994), 3–31.

102 *Victoria Daily Times*, 17 March 1891.

103 *Victoria Daily Times*, 23 September 1893.

104 *Victoria Daily Times*, 22 September 1893; 23 September 1893; 25 September 1893; 26 September 1893; 27 September 1893.

105 *Daily British Colonist*, 6 June 1885.

106 Leier, *Red Flags & Red Tape*, 105.

CHAPTER 2 (pp. 35–63)

1 As Ian MacKay has shown, even among the intellectual, disciplined purveyors of socialism in early twentieth-century Canada, Marxist ideas were intertwined with a belief in evolutionary theory, especially as propounded by Herbert Spencer. Ian McKay, *Reasoning Otherwise: Leftists and the People's Enlightenment in Canada, 1890–1920* (Toronto: Between the Lines, 2008).

2 A rich source for the history of early socialism in BC remains Ross Alfred Johnson, "No Compromise — No Political Trading: The Marxian Socialist Tradition in British Columbia," PhD dissertation, University of British Columbia, 1975.

3 For miners and politics, see Jeremy Mouat, *Roaring Days: Rossland's Mines and the History of British Columbia* (Vancouver: UBC Press, 1995), 88–108; Jeremy Mouat, "The Genesis of Western Exceptionalism: British Columbia's Hard-Rock Miners, 1895–1903," *Canadian Historical Review*, 71/3

228 The Left in British Columbia

(September 1990), 317–345; Allen Seager, "Socialists and Workers: The Western Canadian Coal Miners, 1900–21," *Labour/Le Travail*, 16 (Fall 1985), 23–59.

4 Cited in A. Ross McCormack, *Reformers, Rebels, and Revolutionaries: The Western Canadian Radical Movement, 1899–1919* (Toronto: University of Toronto Press, 1977), 27.

5 Carlos A. Schwantes, *Radical Heritage: Labor, Socialism, and Reform in Washington and British Columbia, 1885–1917* (Vancouver: Douglas & McIntyre, 1979), 166.

6 Paula Wild, *Sointula: Island Utopia* (Madeira Park: Harbour Publishing, 1995), 31. See, also, Gordon Fish, *Dreams of Freedom: Bella Coola, Cape Scott, Sointula* (Victoria: Provincial Archives of British Columbia, 1982).

7 Kevin Wilson, *Practical Dreamers: Communitarianism and Co-operatives on Malcolm Island* (Victoria: British Columbia Institute for Co-operative Studies, 2005).

8 Eugenio F. Biagini, *Liberty, Retrenchment and Reform: Popular Liberalism in the Age of Gladstone, 1860–1880* (Cambridge: Cambridge University Press, 1992); Eugenio F. Biagini and Alastair J. Reid, eds., *Currents of Radicalism: Popular Radicalism, Organised Labour and Party Politics in Britain, 1850–1914* (Cambridge: Cambridge University Press, 1991).

9 John Shepherd, "Labour and Parliament: the Lib.-Labs. as the First Working Class MPs, 1885–1906," in Eugenio F. Biagini and Alastair J. Reid, *Currents of Radicalism*, 187–213; Alastair J. Reid, "Old Unionism Reconsidered: The Radicalism of Robert Knight, 1870–1900," in Biagini and Reid, 187–213; Patrick Joyce, *Visions of the People: Industrial England and the Question of Class 1848–1914* (Cambridge: Cambridge University Press, 1991).

10 Robert A.J. McDonald and Jeremy Mouat, "George Ritchie Maxwell," *Dictionary of Canadian Biography Online*, http://www.biographi.ca, accessed 25 July 2013; Robert A.J. McDonald, *Making Vancouver*, 72–74.

11 Jeremy Mouat, "Christopher Foley," *Dictionary of Canadian Biography Online*, http://www.biographi.ca, accessed 25 July 2013.

12 Mark Leier, "Ralph Smith," *Dictionary of Canadian Biography Online*, http://www.biographi.ca, accessed 25 July 2013.

13 The Liberals were out of power from 1928 to 1933. From 1941 to 1952 the Liberals were the dominant partner in a coalition government with the Conservatives.

14　Jeremy Mouat, *Roaring Days*, 67–108; Eugene Forsey, *Trade Unions in Canada, 1812–1902* (Toronto: University of Toronto Press, 1982), 170–175.

15　John Hinde, *When Coal Was King: Ladysmith and the Coal-Mining Industry of Vancouver Island* (Vancouver: UBC Press, 2003), 93.

16　Paul Phillips, *No Power Greater: A Century of Labour in British Columbia* (Vancouver: BC Federation of Labour/Boag Foundation, 1967), 37–41; Jeremy Mouat, "Frank Rogers," *Dictionary of Canadian Biography Online*, http://www.biographi.ca, accessed 25 July 2013.

17　Robert A.J. McDonald, *Making Vancouver: Class, Status and Social Boundaries, 1863–1913* (Vancouver: UBC Press, 1996), 108–116, 180–186; Robert A.J. McDonald, "Working-Class Vancouver, 1886–1914," *BC Studies*, 69–70 (Spring/Summer 1986), 33–69; James R. Conley, "'Open Shop Means Closed to Union Men': Carpenters and the 1911 Vancouver Building Trades Strike," *BC Studies*, 91–92 (Autumn-Winter, 1991), 127–151; James R. Conley, "Frontier Labourers, Crafts in Crisis and the Western Labour Revolt: The Case of Vancouver, 1900–1919," *Labour/Le Travail*, 23 (Spring 1989), 9–37.

18　Allen Seager, "Workers, Class, and Industrial Conflict in New Westminster, 1900–1930," in Rennie Warburton and David Coburn, eds., *Workers, Capital, and the State in British Columbia: Selected Papers* (Vancouver: UBC Press, 1988), 117–140.

19　Allen Seager and David Roth, "British Columbia and the Mining West: A Ghost of a Chance," in Craig Heron, ed., *The Workers' Revolt in Canada, 1917–1925* (Toronto: University of Toronto Press, 1998), 243.

20　Phillips, 169, 172.

21　Seager and Roth, 246–247.

22　Phillips, 72–74.

23　Elaine Bernard, *The Long Distance Feeling: A History of the Telecommunications Workers Union* (Vancouver: New Star Books, 1982), 56.

24　For Victoria in 1919, see Ben Isitt, "The Search for Solidarity: The Industrial and Political Roots of the Co-operative Commonwealth Federation in British Columbia, 1913–1928," MA thesis, University of Victoria, 2003, 38–71.

25　Gregory S. Kealey, "1919: The Canadian Labour Revolt," *Labour/Le Travail*, 13 (Spring 1984), 32.

26　Kealey, 32–33.

27 Gordon Hak, *Turning Trees into Dollars: The British Columbia Coastal Lumber Industry, 1858–1913* (Toronto: University of Toronto Press, 2000), 47.

28 Hak, *Turning Trees into Dollars*, 116–167; Richard Rajala, "The Forest as Factory: Technological Change and Worker Control in the West Coast Logging Industry," *Labour/Le Travail*, 32 (Fall 1993), 73–104.

29 Gordon Hak, "British Columbia Loggers and the Lumber Workers Industrial Union, 1919–1922," *Labour/Le Travail*, 23 (Spring 1989), 67–90.

30 H.M. Grant, "Solving the Labour Problem at Imperial Oil: Welfare Capitalism in the Canadian Petroleum Industry, 1919–29," *Labour/Le Travail*, 41 (Spring 1998), 69–95.

31 Seager and Roth, 251.

32 The SPC ran three unsuccessful candidates in 1920, winning 3.5 percent of the popular vote. Leftist candidates won roughly 16 percent of the popular vote.

33 Mark Leier, *Where the Fraser River Flows: The Industrial Workers of the World in British Columbia* (Vancouver: New Star Books, 1990); Frank Leonard, *A Thousand Blunders: The Grand Trunk Pacific Railway and Northern British Columbia* (Vancouver: UBC Press, 1995), 92–126.

34 George Hardy, *Those Stormy Years: Memories of the Fight for Freedom on Five Continents* (London: Lawrence & Wishart, 1956), 54.

35 Mark Leier, *Where the Fraser River Flows*; Mark Leier, "Solidarity on Occasion: The Vancouver Free Speech Fights of 1909 and 1912," *Labour/Le Travail*, 23 (Spring 1989), 39–66; Mark Leier, *Red Flags & Red Tape*.

36 Mark Leier, *Red Flags & Red Tape*.

37 Cited in Donald Avery, *'Dangerous Foreigners': European Immigrant Workers and Labour Radicalism in Canada, 1896–1932* (Toronto: McClelland and Stewart, 1979), 53.

38 Gillian Creese, "Exclusion or Solidarity? Vancouver Workers Confront the 'Oriental Problem,'" *BC Studies*, 80 (1988), 24–51. We know too little about the left within Asian-Canadian communities. For insights, see Peter Campbell, "East Meets Left: South Asian Militants and the Socialist Party of Canada in British Columbia, 1904–1914," *International Journal of Canadian Studies*, 20 (Fall 1999), 35–65.

39 For a Canadian overview, see Craig Heron, *Booze: A Distilled History* (Toronto: Between the Lines, 2003).

40 Catherine L. Cleverdon, *The Woman Suffrage Movement in Canada* (Toronto: University of Toronto Press, 1974, original 1950), 84–104. Women's militancy in a coal-mining community during a strike and for female suffrage is addressed in John R. Hinde, "'Stout Ladies and Amazons': Women in the British Columbia Coal-Mining Community of Ladysmith, 1912–14," *BC Studies*, 114 (Summer 1997), 33–57.

41 Marie Campbell, "Sexism in British Columbia Trade Unions, 1900–1920," in Barbara Latham and Cathy Kess, eds., *In Her Own Right: Selected Essays on Women's History in BC* (Victoria: Camosun College, 1980), 167–186.

42 Irene Howard, *The Struggle for Social Justice in British Columbia: Helena Gutteridge, the Unknown Reformer* (Vancouver: UBC Press, 1992), 129.

CHAPTER 3 (pp. 64–92)

1 John Douglas Belshaw and David J. Mitchell, "The Economy since the Great War," in J.M. Johnston, ed., *The Pacific Province: A History of British Columbia* (Vancouver: Douglas & McIntyre, 1996), 321.

2 Paul Phillips, *No Power Greater: A Century of Labour in BC* (Vancouver: BC Federation of Labour/Boag Foundation), 90–91.

3 Cited in Phillips, 94.

4 Phillips, 90.

5 Phillips, 95.

6 There were also two socialist candidates, independent of the CLP banner: William Arthur Pritchard, running in Nanaimo, where no CLP candidate ran; and John David Harrington in Vancouver.

7 Phillips, 99–100; see also, Ben Isitt, "The Search for Solidarity: The Industrial and Political Roots of the Co-operative Commonwealth Federation in British Columbia, 1913–1928," MA thesis, University of Victoria, 2003, 142–177.

8 Phillips, 169.

9 Phillips, 96.

10 The Conservatives won fifteen seats in 1920, based on 31.2 percent of the popular vote, and seventeen seats in 1924 with 29.45 percent of the vote.

11 For a discussion of the "New Liberalism," which embraced an increased role for the state, in a BC context, see James Murton, *Creating a Modern Countryside: Liberalism and Land Resettlement in British Columbia* (Vancouver: UBC Press, 2007).

12 Gordon Hak, "The Socialist and Labourist Impulse in Small-Town British Columbia: Port Alberni and Prince George, 1911–33," *Canadian Historical Review*, 70/4 (December 1989), 636 passim.

13 Hak, 532–533.

14 Phillips, 99.

15 Phillips, 102–103.

16 Jeanne Meyers, "Class and Community in the Fraser Mills Strike, 1931," in Rennie Warburton and David Coburn, eds., *Workers, Capital, and the State in British Columbia* (Vancouver: UBC Press, 1988), 141–160.

17 Cited in Gordon Hak, "Red Wages: Communists and the 1934 Vancouver Island Loggers Strike," *Pacific Northwest Quarterly*, 80/3 (July 1989), 89 passim.

18 Phillips, 103–104; Andrew Parnaby, *Citizen Docker: Making a New Deal on the Vancouver Waterfront, 1919–1939* (Toronto: University of Toronto Press, 2008).

19 Gordon Hak, "On the Fringes: Capital and Labour in the Forest Economies of the Port Alberni and Prince George Districts, British Columbia, 1910–1939," PhD dissertation, Simon Fraser University, 1986, 227–229.

20 Gordon Hak, *Capital and Labour in the British Columbia Forest Industry, 1934–74* (Vancouver: UBC Press, 2007), 71; Andrew Parnaby, "What's the Law Got to Do with It? The IWA and the Politics of State Power in British Columbia, 1935–1939," *Labour/Le Travail*, 44 (Fall 1999), 9–45.

21 Hak, "On the Fringes," 232–234.

22 Phillips, 169.

23 Margaret A. Ormsby, *British Columbia: A History* (Toronto: Macmillan of Canada, 1958), 467.

24 "Regina Manifesto," in Walter D. Young, *The Anatomy of a Party: The National CCF, 1932–61* (Toronto: University of Toronto Press, 1969), 303–313.

25 Christine Price, "'A Very Conservative Radical': Reverend Robert Connell's Encounter with Marxism in the BC CCF," MA thesis, Simon Fraser University, 2006; Peter Campbell, *Canadian Marxists and the Search for a Third Way* (Montreal & Kingston: McGill-Queen's University Press, 1999), 31–72; Dorothy Steeves, *The Compassionate Rebel: Ernest Winch and the Growth of Socialism in Western Canada* (Vancouver: J.J. Douglas, 1977); Young, Walter. "Ideology, Personality and the Origin of the CCF in British Columbia," *BC*

Studies, 32 (Winter 1976–77), 139–162; Patrick George Hill, "A Failure of Unity: Communist Party — CCF Relations in British Columbia, 1935–1939," MA thesis, University of Victoria, 1977.

26 Patrick George Hill, 56. For more on the anti-communism of Angus and Grace MacInnis, see S.P. Lewis, *Grace: The Life of Grace MacInnis* (Madeira Park, BC: Harbour Publishing, 1993).

27 Hak, "On the Fringes," 304.

28 For a provocative debate about the internal workings of the BC CCF in the 1930s, see Robert A.J. McDonald, "'Telford Time' and the Populist Origins of the CCF in British Columbia," *Labour/Le Travail*, 71 (Spring 2013), 87–100; James Naylor, "The British Columbia CCF's Working-Class Moment: Socialism Not Populism," *Labour/Le Travail*, 71 (Spring 2013), 101–121.

29 For cooperation between CCF and CPC women, see Irene Howard, "The Mothers' Council of Vancouver: Holding the Fort for the Unemployed, 1935–1938," *BC Studies*, 69–70 (Spring-Summer 1986), 249–287.

30 Gordon Hak, "The Communists and the Unemployed in the Prince George District, 1930–1935," *BC Studies*, 68 (Winter 1985–86), 58, 60.

31 John Richards, *Retooling the Welfare State: What's Right, What's Wrong, What's to Be Done*, Policy Study 31 (Toronto: C.D. Howe Institute, 1997), 45. See, also, James Naylor, "Canadian Labour Politics and the British Model, 1920–50," in Phillip Buckner and R. Douglas Francis, eds., *Canada and the British World: Culture, Migration, and Identity* (Vancouver: UBC Press, 2006), 288–308. The British influence on British Columbia politics generally is stated bluntly by Nelson Wiseman: "British immigrants were the most important group in the political making of BC." Nelson Wiseman, *In Search of Canadian Political Culture* (Vancouver: UBC Press, 2007), 242.

32 Increasingly, citizens expected the state to help them in times of need, not out of charity, but because they had honourably fulfilled their duty to society. This was especially true for those who had served their country during the First World War. The notion of a contract between citizens and the state gathered strength in the 1920s and became more fully realized during the difficult years of the 1930s. Rather than the needy appealing to governments with cap in hand asking for charity, a humiliation in the culture of worker independence, the claim was now made in terms of a contract. Thoughts about government action were also gendered, with the intent of propping up the role of men in the patriarchal family. Nancy Christie, *Engendering the State: Family, Work, and Welfare in Canada* (Toronto: University of Toronto

Press, 2000); Lara Campbell, "'We Who Have Wallowed in the Mud of Flanders': First World War Veterans, Unemployment and the Development of Social Welfare in Canada, 1929–1939," *Journal of the Canadian Historical Association* (2000), 125–149; Andrew Parnaby, *Citizen Docker*.

33 Margaret A. Ormsby, "T. Dufferin Pattullo and the Little New Deal," *Canadian Historical Review*, 43/4 (December 1962), 277–297; Allan Irving, "The Development of a Provincial Welfare State: British Columbia, 1900–1939, in Allan Moscovitch and Jim Albert, eds., *The Benevolent State: The Growth of Welfare in Canada* (Toronto: Garamond Press, 1987), 155–174; Margaret Andrews, "The Course of Medical Opinion on State Health Insurance in British Columbia, 1919–1939," *Histoire sociale/Social History*, 31 (May 1983), 131–143; Allan Irving, "The Doctors Versus the Expert: Harry Morris Cassidy and the British Columbia Health Insurance Dispute of the 1930s," *BC Studies*, 78 (Summer 1988), 53–79; Robin Fisher, "The Decline of Reform: British Columbia Politics in the 1930s," *Journal of Canadian Studies*, 25/3 (Fall 1990), 74–89.

34 The BC CCF also did well in the 1935 federal election. They won three of thirteen federal ridings with 33.6 percent of the popular vote. No other party secured as many votes in the province. John Herd Thompson with Allen Seager, *Canada 1922–1939: Decades of Discord* (Toronto: McClelland and Stewart, 1985), 337.

35 Patricia E. Roy, *The Oriental Question: Consolidating a White Man's Province, 1914–41* (Vancouver: UBC Press, 2003), 67.

36 Roy, 91.

37 Roy, 156.

38 Roy, 153–162.

39 Irene Howard, "The Mothers' Council of Vancouver," 249–287.

40 Joan Sangster, *Dreams of Equality: Women on the Canadian Left, 1920–1950* (Toronto: McClelland & Stewart, 1989), 114–121.

41 Ann Porter, *Gendered States: Women, Unemployment Insurance, and the Political Economy of the Welfare State in Canada, 1945–1997* (Toronto: University of Toronto Press, 2003).

42 Angus McLaren and Arlene Tigar McLaren, *The Bedroom and the State: The Changing Practices and Politics of Contraception and Abortion in Canada, 1880–1980* (Toronto: McClelland and Stewart, 1986), 51.

43 McLaren and McLaren, 58–66, 73.

CHAPTER 4 (pp. 93–112)

1 John Douglas Belshaw and David J. Mitchell, "The Economy since the Great War," in J.M. Johnston, ed., *The Pacific Province: A History of British Columbia* (Vancouver: Douglas & McIntyre, 1996), 321.

2 Paul Phillips, *No Power Greater: A Century of Labour in British Columbia* (Vancouver: BC Federation of Labour/Boag Foundation, 1967), 169, 172.

3 Phillips, 129.

4 There were critics of government support for collective bargaining. They argued that, under the new system, workers relinquished the right to strike during the time of the collective agreement, thus taking away the most potent weapon workers had to deal with grievances, namely, job action.

  Unions also became more secure financially in the 1940s. The pattern-setting Rand arbitration decision, dealing with a strike in Ontario in 1945, set out that all workers at a union site had to pay union dues, even if they did not belong to the union. The argument was that anti-union workers also enjoyed the benefits secured by the union, and as such should pay dues. Since now everyone in a bargaining unit was paying dues, it was a simple administrative matter for company payroll departments to deduct union dues from each worker's pay cheque and then turn the money over to the union. This was called either the Rand formula or check-off. For unions it meant a guaranteed, predictable revenue stream. There were critics here, too. Without personally collecting dues, it was argued, union leaders would become estranged from workers on the shop floor, thus establishing a bureaucracy and weakening worker participation in the life of a union. But for the most part it was seen a positive step that made unions stronger.

5 Gordon Hak, *Capital and Labour in the British Columbia Forest Industry, 1934–74* (Vancouver: UBC Press, 2007), 83–87.

6 Phillips, 171.

7 Irving Abella, "Communism and Anti-Communism in the British Columbia Labour Movement: 1940–1948," in David Jay Bercuson, ed., *Western Perspectives I: Papers of the Western Canadian Studies Conference, 1973* (Toronto: Holt, Rinehart and Winston, 1974), 88.

8 Phillips, 144; Irving Martin Abella, *Nationalism, Communism, and Canadian Labour: The CIO, the Communist Party, and the Canadian Congress of Labour, 1935–1956* (Toronto: University of Toronto Press, 1973), 11–138; Abella, Communism and Anti-Communism," 88–100.

9 Abella, *Nationalism, Communism, and Canadian Labour*, 11–138; Hak, *Capital and Labour*, 101–108.

10 Martin Robin, *Pillars of Profit: The Company Province, 1934–1972* (Toronto: McClelland and Stewart, 1973), 73–74.

11 Alicja Muszynski, *Cheap Wage Labour: Race and Gender in the Fisheries of British Columbia* (Montreal and Kingston: McGill-Queen's Press, 1996), 202–204.

12 Hak, *Capital and Labour*, 81–82.

13 Mark Leier, "Solidarity on Occasion: The Vancouver Free Speech Fights of 1909 and 1912," *Labour/Le Travail*, 23 (1989), 39–66.

14 For an introduction to the history of human rights in Canada, see Ross Lambertson, *Repression and Resistance: Canadian Human Rights Activists 1930–1960* (Toronto: University of Toronto Press, 2005); Dominique Clément, *Canada's Rights Revolution: Social Movements and Social Change, 1937–82* (Vancouver: UBC Press, 2008); Janet Miron, ed., *A History of Human Rights in Canada: Essential Issues* (Toronto: Canadian Scholars' Press, 2009).

15 The Universal Declaration of Human Rights, as adopted at the UN on 10 December 1948, is found in Gary Teeple, *The Riddle of Human Rights* (Aurora, Ontario: Garamond Press, 2005), 213–218.

16 Sangster, 198, 212.

17 Gordon Hak, "Populism and the Social Credit Breakthrough in British Columbia," *Canadian Historical Review*, 85/2 (June 2004), 277–296.

CHAPTER 5 (pp. 113–145)

1 Jean Barman, *The West beyond the West: A History of British Columbia* (Toronto: University of Toronto, 1991), 375.

2 Ken Drushka, HR: *A Biography of H.R. MacMillan* (Madeira Park, BC: Harbour Publishing, 1995), 303–304.

3 Gordon Hak, *Capital and Labour in the British Columbia Forest Industry, 1934–74* (Vancouver: UBC Press, 2007), 42–66.

4 Paul Phillips, *No Power Greater: A Century of Labour in British Columbia* (Vancouver: BC Federation of Labour/Boag Foundation, 1967), 171; Ben Isitt, *Militant Minority: British Columbia Workers and the Rise of a New Left, 1948–1972* (Toronto: University of Toronto Press, 2011), 206.

5 Sara Slinn, "Restructuring Reality So That the Law Will Follow: British Columbia Teachers' Quest for Collective Bargaining Rights," *Labour/Le Travail*, 68 (Fall 2011), 35–77.

6 Phillips, 157.

7 Bruce McLean, 'A Union Amongst Government Employees': A History of the BC Government Employees Union, 1919–1979 (Burnaby: BCGEU, 1979); Patricia G. Webb, The Heart of Health Care, The Story of the Hospital Employees' Union: The First 50 Years (Vancouver: HEU, 1994); Terry Wotherspoon, "Occupational Divisions and Struggles for Unity Among British Columbia's Public School Teachers," BC Studies, 107 (Autumn 1995), 30–59; Geoff Meggs and Rod Mickleburgh, The Art of the Impossible: Dave Barrett and the NDP in Power, 1972–1975 (Madeira Park, BC: Harbour Publishing, 2012), 170–173.

8 Phillips, 149–153.

9 Hak, 108.

10 Martin Robin, Pillars of Profit: The Company Province 1934–1972 (Toronto: McClelland and Stewart, 1973), 215.

11 Hak, 158–164.

12 Walter D. Young, The Anatomy of a Party: The National CCF, 1932–61 (Toronto: University of Toronto Press, 1969), 127–130; 313–317.

13 Cited in Hak, 142.

14 Cited in Hak, 165.

15 Cited in Hak, 160, 164.

16 Phillips, 146–147; Judy Fudge and Eric Tucker, "'Everybody knows what a picket line means': Picketing before the British Columbia Court of Appeal," BC Studies, 162 (Summer 2009), 53–79.

17 Robin, 216.

18 David J. Mitchell, W.A.C.: Bennett and the Rise of British Columbia (Vancouver: Douglas & McIntyre, 1983), 360–361.

19 Norman Penner, Canadian Communism: The Stalin Years and Beyond (Toronto: Methuen, 1988), 237.

20 Ian McDonald, "Class Conflict and Political Factionalism: A History of Local 213 of the International Brotherhood of Electrical Workers, 1901–1961," MA thesis, Simon Fraser University, 1986, 160.

21 See Peter E. Newell, The Impossibilists: A Brief Profile of the Socialist Party of Canada (London: Athena Press, 2008).

22 McDonald, "Class Conflict and Political Factionalism," 181–222.

23 Hak, 110.

24 Hak, 108.

25 Dorothy June Roberts, "Doctrine and Disunity in the British Columbia Section of the CCF, 1932–1956," MA thesis, University of Victoria, 1972, 94–115. See too, Benjamin Isitt, "Confronting the Cold War: The 1950 Vancouver Convention of the Co-operative Commonwealth Federation," *Canadian Historical Review*, 91/3 (September 2010), 465–501.

26 Hak, 115.

27 For a famous critique of American liberal capitalism from a conservative perspective, see George Grant, *Lament for a Nation: The Defeat of Canadian Nationalism* (Ottawa: Carleton University Press, 1995, original 1965).

28 Hak, 116–123.

29 Bryan D. Palmer, *Working-Class Experience: Rethinking the History of Canadian Labour, 1880–1991* (Toronto: McClelland & Stewart, 1992), 320.

30 William Beeching and Phyllis Clarke, eds., *Yours in the Struggle: Reminiscences of Tim Buck* (Toronto: NC Press, 1977), 366.

31 Hak, 116.

32 Kari Levitt, *Silent Surrender: The Multinational Corporation in Canada* (Toronto: Macmillan, 1970).

33 Mel Watkins, "A Staple Theory of Economic Growth," in W.T. Easterbrook and M.H. Watkins, eds., *Approaches to Canadian Economic History* (Toronto: McClelland and Stewart, 1967), 49–73.

34 Patricia Marchak, *Green Gold: The Forest Industry in British Columbia* (Vancouver: UBC Press, 1983); Marchak, "A Changing Global Context for British Columbia's Forest Industry," in Trevor J.Barnes and Roger Hayter, eds., *Troubles in the Rainforest: British Columbia's Forest Economy in Transition*, in Canadian Western Geographical Series, vol. 33. (Victoria: Western Geographical Press, 1997), 149–164.

35 John Bullen, "The Ontario Waffle and the Struggle for an Independent Socialist Canada: Conflict within the NDP," *Canadian Historical Review*, VXIV, 2 (1983), 193.

36 Bullen, 194.

37 Judy Rebick, *Ten Thousand Roses: The Making of a Feminist Revolution* (Toronto: Penguin Canada, 2005), 18.

38 Cited in Hak, 185.

39 For a discussion of Vancouver's freeway debate of 1969, see Will Langford, "'Is Sutton Brown God?' Planning and Expertise and the Local State in Vancouver, 1952–73," *BC Studies*, 173 (Spring 2012), 11–39.

40 Discussion of continuities between the Old and New Lefts in BC is found in Ben Isitt, *Militant Minority: British Columbia Workers and the Rise of a New Left, 1948–1972* (Toronto: University of Toronto Press, 2011).

41 Hak, 190–191. For Canada see Bryan D. Palmer, "Wildcat Workers in the 1960s: The Unruly Face of Class Struggle," in Bryan D. Palmer and Joan Sangster, eds., *Labouring Canada: Class, Gender, and Race in Canadian Working-Class History* (Don Mills: Oxford University Press, 2008), 373–394.

42 Tom Hayden, "The Way We Were and the Future of the Port Huron Statement," in Dimitrios Roussopoulos, ed., *The New Left: Legacy and Continuity* (Montreal: Black Rose Books, 2007), 130–156.

43 Hugh Johnston, *Radical Campus: Making Simon Fraser University* (Vancouver: Douglas & McIntyre, 2005), 255–329; Ian Milligan, "Coming off the Mountain: Forging an Outward-Looking New Left at Simon Fraser University," *BC Studies*, 171 (Autumn 2011), 69–91; Doug Owram, *Born at the Right Time: A History of the Baby-Boom Generation* (Toronto: University of Toronto Press, 1996), 242–247.

44 *The Ubyssey*, Vancouver, 25 October 1968.

45 Douglas Owram, *Born at the Right Time*, 278.

46 Christabelle Sethna and Steve Hewitt, "Clandestine Operations: The Vancouver Women's Caucus, the Abortion Caravan, and the RCMP," *Canadian Historical Review*, 90/3 (September 2009), 463–495.

47 Judy Rebick, *Ten Thousand Roses*, 35–46; Ann Thomson, *Winning Choice on Abortion: How British Columbian Feminists Won the Battles of the 1970s and 1980s* (Victoria: Trafford Publishing, 2004), 1–76.

48 Hak, *Capital and Labour*, 167–174.

49 Rex Weyler, *Greenpeace: How a Group of Ecologists, Journalists and Visionaries Changed the World* (Vancouver: Raincoast Books, 2004), 1–137; Frank Zelko, "Making Greenpeace: The Development of Direct Action Environmentalism in British Columbia," *BC Studies*, 142/143 (Summer/Autumn 2004), 197–239; Jim Bohlen, *Making Waves: The Origins and Future of Greenpeace* (Montreal: Black Rose Books, 2001).

50 James Harding, "The New Left in British Columbia," *Our Generation*, 7/2 (June–July 1970), 39.

51 Tom Warner, *Never Going Back: A History of Queer Activism in Canada* (Toronto: University of Toronto Press, 2002), 73.

52 For a recent account of the Barrett years, see Geoff Meggs and Rod Mickleburgh, *The Art of the Impossible: Dave Barrett and the NDP in Power, 1972–1975* (Madeira Park, BC: Harbour Publishing, 2012).

53 Barman, 295.

54 Isitt, *Militant Minority*, 186.

55 Recently Robert McDonald has interpreted the leadership struggle between Barrett and Berger as a struggle between shifting notions of modernity within the party. Robert McDonald, "Modernity and the Political Left: Robert Strachan, Thomas Berger, and Leadership of the Provincial NDP, 1963–69," paper presented at the BC Studies Conference, Kelowna, 6 May 2011.

56 Rennie Warburton and David Coburn, "The Rise of Non-Manual Work in British Columbia," *BC Studies*, 59 (Autumn 1983), 5–27.

57 Philip Resnick, "Social Democracy in Power: The Case of British Columbia," *BC Studies*, 34 (Summer 1977), 3–20.

58 Andrew Petter, "Sausage Making in British Columbia's NDP Government: The Creation of the Land Commission Act, August 1972–April 1973," *BC Studies*, 65 (Spring 1985), 3–33; Raymond W. Payne, "Corporate Power, Interest Groups and the Development of Mining Policy in British Columbia, 1972–77," *BC Studies*, 54 (Summer 1982), 3–37; Nükhet Kardam, "Interest Group Power and Government Regulation: The Cases of the Mining and Insurance Industries During the Period of the New Democratic Party Government in British Columbia, 1972–75," *BC Studies*, 60 (Winter 1983–84), 48–74.

59 Alan F.J. Artibise, "'A Worthy, if Unlikely Enterprise': The Labour Relations Board and the Evolution of Labour Policy and Practice in British Columbia, 1973–1980," *BC Studies*, 56 (Winter 1982–83), 3–43.

60 Allen Garr, *Tough Guy: Bill Bennett and the Taking of British Columbia* (Toronto: Key Porter Books, 1985), 26–29; G.L. Kristianson, "The Non-partisan Approach to BC Politics: The Search for a Unity Party, 1972–1975," *BC Studies*, 33 (Spring 1977), 13–29.

61 Meggs and Mickleburgh, 236–248.

62 Philip Van Huizen, "'Panic Park': Environmental Protest and the Politics of Parks in British Columbia's Skagit Valley," *BC Studies*, 170 (Summer 2011), 67–92.

63 Hak, 184.

64 BC Ministry of Labour, *Annual Report 1976* (Victoria: Queen's Printer, 1977).

CHAPTER 6 (pp. 146–169)

1 Stan Persky, *Bennett II: The Decline & Stumbling of Social Credit Government in British Columbia* (Vancouver: New Star Books, 1983), 253.

2 Stan Persky, *Son of Socred: Has Bill Bennett's Government Gotten BC Moving Again?* (Vancouver: New Star Books, 1979), 30–31.

3 Persky, *Son of Socred*, 289–291.

4 British Columbia, Ministry of Labour, *Annual Reports*, 1980–82 (Victoria: Queen's Printer, 1980–82).

5 Norman Ruff, "Social Credit as Employer," in Warren Magnusson, William K. Carroll, Charles Boyle, Monika Langer, and R.B.J. Walker, eds., *The New Reality: The Politics of Restraint in British Columbia* (Vancouver: New Star Books, 1984), 154.

6 For a Fraser Institute perspective on unionism in the public sector, see Sandra Christensen, *Unions and the Public Interest: Collective Bargaining in the Government Sector* (Vancouver: Fraser Institute, 1980).

7 Stan Persky, *Bennett II*, 107–129.

8 For a structural perspective on the roots of Solidarity, see Michael Howlett and Keith Brownsey, "The Old Reality and the New Reality: Party Politics and Public Policy in British Columbia 1941–1987," *Studies in Political Economy*, 25 (Spring 1988), 141–176. For an interpretation using Gramscian concepts, see William Carroll and R.S. Ratner, "Social Democracy, Neo-Conservatism and Hegemonic Crisis in British Columbia," *Critical Sociology*, 16/1 (Spring 1989), 29–53.

9 Ruff, 155.

10 William K. Carroll, "The Solidarity Coalition," in Warren Magnusson, William K. Carroll, Charles Boyle, Monika Langer, and R.B.J. Walker, eds., *The New Reality: The Politics of Restraint in British Columbia*, (Vancouver: New Star Books, 1984), 97.

11 Bryan D. Palmer, *Solidarity: The Rise and Fall of an Opposition in British Columbia* (Vancouver: New Star, 1987), 32.

12 Carroll, "The Solidarity Coalition," 98.

13 Jack Munro and Jane O'Hara, *Union Jack: Labour Leader Jack Munro* (Vancouver: Douglas & McIntyre, 1988), 7.

14 Carroll, 101.

15 The declaration is reprinted in full in Appendix B, *The New Reality*, 286–287.

16 *The New Reality*, 287.

17 According to Bob Plecas, a high-ranking BC civil servant in the 1980s, Bennett "had known from the start of this fight that the conclusion would be reached only if the public- and private-sector unions could be split." Bob Plecas, *Bill Bennett: A Mandarin's View* (Vancouver: Douglas & McIntyre, 2006), 226.

18 For interpretations of Solidarity, see Ted Richmond and John Shields, "Reflections on Resistance to Neoliberalism: Looking Back on Solidarity in 1983 British Columbia," *Socialist Studies/Études socialistes*, 7/1–2 (Spring/Fall 2011), 216–237.

19 *Sun*, Vancouver, 21 January 1983; Ann Hansen, *Direct Action: Memoirs of an Urban Guerilla* (Toronto: Between the Lines, 2001); http://encyclopedia.the freedictionary.com/Squamish+Five, accessed 24 July 2013.

20 Jack Munro and Jane O'Hara, *Union Jack*, 153–174; Bruce Elphinstone, "The IWA on Strike: Drawing the Line," *New Directions*, 2/4 (February/March 1987), 20–23.

21 Jimmy Pattison with Paul Grescoe, *Jimmy: An Autobiography* (Toronto: Seal Books, McClelland-Bantam, 1987), 246–249; Bob Plecas, *Bill Bennett: A Mandarin's View*, 248. For a critique of the Expo project from the left, see Larry Kuehn, "The Bad BCers' Guide to Expo," *New Directions*, 1/5 (April/May 1986), 9–13.

22 Ken Novakowski, "Gaining Full Bargaining Rights," *Teacher Newsmagazine*, 12/6 (April 2000), 5.

23 Ben Isitt, *Militant Minority: British Columbia Workers and the Rise of a New Left, 1948–1972* (Toronto: University of Toronto Press, 2011), 66–67; 125–129.

24 Ann Thomson, *Winning Choice on Abortion: How Feminist British Columbian and Canadian Feminists Won the Battles of the 1970s and 1980s*. (Victoria: Trafford Publishing, 2004), 236; Gary Mason and Keith Baldrey, *Fantasyland: Inside the Reign of Bill Vander Zalm* (Toronto: McGraw-Hill Ryerson, 1989), 175–196.

25 Tom Warner, *Never Going Back: A History of Queer Activism in Canada* (Toronto: University of Toronto Press, 2002), 59–78.

26 Warner, 159, 163; Robb Atkinson, "Silence Equals Death; Action Equals Life," *New Directions*, 5/2 (November/December 1989), 9–11.

27 Mason and Baldrey, 316.

28 Warner, 204–205. Changing public opinion and favourable Supreme Court decisions based on the Charter of Rights and Freedoms led to greater equality rights for LGBT people in 1995, recognition of same-sex marriage in BC in 2003, and federal sanction of same-sex marriage in 2005. See Jim Egan, *Challenging the Conspiracy of Silence: My Life as a Canadian Gay Activist*, compiled and edited by Donald W. McLeod (Toronto: The Canadian Lesbian and Gay Archives and Homewood Books, 1998); Sylvain Larocque, *Gay Marriage: The Story of a Canadian Social Revolution*, tr. Robert Chodos, Louisa Blair, and Benjamin Waterhouse (Toronto: James Lorimer & Company, 2006); J. Scott Matthews, "The Political Foundations of Support for Same-Sex Marriage in Canada," *Canadian Journal of Political Science*, 38/4 (December 2005), 841–866.

29 In 1986 the British Columbia section of the International Woodworkers of America withdrew from the international union based in the United States, creating IWA-Canada, a national union. The IWA was responding to economic circumstances: Canadian workers, because of productivity levels and the lower value of the Canadian dollar, did not have to take the concessions being taken by American IWA members; nor were they willing to take direction from an American leadership forced into a defensive negotiating position. According to Jane O'Hara, for BC IWA leader Jack Munro, "the pull-out was not so much a gesture of nationalism as a means of survival heading into the twenty-first century." To quote Munro: "To this day, I'm still a supporter of international unions, if they work to everyone's benefit. When we decided to break away, it wasn't because I was on some Canadian nationalist crusade." Jack Munro and Jane O'Hara, *Union Jack: Labour Leader Jack Munro* (Vancouver: Douglas & McIntyre, 1988), 176. For Munro's account of the breakaway, see pp. 174–182.

30 Robert Wright, *Virtual Sovereignty: Nationalism, Culture and the Canadian Question* (Toronto: Canadian Scholars' Press, 2004), 153–191.

31 A right-wing party called the Reform Party of British Columbia (Reform BC) was founded in 1983. It was active in provincial politics but it was not associated with the Reform Party of Canada.

32 Trevor Harrison, *Of Passionate Intensity: Right-Wing Populism and the Reform Party of Canada* (Toronto: University of Toronto Press, 1995), 81–138.

33 Elections Canada, "General Information: Official Reports: Thirty-sixth General Election 1997 — Official Voting Results — Synopsis," www.elections. ca, accessed 24 July 2013.

34 Harrison, 208. See also Tom Flanagan, *Waiting for the Wave: The Reform Party and Preston Manning* (Toronto: Stoddart, 1995).

35 Harrison, 210.

36 For critiques of the role of the provincial press in spreading right-wing ideology and maintaining a constant attack on the NDP, see Mike Harcourt with Wayne Skene, *Mike Harcourt: A Measure of Defiance* (Vancouver: Douglas & McIntyre, 1996), 164–185; Judy Tyabji Wilson, *Daggers Unsheathed: The Political Assassination of Glen Clark* (Surrey: Heritage House, 2002), 296–303.

37 The Pulp and Paper Workers of Canada, Local 4, and the Canadian Smelter and Allied Workers Union were early supporters of environmentalism.

38 Elizabeth May, *Paradise Won: The Struggle for South Moresby* (Toronto: McClelland and Stewart, 1990). See, also, Elizabeth May, "Brian Mulroney and the Environment," in Raymond B. Blake, ed., *Transforming the Nation: Canada and Brian Mulroney* (Montreal and Kingston: McGill-Queen's University Press, 207), 381–392.

39 Paul George, *Big Trees Not Stumps: 25 Years of Campaigning to Save Wilderness with the Wilderness Committee* (Vancouver: Western Canada Wilderness Committee, 2006). Other flashpoints in the 1980s included the Stein Valley, an undeveloped watershed near Lytton, which became a provincial park in 1995, the forests of the Valhalla Range of the Selkirk Mountains, and the Carmanah Valley on the west coast of Vancouver Island. The Valhalla became an official park in 1987 and the Carmanah Valley achieved the same status in 1990.

CHAPTER 7 (pp. 170–203)

The following were accessed, unless otherwise noted, in April 2011 online at the following site: <http://www.proquest.com.ezproxy.viu.ca/>: *Maclean's; Canadian Dimension; This Magazine; Briar Patch; Enviromation; Canadian Press Newswire; Canadian Press; Our Times; Daily Commercial News and Construction Record; Alternatives Journal; Natural Life; Report on Business Magazine; Windspeaker*.

1 In the 1991 election the NDP won fifty-one seats with 40.71 percent of the popular vote; the Liberal Party took 33.25 percent of the popular vote and won seventeen seats; and the disintegrating Social Credit party won seven seats with 24.05 percent of the popular vote. In 1996 the NDP won thirty-nine seats with 39.4 percent of the popular vote, while the British Columbia Liberal Party, now a coalition of federal Liberals, federal Conservatives and Reformers, provincial Liberals and former Social Crediters, a party with no organizational links to the federal Liberal Party, won thirty-three seats with 41.82 percent of the popular vote.

2 Bryan Evans, "The New Democratic Party in the Era of Neoliberalism," in Stephanie Ross and Larry Savage, eds., *Rethinking the Politics of Labour in Canada* (Halifax: Fernwood Publishing, 2012), 54–56.

3 A Harcourt biographer describes him as a Liberal with social democratic leanings, a description that Harcourt does not deny. Daniel Gawthrop, *Highwire Act: Power, Pragmatism, and the Harcourt Legacy* (Vancouver: New Star Books, 1996), 23; Mike Harcourt with Wayne Skene, *Mike Harcourt: A Measure of Defiance* (Vancouver: Douglas & McIntyre, 1996).

4 Rod Mickleburgh, "Dosanjh Gamble Could Ultimately Lead to Cabinet Post," *The Globe and Mail*, 30 June 2004.

5 Benjamin Cashore, George Hoberg, Michael Howlett, Jeremy Rayner, and Jeremy Wilson, *In Search of Sustainability: British Columbia Forest Policy in the 1990s* (Vancouver: UBC Press, 2001), 26.

6 Jeremy Wilson, *Talk and Log: Wilderness Politics in British Columbia, 1965–96* (Vancouver: UBC Press, 1998), 262–300; Gawthrop, 155–197; Tzeporah Berman with Mark Leiren-Young, *This Crazy Time: Living Our Environmental Challenge* (Toronto: Alfred A. Knopf Canada, 2011), 103.

7 Kim Goldberg, "Harcourt's Tangled Web (Premier Harcourt's Environmental and Political Woes)," *Canadian Dimension*, 29/1 (February 1995), 16.

8 Ronald B. Hatch, "The Clayoquot Show Trials," in Tzeporah Berman, et. al., *Clayoquot & Dissent* (Vancouver: Ronsdale Press, 1994), 105–153.

9 Mark Nichols, "The World is Watching," *Maclean's*, 106/33 (16 August 1993), 22–27; Ivan Bulic, "Clayoquot Summer: Reality in the Black Hole (Clayoquot Peace Camp)," *Canadian Dimension*, 28/1 (January 1994), 34; Kim Goldberg, "Clayoquot Collusion: MacMillan Bloedel, the NDP and a Kangaroo Court Put the Right to Dissent on Trial," *This Magazine*, 27/8 (April/May 1994), 20–21; Gabriel Haythornthwaite, "The Clayoquot Legacy: The

Future of Environmental Activism," *Canadian Dimension*, 33/1 (February 1999), 28; Valerie Langer, "Echoes of Clayoquot Sound," *Briar Patch*, 32/6 (July/August 2003), 19–20.

10 Berman, 103–106.

11 W.T. Stanbury, *Environmental Groups and the International Conflict Over Forests of British Columbia, 1990–2000* (Vancouver: SFU-UBC Centre for the Study of Government and Business, 2000).

12 British Columbia, Ministry of Labour, *Annual Report 1982–83* (Victoria: Queen's Printer, 1983), 73; *Annual Report 1999–2000*, 43; Jennifer Patterson, "Union Says New BC Coastal Forest Mills Contract Best in Canada," *Canadian Press Newswire*, 1 August 1997.

13 Gabriel Haythornthwaite, "The Clayoquot Legacy: The Future of Environmental Activism," *Canadian Dimension*, 33/1 (February 1999), 28.

14 Ian Bailey, "Loggers Borrow 'Green' Tactics," *Canadian Press Newswire*, 6 July 1997; Larry Martel, "Loggers vs. Greenpeace: Corporate Blackmail," *Canadian Dimension*, 31/5 (September 1997), 33–34; Andrew Neufeld and Andrew Parnaby, *The IWA in Canada: The Life and Times of an Industrial Union* (Vancouver: IWA Canada/New Star Books, 2000), 288–289.

15 Berman, 72–73.

16 "BC Loggers Assault Protesters [Elaho Valley]," *Natural Life*, 70 (November/December 1999); "Confrontations in Elaho Valley Seem Likely to Continue for Foreseeable Future," *Canadian Press NewsWire*, 13 October 2000.

17 Gabriel Haythornthwaite, "The Clayoquot Legacy: The Future of Environmental Activism," *Canadian Dimension*, 33/1 (February 1999), 28–30. See also, Joseph G. Moore, "Two Struggles Into One? Labour and Environmental Movement Relations and the Challenge to Capitalist Forestry in British Columbia, 1900–2000," PhD dissertation, McMaster University, 2002, 281–347, 392–461.

18 Michael M'Gonigle, "Reinventing British Columbia: Towards a New Political Economy in the Forest," in Trevor J. Barnes and Roger Hayter, eds., *Troubles in the Rainforest: British Columbia's Forest Economy in Transition*, Canadian Western Geographical Series, Volume 33 (Victoria: University of Victoria, Department of Geography, Western Geographical Press, 1997), 48.

19 James MacKinnon, "Green Machine: Green Politics is On the Rise across the Globe. And It's Come to BC, Where Greens Beat the NDP in a By-Election Last Month," *This Magazine*, 33/4 (January/February 2000), 27;

Cindy Harnett, "Poised to Scoop Voters Disillusioned with the NDP, the Green Party Faces Its Own Ugly, Internal Battle for Leadership," *Canadian Press Newswire*, 7 February 2000; "Green Party Names New Interim Leader, Schedules Fall Leadership Convention," *Canadian Press Newswire*, 29 March 2000; "Accusations Fly After Longtime BC Green Party Leader Ousted," *Canadian Press Newswire*, 20 March 2000; Kim Goldberg, "Green Party Coup," *Canadian Dimension*, 34/4 (July/August 2000), 10.

20 Debra J. Salazar and Donald K. Alper, "Beyond the Politics of Left and Right: Beliefs and Values of Environmental Activists in British Columbia," *BC Studies*, 121 (Spring 1999), 5–34; Salazar and Alper, "Reconciling Environmentalism and the Left: Perspectives on Democracy and Social Justice in British Columbia's Environmental Movement," *Canadian Journal of Political Science*, 35/3 (September 2002), 527–566.

21 British Columbia, Ministry of Finance and Corporate Relations, *BC Stats Business Indicators*, 99/6 (June 1999), 4, http://www.bcstats.gov.bc.ca, accessed 26 July 2013.

22 British Columbia, Ministry of Finance and Corporate Relations, BC Stats, *Business Indicators*, 99/6 (June 1999), 3, http://www.bcstats.gov.bc.ca, accessed 26 July 2013.

23 Denise Kellahan, "Unions on the Menu: Organizing in BC's Service Sector," *Our Times*, 16/2 (March/April 1997), 24–30; Ian Bailey, "Starbucks Deal Could Perk Up Conditions for All Workers," *Canadian Press Newswire*, 11 July 1997.

24 Andrew Jackson, "Solidarity Forever? Trends in Canadian Union Density," *Studies in Political Economy*, 74 (Autumn 2004), 141; Tom Sandborn, "The Decade's Top Labour Stories in BC," *The Tyee*, 6 September, 2010; British Columbia, A Guide to the BC Economy and Labour Market, 2010, www.guidetobceconomy.org/Library/GTBCE_2010.pdf, accessed 18 May 2011.

25 British Columbia, Ministry of Finance and Corporate Relations, *BC Stats Business Indicators*, 99/6 (June 1999), 4, www.bcstats.gov.bc.ca, accessed 26 July 2013; British Columbia, BC Stats, *Infoline*, 04/09 (4 March 2004), 2, www.bcstats.gov.bc.ca/releases/info2004/in0409.pdf, accessed 25 July 2013.

26 British Columbia, BC Stats, *Infoline Report*, 10/01 (8 January 2010), 1, www.bcstats.gov.bc.ca/releases/info2010/on1001.pdf, accessed 25 July 2013.

27 Leo Panitch and Donald Swartz, *From Consent to Coercion: The Assault on Trade Union Freedoms*, 3rd ed. (Aurora: Garamond Press, 2003), 203–207;

Thomas Fleming, *Worlds Apart: British Columbia Schools, Politics, and Labour Relations Before and After 1972* (Mill Bay, BC: Bendall Books, 2011), 80.

28 Panitch and Swartz, 207–208.

29 Ken MacQueen, "BC's Black Thursday," *Maclean's*, 28 January 2002; 11 February 2002; Kim Goldberg, "BC's Black Thursday and the Fightback," *Canadian Dimension*, 36/2 (March/April 2002), 7; Donna Harrison, "BC's Protracted Class War," *Canadian Dimension*, 36/2 (March/April 2002), 12–13; Kim Goldberg, "Pacific Edge: Referendum & Dumber in BC," *Canadian Dimension*, 36/3 (May/June 2002), 4; Kimball Cariou, "BC's Fight Back," *Canadian Dimension*, 36/4 (July/August 2002), 8–9; David Camfield, "Neoliberalism and Working-Class Resistance in British Columbia: The Hospital Employees' Union Struggle, 2002–2004," *Labour/Le Travail*, 57 (Spring 2006), 9–41; Tiffany Crawford, "BC Government, Health Union Agree to Cap Layoffs, Avert General Strike," *Canadian Press Newswire*, 3 May 2004; Steve Hunt, "Speaking of Solidarity," *Our Times*, 23/3 (June/July 2004), 18–22. For more recent events, see Craig McInnes, "Laid-off Health Care Workers Face EI Clawback," *Vancouver Sun*, 25 September 2012; Katherine Dedyna, "Hospital Workers Fight Clawback of Employment Insurance Money," *Times Colonist*, Victoria, 4 January 2013.

30 Amy Carmichael, "Illegally Striking Teachers Vote to Go Back to Work After Two-Week Walkout," *Canadian Press Newswire*, 24 October 2005; Nancy Knickerbocker, "Doing the Right Thing," *Our Times*, 24/5 (November 2005), 40; Shane Gunster, "Listening to Labour: Mainstream Media, Talk Radio, and the 2005 BC Teachers Strike," *Canadian Journal of Communication*, 33/4 (2008), 661–684.

31 Tom Barrett, "Tale of Two Strikes," *The Tyee*, 27 July 2007, accessed 24 July 2013.

32 Tom Sandborn, "The View from a HandyDart Driver's Seat," *The Tyee*, 12 November 2009, accessed 24 July 2013.

33 Minor parties on the left were not contenders. While the NDP garnered 731,719 votes in 2005 and the Green Party 161,858, the environmentalist and socialist Work Less Party secured 1,642 votes running eleven candidates, the People's Front won 383 votes with five candidates, and the three Communist Party candidates received 244 votes. The 2009 results were similar.

34 Bill Tieleman, "NDP Needs Some Class!" *The Tyee*, 21 March 2008, accessed 24 July 2013; Bill Tieleman, "Sihota's Soft Path," *The Tyee*, 24 November

2009, accessed 24 July 2013; Bill Tieleman, "Why Carole James is Too Nice to Business," *The Tyee*, 28 September 2010, accessed 24 July 2013.

35 David Schreck, "Biggest Tax Shift in BC History: Why Did Campbell Do It?" *The Tyee*, 17 August 2009, accessed 24 July 2013; Bill Tieleman, "Tax Revolt! HST Hatred Keeps Growing," *The Tyee*, 11 August 2009, accessed 24 July 2013; Andrew MacLeod, "Who Are the NDP's 13 Dissidents?" *The Tyee*, 4 December 2010, accessed 24 July 2013.

36 The 2013 election results, as of June 5, 2013, were as follows: the BC Liberals 49 seats (44.14 percent of the popular vote), the NDP 34 seats (39.71 percent of the popular vote), and the Greens 1 seat (8.13 percent of the popular vote). One Independent was also elected, and though they did not win a seat, the Conservative Party took 4.76 percent of the popular vote.

37 Rex Weyler, "To Save our Ecology, We Must Move Beyond Hope," *The Tyee*, 10 August 2012, accessed 12 August 2012. See also, David Suzuki, "The Fundamental Failure of Environmentalism," *Straight.com*, 1 May 2012, accessed 27 September 2012.

38 *Vancouver Sun*, 15 December 2012.

39 James Keller, "Former Greens Say Leader Jim Harris Moving Party Too Far to the Right," *Canadian Press Newswire*, 11 December 2005.

40 Kathryn Harrison, "Environmental Protection in British Columbia: Post-material Values, Organized Interests, and Party Politics," in R.K. Carty, ed., *Politics, Policy, and Government in British Columbia* (Vancouver: UBC Press, 1996), 290–309.

41 Andrew MacLeod, "Elizabeth May's Political Progress in BC," *The Tyee*, 6 July 2010, accessed 24 July 2013.

42 Marc Lee, "Can the NDP Deal with BC's Economic Challenges," *Vancouver Sun*, 20 April 2009, A11.

43 Tom Barrett, "How Fair is BC's New Carbon Tax?" *The Tyee*, 20 February 2008, accessed 24 July 2013; Tom Barrett, "Don't Call Him Mr. Carbon Tax," *The Tyee*, 6 March 2008, accessed 24 July 2013; Andrew MacLeod, "The Carbon Campaign of '09," *The Tyee*, 5 June 2008, accessed 24 July 2013; Tom Barrett, "A Carbon Tax Backlash?" *The Tyee*, 23 June 2008, accessed 24 July 2013; Tom Barrett, "Carbon Tax Whacks the Poor, Later," *The Tyee*, 30 October 2008, accessed 24 July 2013; Bill Tieleman, "Furious Rebuke to Suzuki, Berman," *The Tyee*, 21 April 2009, accessed 24 July 2013; Michael M'Gonigle and Blake Anderson, "Beyond the Carbon Tax," 30 April 2009,

accessed 24 July 2013; Bill Tieleman, "How I 'Demonized' David Suzuki," *The Tyee*, 9 June 2009, accessed 24 July 2013; Bill Tieleman, "Axe the Gas Tax Won Votes for NDP," *The Tyee*, 16 June 2009, accessed 24 July 2013; Bill Tieleman, "Carbon Tax Hike Booed: Poll," *The Tyee*, 7 July 2009, accessed 24 July 2013.

44 *Globe and Mail*, 23 April 2013.

45 Steve Mertl, "Environmentalists, Unions, Challenge BC Raw Log Export Program," *Canadian Press Newswire*, 20 November 2002; Daniel Tatroff, "Clear-Cut Thinking: BC Unions at Loggerheads," *Our Times*, 12/3 (September/October 1993), 26–29.

46 Kate Leslie, "From Enemy to Ally: Labour and Environmental Activists in BC," *Our Times*, 23/5 (October/November 2004), 14–19.

47 Richard A. Rajala, *Up-Coast: Forest and Industry on British Columbia's North Coast, 1870–2005* (Victoria: Royal BC Museum, 2006), 241.

48 Carole Pearson, "Old Growth Trees & New Coalitions: BC Forest Workers and Environmentalists," *Our Times*, 26/5 (October/November 2007), 23 passim. For environmentalism within the IWA, see Andrew Neufeld and Andrew Parnaby, *The IWA in Canada: The Life and Times of an Industrial Union* (Vancouver: IWA Canada/New Star Books, 2000), 268–299.

49 Colleen Kimmett, "Greens and Labour: Make Work Not War!" *The Tyee*, 25 September 2012, accessed 24 July 2013.

50 Kai Nagata, "Manning's Map to Victory," *The Tyee*, 11 March 2013, accessed 15 March 2013.

51 Unionization itself in First Nations communities has been controversial. In 1999, for example, eighty-five Kamloops Indian Band employees sought to be represented by the BC Government and Services Employees' Union (BCGEU), but the band leaders responded that confrontation was foreign to Shuswap culture. In the end, the two sides worked out a satisfactory agreement. Paul Barnsley, "Band, Union Meet Half Way in Negotiations," *Windspeaker*, 17/2 (June 1999), 7. See also, Janet Mary Nicol, "'Unions Aren't Native': The Muckamuck Restaurant Labour Dispute, Vancouver, BC (1978–1983), *Labour/Le Travail*, 40 (1997), 249.

52 In 2008, there was a clash between greens and an Indigenous enterprise when MaMook Natural Resources, in partnership with Coulson Forest Products, began preparing to log an area in Clayoquot Sound. The Aboriginal people, now with some control over their traditional lands, wanted to log in a sus-

tainable way to provide jobs and economic development for their communities. Environmentalists rallied to stop the logging. Greenpeace, ForestEthics, the Sierra Club, the WCWC, the Watershed Watch Salmon Society, the federal Green Party, and the Natural Resources Defense Council wanted to protect the pristine forests that had been saved by an environmentalist-First Nations alliance in the early 1990s. Eventually a compromise was reached. Keven Drews, "Environmentalists Issue Ultimatum over Logging in BC's Clayoquot Sound," *The Canadian Press*, 27 July 2008; Drews, "Environmentalists Renew Calls for Opposition to Development in Clayoquot Sound," *The Canadian Press*, 3 August 2008; Konrad Yakabuski, "Woods War II," *Report on Business Magazine* (September 2008), 54; *Vancouver Sun*, 24 September 2008. In 2011 logging in Clayoquot Sound that involved First Nations loggers was proceeding and remained controversial with environmentalists. See Mark Hume, "The Sound and the Fury," *The Globe and Mail*, 11 April 2011.

53 Naomi Klein, *No Logo: Taking Aim at the Brand Bullies* (Toronto: Knopf Canada, 2000), xix.

54 Klein, 269.

55 *Financial Post Magazine* (December 1995), 59–63.

56 Klein, 445–446.

57 Joel Bakan, "The Significance of the APEC Affair," in W. Wesley Pue, ed., *Pepper in Our Eyes: The APEC Affair* (Vancouver: UBC Press, 2000), 80. UBC professor Joel Bakan made a significant contribution to the international anti-corporate movement with his book *The Corporation: The Pathological Pursuit of Profit and Power* (Toronto: Penguin Canada, 2004), and the accompanying documentary film, *The Corporation*, 2003.

58 Naomi Klein, *Fences and Windows: Dispatches from the Front Lines of the Globalization Debate* (Toronto: Vintage Canada, 2002), 228.

59 Klein, *Fences and Windows*, 229.

60 Victor Olson, "Nothing to Lose: The New Politics Initiative," *Canadian Dimension*, 35/4 (July/August 2001), 15–16.

61 Geoff Dembicki, "Who Are the Protesters?" *The Tyee*, 2 February 2010, accessed 24 July 2013.

62 Geoff Dembicki, "Arrests, Beatings as Saturday Protest Turns Violent," *The Tyee*, 13 February 2010, accessed 24 July 2013.

63 *Vancouver Sun*, 6 December 2011, C1.

64 *The Globe and Mail*, 5 October 2011, A12; 22 December 2012, A10, A11.

65 *The Navigator*, Nanaimo, 43/5 (Nov. 2–Nov. 15, 2011), 10.

66 Indigenous understandings of modern political and environmental problems offer an alternative approach to Enlightenment thinking, and these ideas about environmental sustainability, human relationships with nature, science, and community may become more evident in the left. See Umeek (E. Richard Atleo), *The Principles of Tsawalk: An Indigenous Approach to Global Crisis* (Vancouver: UBC Press, 2011).

CONCLUSION (pp. 197–203)

1 *Nanaimo Free Press*, 22 January 1892.

2 See, also, Nelson Wiseman and Benjamin Isitt, "Social Democracy in Twentieth-Century Canada: An Interpretive Framework," *Canadian Journal of Political Science*, 40/3 (September 2007), 567–589.

3 Tom Fletcher, "BCTF Digs In for Endless War," *Saanich News*, 29 May 2013, A8.

4 Richard Littlemore, "Union 2.0," *Report on Business, Globe and Mail*, 29/9 (April 2013), 47–52.

5 Benjamin Isitt, *Militant Minority: British Columbia Workers and the Rise of a New Left, 1948–1972* (Toronto: University of Toronto Press, 2011), 123–131.

6 Naomi Klein, "Capitalism vs. the Climate," Part III of III, *The CCPA Monitor*, 18/10 (April 2012), 21. For the other two parts in the series, see *The CCPA Monitor*, 18/8 (February 2012), 10–12; and 18/9 (March 2012), 8–10.

Bibliography

NEWSPAPERS: LATE 19TH CENTURY

- *British Colonist*, Victoria
- *Daily Columbian*, New Westminster
- *Daily British Colonist*, Victoria
- *Daily Globe*, St. Paul Minnesota
- *Daily News-Advertiser*, Vancouver
- *The Eugene City Guard*
- *Los Angeles Daily Herald*
- *Morning Ledger*, New Westminster
- *Nanaimo Free Press*
- *The Truth*, New Westminster
- *Times Colonist*, Victoria
- *Vancouver Daily World*
- *Vancouver News*
- *Victoria Daily Colonist*
- *Victoria Daily Times*

PERIODICALS AND NEWSPAPERS
(electronic and hardcopy): 20th century and 21st century

- *2006 Census Fast Facts*, British Columbia Government, Victoria

- Annual Reports, British Columbia, Ministry of Labour, 1976–2000

- *BC Stats*, British Columbia Government, Victoria

- *BC Stats Business Indicators*, British Columbia, Ministry of Finance and Corporate Relations, Victoria

- *Briar Patch*

- *Canadian Dimension*

- *Canadian Press Newswire*

- *Financial Post Magazine*

- *thefreedictionary.com*

- *The Globe and Mail*

- *Infoline Report, BC Stats*, Victoria

- *Maclean's*, Toronto

- *Nanaimo Free Press*

- *Natural Life*

- *The Navigator*, Nanaimo

- *New Directions*

- *Our Times*

- *Report on Business*

- *Saanich News*

- *Straight.com.*

- *Teacher Newsmagazine*

- *This Magazine*

- *The Tyee*, Vancouver

- *The Ubyssey*, Vancouver

- *Vancouver Sun*

- *Windspeaker*

BOOKS AND ARTICLES

Abella, Irving. "Communism and Anti-Communism in the British Columbia Labour Movement: 1940–1948." In David Jay Bercuson, ed. *Western Perspectives I: Papers of the Western Canadian Studies Conference, 1973*. Toronto: Holt, Rinehart and Winston, 1974, 88–100.

———. *Nationalism, Communism, and Canadian Labour: The CIO, the Communist Party, and the Canadian Congress of Labour, 1935–1956*. Toronto: University of Toronto Press, 1973.

Andrews, Margaret. "The Course of Medical Opinion on State Health Insurance In British Columbia, 1919–1939." *Histoire sociale/Social History*, 31 (May 1983), 131–143.

Artibise, Alan F.J. "'A Worthy, if Unlikely Enterprise': The Labour Relations Board and the Evolution of Labour Policy and Practice in British Columbia, 1973–1980." *BC Studies*, 56 (Winter 1982–83), 3–43.

Ashby, Daryl. *John Muir: West Coast Pioneer*. Vancouver: Ronsdale Press, 2005.

Avery, Donald. *'Dangerous Foreigners': European Immigrant Workers and Labour Radicalism in Canada, 1896–1932*. Toronto: McClelland and Stewart, 1975.

Baird, Irene. *Waste Heritage*. Toronto: Macmillan of Canada, 1973 [original 1939].

Bakan, Joel. *The Corporation: The Pathological Pursuit of Profit and Power*. Toronto: Penguin Canada, 2004.

———. "The Significance of the APEC Affair." In W. Wesley Pue, ed. *Pepper in Our Eyes: The APEC Affair*. Vancouver: UBC Press, 2000, 77–84.

Barman, Jean. *The West beyond the West: A History of British Columbia*. Toronto: University of Toronto Press, 1991.

Baskerville, Peter and Eric W. Sager. *Unwilling Idlers: The Urban Unemployed and Their Families in Late Victorian Canada*. Toronto: University of Toronto Press, 1998.

Baum, Gregory and Duncan Cameron. *Ethics and Economics: Canada's Catholic Bishops on the Economic Crisis*. Toronto: James Lorimer & Company, 1985.

Beeching, William and Phyllis Clarke, eds. *Yours in the Struggle: Reminiscences of Tim Buck*. Toronto: NC Press, 1977.

Belshaw, John Douglas and David J. Mitchell. "The Economy since the Great War." In J.M. Johnston, ed. *The Pacific Province: A History of British Columbia*. Vancouver: Douglas & McIntyre, 1996, 313–342.

Berman, Tzeporah, et. al. *Clayoquot & Dissent*. Vancouver: Ronsdale Press, 1994.

Berman, Tzeporah with Mark Leiren-Young. *This Crazy Time: Living Our Environmental Challenge*. Toronto: Alfred A. Knopf Canada, 2011.

Bernard, Elaine. *The Long Distance Feeling: A History of the Telecommunications Union*. Vancouver: New Star Books, 1982.

Biagini, Eugenio F. *Liberty, Retrenchment and Reform: Popular Liberalism in the Age of Gladstone, 1860–1880*. Cambridge: Cambridge University Press, 1992.

Biagini, Eugenio F. and Alastair J. Reid, eds. *Currents of Radicalism: Popular Radicalism, Organised Labour and Party Politics in Britain, 1850–1914*. Cambridge: Cambridge University Press, 1991.

Birney, Earle. *Down the Long Table*. Toronto: McClelland and Stewart, 1975 [original, 1955].

Blake, Donald E. "Value Conflicts in Lotusland: British Columbia Political Culture." In R.K. Carty, ed. *Politics, Policy, and Government in British Columbia*. Vancouver: UBC Press, 1996, 3–17.

Bohlen, Jim. *Making Waves: The Origins and Future of Greenpeace*. Montreal: Black Rose Books, 2001.

Boucher, Geoff. *The Charmed Circle of Ideology: A Critique of Laclau and Mouffe, Butler and Žižek*. Melbourne: re:press, 2008.

Bray, Bonita. "Against All Odds: The Progressive Arts Club's Production of *Waiting for Lefty.*" *Journal of Canadian Studies*, 25/3 (Fall 1990), 106–122.

Bridge, William Frederick. *An Account of the Descendants of John Bridge, Cambridge, 1632*. Boston: Cushing, 1884.

British Columbia, Ministry of Labour. *Annual Reports*, 1976–2000. Victoria: Queen's Printer, 1977–2001.

Bullen, John. "The Ontario Waffle and the Struggle for an Independent Socialist Canada: Conflict Within the NDP." *Canadian Historical Review*, 64/2 (1983), 188–215.

Burrows, James K. "'A Much-Needed Class of Labour': The Economy and Income of the Southern Interior Plateau Indians, 1897–1910." *BC Studies*, 71 (Autumn 1986), 27–46.

Cameron, Elspeth. *Earle Birney: A Life*. Toronto: Viking/Penguin, 1994.

Camfield, David. "Neoliberalism and Working-Class Resistance in British Columbia: The Hospital Employees' Union Struggle, 2002–2004." *Labour/Le Travail*, 57 (Spring 2006), 9–41.

Campbell, Lara. "'We Who Have Wallowed in the Mud of Flanders': First World War Veterans, Unemployment and the Development of Social Welfare in Canada, 1929–1939." *Journal of the Canadian Historical Association* (2000), 125–149.

Campbell, Marie. "Sexism in British Columbia Trade Unions, 1900–1920." In Barbara Latham and Cathy Kess, eds. *In Her Own Right: Selected Essays on Women's History in BC*. Victoria: Camosun College, 1980, 167–86.

Campbell, Peter. *Canadian Marxists and the Search for a Third Way*. Montreal & Kingston: McGill-Queen's University Press, 1999.

———. "East Meets Left: South Asian Militants and the Socialist Party of Canada in British Columbia, 1904–1914." *International Journal of Canadian Studies*, 20 (Fall 1999), 35–65.

Careless, Ric. *To Save the Wild Earth: Field Notes from the Environmental Frontline*. Vancouver: Raincoast Books, 1997.

Carroll, William and R.S. Ratner. "Social Democracy, Neo-Conservatism and Hegemonic Crisis in British Columbia." *Critical Sociology Critical Sociology*, 16/1 (Spring 1989), 29–53.

Carroll, William. "The Solidarity Coalition." In Warren Magnusson, William K. Carroll, Charles Boyle, Monika Langer, and R.B.J. Walker, eds. *The New Reality: The Politics of Restraint in British Columbia*. Vancouver: New Star Books, 1983, 94–113.

Carty, R.K., ed. *Politics, Policy, and Government in British Columbia*. Vancouver: UBC Press, 1996.

Cashore, Benjamin, George Hoberg, Michael Howlett, Jeremy Rayner, and Jeremy Wilson. *The Search for Sustainability: British Columbia Forest Policy in the 1990s*. Vancouver: UBC Press, 2001.

Christensen, Sandra. *Unions and the Public Interest: Collective Bargaining in the Government Sector*. Vancouver: Fraser Institute, 1980.

Christie, Nancy. *Engendering the State: Family, Work, and Welfare in Canada*. Toronto: University of Toronto Press, 2000.

Clément, Dominique. *Canada's Rights Revolution: Social Movements and Social Change, 1937–82*. Vancouver: UBC Press, 2008.

———. "Human Rights Law and Sexual Discrimination in British Columbia, 1953–84." In *The West and Beyond: New Perspectives on an Imagined Region*. Edmonton: Athabasca University Press, 2010, 297–325.

Cleverdon, Catherine L. *The Woman Suffrage Movement in Canada*. Toronto: University of Toronto Press, 1974 [original 1950].

Conley, James R. "Frontier Labourers, Crafts in Crisis and the Western Labour Revolt: The Case of Vancouver, 1900–1919." *Labour/Le Travail*, 23 (Spring 1989), 9–37.

———. "'Open Shop Means Closed to Union Men': Carpenters and the 1911 Vancouver Building Trades Strike." *BC Studies*, 91–92 (Autumn-Winter, 1991–92), 127–151.

Cook, Ramsay. "Henry George and the Poverty of Canadian Progress." *Historical Papers*. Canadian Historical Association, 12/1 (1977), 142–156.

———. *The Regenerators: Social Criticism in Late Victorian English Canada*. Toronto: University of Toronto Press, 1985.

Creese, Gillian. "Exclusion or Solidarity? Vancouver Workers Confront the 'Oriental Problem.'" *BC Studies*, 80 (1988), 24–51.

Critchley, Simon and Oliver Marchart. *Laclau: A Critical Reader*. London: Routledge, 2004.

Drushka, Ken. *HR: A Biography of H.R. MacMillan*. Madeira Park, BC: Harbour Publishing, 1995.

Egan, Jim. *Challenging the Conspiracy of Silence: My Life as a Canadian Gay Activist*. Compiled and edited by Donald W. McLeod. Toronto: The Canadian Lesbian and Gay Archives and Homewood Books, 1998.

Elections British Columbia. *Electoral History of British Columbia, 1871–1986*. Victoria: Legislative Library, 1988.

———. *Electoral History of British Columbia Supplement, 1987–2001*. Victoria: Legislative Library, 2002.

Elections Canada. "General Information: Official Reports: Thirty-sixth General Election 1997 — Official Voting Results — Synopsis," http://www.elections.ca, accessed 24 July 2013.

Eley, Geoff. *Forging Democracy: The History of the Left in Europe, 1850–2000*. Oxford: Oxford University Press, 2002.

Eley, Geoff and Keith Nield. *The Future of Class in History: What's Left of the Social?* Ann Arbor: University of Michigan Press, 2007.

Evans, Bryan. "The New Democratic Party in the Era of Neoliberalism." In Stephanie Ross and Larry Savage, eds. *Rethinking the Politics of Labour in Canada*. Halifax: Fernwood Publishing, 2012, 54–56.

Fetherling, Douglas. *The Gentle Anarchist: A Life of George Woodcock*. Vancouver: Douglas & McIntyre, 1998.

Fish, Gordon. *Dreams of Freedom: Bella Coola, Cape Scott, Sointula*. Victoria: Provincial Archives of British Columbia, 1982.

Fisher, Robin. "The Decline of Reform: British Columbia Politics in the 1930s." *Journal of Canadian Studies*, 25/3 (Fall 1990), 74–89.

Flanagan, Tom. *Waiting for the Wave: The Reform Party and Preston Manning*. Toronto: Stoddart, 1995.

Fleming, Thomas. *Worlds Apart: British Columbia Schools, Politics, and Labour Relations Before and After 1972*. Mill Bay, BC: Bendall Books, 2011.

Forsey, Eugene. *Trade Unions in Canada, 1812–1902*. Toronto: University of Toronto Press, 1982.

Francis, Daniel. *L.D.: Mayor Louis Taylor and the Rise of Vancouver*. Vancouver: Arsenal Press, 2004.

Fudge, Judy and Eric Tucker. "'Everybody knows what a picket line means': Picketing before the British Columbia Court of Appeal." *BC Studies*, 162 (Summer 2009), 53–79.

Garr, Allen. *Tough Guy: Bill Bennett and the Taking of British Columbia*. Toronto: Key Porter Books, 1985.

Gawthorp, Daniel. *Highwire Act: Power, Pragmatism, and the Harcourt Legacy*. Vancouver: New Star Books, 1996.

Goutor, David. *Guarding the Gates: The Canadian Labour Movement and Immigration, 1872–1934*. Vancouver: UBC Press, 2007.

Grant, George. *Lament for a Nation: The Defeat of Canadian Nationalism*. Ottawa: Carleton University Press, 1995, original 1965.

Grant, H.M. "Solving the Labour Problem at Imperial Oil: Welfare Capitalism in the Canadian Petroleum Industry, 1919–29." *Labour/Le Travail*, 41 (Spring 1998), 69–95.

Grove, Alan and Ross Lambertson. "Pawns of the Powerful: The Politics of Litigation in the Union Colliery Case." *BC Studies*, 103 (Autumn 1994), 3–31.

Gunster, Shane. "Listening to Labour: Mainstream Media, Talk Radio, and the 2005 BC Teachers Strike," *Canadian Journal of Communications*, 33/4 (2008), 661–684.

Hak, Gordon. "British Columbia Loggers and the Lumber Workers Industrial Union, 1919–1922." *Labour/Le Travail*, 23 (Spring 1989), 67–90.

———. *Capital and Labour in the British Columbia Forest Industry, 1934–1974*. Vancouver: UBC Press, 2007.

———. "The Communists and the Unemployed in the Prince George District, 1930–1935." *BC Studies*, 68 (Winter 1985–86), 45–61.

———. "Populism and the Social Credit Breakthrough in British Columbia." *Canadian Historical Review*, 85/2 (June 2004), 277–296.

———. "Red Wages: Communists and the 1934 Vancouver Island Loggers Strike." *Pacific Northwest Quarterly*, 80/3 (July 1989), 82–90.

———. "The Socialist and Labourist Impulse in Small-Town British Columbia: Port Alberni and Prince George, 1911–33." *Canadian Historical Review*, LXX/4 (December 1989), 519–542.

———. *Turning Trees into Dollars: The British Columbia Coastal Lumber Industry, 1858–1913*. Toronto: University of Toronto Press, 2000.

Hansen, Ann. *Direct Action: Memoirs of an Urban Guerilla*. Toronto: Between the Lines, 2001.

Harcourt, Mike with Wayne Skene. *Mike Harcourt: A Measure of Defiance*. Vancouver: Douglas & McIntyre, 1996.

Harding, James. "The New Left in British Columbia." *Our Generation*, 7/2 (June–July 1970), 21–44.

Hardt, Michael and Antonio Negri. *Empire*. Cambridge: Harvard University Press, 2000.

———. *Multitude: War and Democracy in the Age of Empire*. New York: Penguin Books, 2004.

Hardy, George. *Those Stormy Years: Memories of the Fight for Freedom on Five Continents*. London: Lawrence & Wishart, 1956.

Harris, Cole. *Making Native Space: Colonialism, Resistance, and Reserves in British Columbia*. Vancouver: UBC Press, 2002.

Harrison, Kathryn. "Environmental Protection in British Columbia: Postmaterial Values, Organized Interests, and Party Politics." In R.K. Carty, ed. *Politics, Policy, and Government in British Columbia*. Vancouver: UBC Press, 1996, 290–309.

Harrison, Trevor. *Of Passionate Intensity: Right-Wing Populism and the Reform Party of Canada*. Toronto: University of Toronto Press, 1995.

Harvey, David. *A Brief History of Neoliberalism*. Oxford: Oxford University Press, 2005.

Hayden, Tom. "The Way We Were and the Future of the Port Huron Statement." In Dimitrios Roussopoulos, ed., *The New Left: Legacy and Continuity*. Montreal: Black Rose Books, 2007, 130–156.

Heron, Craig. *Booze: A Distilled History*. Toronto: Between the Lines, 2003.

Heron, Craig and Steve Penfold. *The Workers' Festival: A History of Labour Day in Canada*. Toronto: University of Toronto Press, 2005.

Hinde, John R. "'Stout Ladies and Amazons': Women in the British Columbia Coal-Mining Community of Ladysmith, 1912–1914." *BC Studies*, 114 (Summer 1997), 33–57.

———. *When Coal Was King: Ladysmith and the Coal-Mining Industry of Vancouver Island*. Vancouver: UBC Press, 2003.

Hoberg, George. "The Politics of Sustainability: Forest Policy in British Columbia." In R.K. Carty, ed. *Politics, Policy, and Government in British Columbia*. Vancouver: UBC Press, 1996, 272–289.

Howard, Irene. "The Mothers' Council of Vancouver: Holding the Fort for the Unemployed, 1935–1938." *BC Studies*, 69–70 (Spring–Summer 1986), 249–287.

———. *The Struggle for Social Justice in British Columbia: Helena Gutteridge, the Unknown Reformer*. Vancouver: UBC Press, 1992.

Howlett, Michael and Keith Brownsey. "The Old Reality and New Reality: Party Politics and Public Policy in British Columbia 1941–1987." *Studies in Political Economy*, 25 (Spring 1988), 141–176.

Huizen, Philip Van. "'Panic Park': Environmental Protest and the Politics of Parks in British Columbia's Skagit Valley." *BC Studies*, 170 (Summer 2011), 67–92.

Inglehart, Ronald. *The Silent Revolution: Changing Values and Political Styles Among Western Publics*. Princeton: Princeton University Press, 1977.

Irving, Allan. "The Development of a Provincial Welfare State: British Columbia, 1900–1939." In Allan Moscovitch and Jim Albert, eds. *The Benevolent State: The Growth of Welfare in Canada*. Toronto: Garamond Press, 1987, 155–174.

———. "The Doctors Versus the Expert: Harry Morris Cassidy and the British Columbia Healthy Insurance Dispute of the 1930s." *BC Studies*, 78 (Summer 1988), 53–79.

Isitt, Ben. "Confronting the Cold War: The 1950 Vancouver Convention of the Co-operative Commonwealth Federation." *Canadian Historical Review*, 91/3 (September 2010), 465–501.

———. *From Victoria to Vladivostok: Canada's Siberian Expedition, 1917–19*. Vancouver: UBC Press, 2010.

———. *Militant Minority: British Columbia Workers and the Rise of a New Left, 1948–1972*. Toronto: University of Toronto Press, 2011.

George, Paul. *Big Trees Not Big Stumps: 25 Years of Campaigning to Save Wilderness with the Wilderness Committee*. Vancouver: Western Canada Wilderness Committee, 2006.

Jackson, Andrew. "Solidarity Forever? Trends in Canadian Union Density." *Studies in Political Economy*, 74 (Autumn 2004), 124–146.

Johnston, Hugh. *Radical Campus: Making Simon Fraser University*. Vancouver: Douglas & McIntyre, 2005, 255–329.

Joyce, Patrick. *Visions of the People: Industrial England and the Question of Class, 1848–1914*. Cambridge: Cambridge University Press, 1991.

Kardam, Nükhet. "Interest Group Power and Government Regulation: The Cases of the Mining and Insurance Industries During the Period of the New Democratic Party Government in British Columbia, 1972–75." *BC Studies*, 60 (Winter 1983–84), 48–74.

Kealey, Gregory S. "1919: The Canadian Labour Revolt." *Labour/Le Travail*, 13 (Spring 1984), 11–44.

———. *Toronto Workers Respond to Industrial Capitalism, 1867–1892*. Toronto: University of Toronto Press, 1980.

Kew, Michael. "Making Indians." In *Workers, Capital, and the State in British Columbia: Selected Papers*. Vancouver: UBC Press, 1988, 24–34.

Klein, Naomi. "Capitalism vs. the Climate." *The CCPA Monitor*, 18/10 (April 2012), 19–22; 18/8 (February 2012), 10–12; 18/9 (March 2012), 8–10.

———. *Fences and Windows: Dispatches from the Front Lines of the Globalization Debate*. Toronto: Vintage Canada, 2002.

———. *No Logo: Taking Aim at the Brand Bullies*. Toronto: Knopf Canada, 2000.

Knight, Rolf. *Indians at Work*, 2nd ed. Vancouver: New Star Books, 1996.

Kristianson, G.L. "The Non-partisan Approach to BC Politics: The Search for a Unity Party, 1972–1975." *BC Studies*, 33 (Spring 1977), 13–29.

Laclau, Ernesto. *On Populist Reason*. London: Verso, 2007.

Laclau, Ernesto and Chantal Mouffe. *Hegemony and Socialist Strategy: Towards a Radical Democratic Politics*, 2nd ed. London: Verso, 2001.

Lambertson, Ross. *Repression and Resistance: Canadian Human Rights Activists 1930–1960*. Toronto: University of Toronto Press, 2005.

Langford, Will. "Is Sutton Brown God? Planning and Expertise and the Local State in Vancouver, 1952–1973." *BC Studies*, 173 (Spring 2012), 11–39.

Larocque, Sylvain. *Gay Marriage: The Story of a Canadian Social Revolution*. Tr. Robert Chodos, Louisa Blair, and Benjamin Waterhouse. Toronto: James Lorimer & Company, 2006.

Leier, Mark. "Ralph Smith." *Dictionary of Canadian Biography Online*. http:// www.biographi.ca, accessed 25 July 2013.

——. *Red Flags & Red Tape: The Making of a Labour Bureaucracy*. Toronto: University of Toronto Press, 1995.

——. "Solidarity on Occasion: The Vancouver Free Speech Fights of 1909 and 1912." *Labour/Le Travail*, 23 (1989), 39–66.

——: *Where the Fraser River Flows: The Industrial Workers of the World in British Columbia*. Vancouver: New Star Books, 1990.

Leonard, Frank. *A Thousand Blunders: The Grand Trunk Pacific Railway and Northern British Columbia*. Vancouver: UBC Press, 1995.

Levitt, Kari. *Silent Surrender: The Multinational Corporation in Canada*. Toronto: Macmillan, 1970.

Lewis, S.P. *Grace: The Life of Grace MacInnis*. Madeira Park, BC: Harbour Publishing, 1993.

Liversedge, Ronald. *Recollections of the On to Ottawa Trek*. Ed. Victor Hoar. Toronto: McClelland and Stewart, 1973.

Livesay, Dorothy. *Right Hand Left Hand*. Erin, Ontario: Press Porcepic, 1977.

Lutz, John. "After the Fur Trade: The Aboriginal Labouring Class of British Columbia, 1849–1890." *Journal of the Canadian Historical Association* (1992), 69–94.

——. *Makúk: A New History of Aboriginal-White Relations*. Vancouver: UBC Press, 2008.

Marchak, Patricia. "A Changing Global Context for British Columbia's Forest Industry." In Trevor J. Barnes and Roger Hayter, eds. *Troubles in the Rainforest: British Columbia's Forest Economy in Transition*. Canadian Western Geographical Series, vol. 33. Victoria: Western Geographical Press, 1997, 147–164.

——. *Green Gold: The Forest Industry in British Columbia*. Vancouver: UBC Press, 1983.

Mason, Gary and Keith Baldrey. *Fantasyland: Inside the Reign of Bill Vander Zalm*. Toronto: McGraw-Hill Ryerson, 1989.

Matthews, J. Scott. "The Political Foundations of Support for Same-Sex Marriage in Canada." *Canadian Journal of Political Science*, 38/4 (December 2005), 841–866.

May, Elizabeth. "Brian Mulroney and the Environment." In Raymond B. Blake, ed. *Transforming the Nation: Canada and Brian Mulroney*. Montreal and Kingston: McGill-Queen's University Press, 2007, 381–392.

———. *Paradise Won: The Struggle for South Moresby*. Toronto: McClelland and Stewart, 1990.

McCormack, A. Ross. *Reformers, Rebels, and Revolutionaries: The Western Canadian Radical Movement, 1899–1919*. Toronto: University of Toronto Press, 1977.

McDonald, Robert A.J. *Making Vancouver: Class, Status, and Social Boundaries, 1863–1913*. Vancouver: UBC Press, 1996.

———. "Working-Class Vancouver, 1886–1914." *BC Studies*, 69/70 (Spring/Summer 1986), 33–69.

McDonald, Robert A.J. "'Telford Time' and the Populist Origins of the CCF in British Columbia," *Labour/Le Travail*, 71 (Spring 2013), 87–100.

McDonald, Robert A.J. and Jeremy Mouat. "George Ritchie Maxwell." *Dictionary of Canadian Biography Online*. accessed 25 July 2013.

M'Gonigle, Michael. "Reinventing British Columbia: Towards a New Political Economy in the Forest." In Trevor J. Barnes and Roger Hayter, eds. *Troubles in the Rainforest: British Columbia's Forest Economy in Transition*. Canadian Western Geographical Series, Volume 33. Victoria: University of Victoria, Department of Geography, Western Geographical Press, 1997, 37–50.

McKay, Ian. *Reasoning Otherwise: Leftists and the People's Enlightenment in Canada, 1890–1920*. Toronto: Between the Lines, 2008.

———. *Rebels, Reds, Radicals: Rethinking Canada's Left History*. Toronto: Between the Lines, 2005.

McLaren, Angus and Arlene Tigar McLaren. *The Bedroom and the State: The Changing Practices and Politics of Contraception and Abortion in Canada, 1880–1980*. Toronto: McClelland and Stewart, 1986.

McLean, Bruce. *'A Union Amongst Government Employees': A History of the BC Government Employees Union, 1919–1979*. Burnaby: BCGEU, 1979.

Meggs, Geoff and Rod Mickleburgh. *The Art of the Impossible: Dave Barrett and the NDP in Power, 1972–1975*. Madeira Park, BC: Harbour Publishing, 2012.

Meyers, Jeanne. "Class and Community in the Fraser Mills Strike, 1931." In Rennie Warburton and David Coburn, eds. *Workers, Capital, and the State in British Columbia*. Vancouver: UBC Press, 1988, 141–160.

Milligan, Ian. "Coming off the Mountain: Forging an Outward-Looking New Left at Simon Fraser University." *BC Studies*, 171 (Autumn 2011), 69–91.

Miron, Janet, ed. *A History of Human Rights in Canada: Essential Issues*. Toronto: Canadian Scholars' Press, 2009.

Mitchell, David J. *W.A.C.: Bennett and the Rise of British Columbia*. Vancouver: Douglas & McIntyre, 1983.

Mouat, Jeremy. "Christopher Foley." *Dictionary of Canadian Biography Online*, accessed 25 July 2013.

——. "Frank Rogers." *Dictionary of Canadian Biography Online*. accessed 25 July 2013.

——. "The Genesis of Western Exceptionalism: British Columbia's Hard-Rock Miners, 1895–1903." *Canadian Historical Review*, 71/3 (September 1990), 317–345.

——. "The Politics of Coal: A Study of the Wellington Miners' Strike of 1890–91." *BC Studies*, 77 (Spring 1988), 3–29.

——. *Roaring Days: Rossland's Mines and the History of British Columbia*. Vancouver: UBC Press, 1995.

Munro, Jack and Jane O'Hara. *Union Jack: Labour Leader Jack Munro*. Vancouver: Douglas & McIntyre, 1988.

Murton, James. *Creating a Modern Countryside: Liberalism and Land Resettlement in British Columbia*. Vancouver: UBC Press, 2007.

Muszynski, Alicja. *Cheap Wage Labour: Race and Gender in the Fisheries of British Columbia*. Montreal and Kingston: McGill-Queen's Press, 1996.

Naylor, James. "The British Columbia CCF's Working-Class Moment: Socialism Not Populism." *Labour/Le Travail*, 71 (Spring 2013), 101–121.

——. "Canadian Labour Politics and the British Model, 1920–50." In Phillip Buckner, and R. Douglas Francis, eds. *Canada and the British World: Culture, Migration, and Identity*. Vancouver: UBC Press, 2006, 288–308.

Neufeld, Andrew and Andrew Parnaby. *The IWA in Canada: The Life and Times of an Industrial Union*. Vancouver: IWA Canada/New Star Books, 2000.

Newell, Peter E. *The Impossibilists: A Brief Profile of the Socialist Party of Canada*. London: Athena Press, 2008.

Nicol, Janet Mary. "'Unions Aren't Native': The Muckamuck Restaurant Labour Dispute, Vancouver, BC (1978–1983)." *Labour/Le Travail*, 40 (1997), 235–251.

Northrup, David. *Indentured Labor in the Age of Imperialism*. Cambridge: Cambridge University Press, 1995.

Ormsby, Margaret. *British Columbia: A History*. Toronto: Macmillan of Canada, 1958.

——. "T. Dufferin Pattullo and the Little New Deal." *Canadian Historical Review*, 43/4 (December 1962), 277–297.

Owram, Doug. *Born at the Right Time: A History of the Baby-Boom Generation*. Toronto: University of Toronto Press, 1996.

Palmer, Bryan D. *Solidarity: The Rise and Fall of an Opposition in British Columbia*. Vancouver: New Star, 1987.

——. "Wildcat Workers in the 1960s: The Unruly Face of Class Struggle." In Bryan D. Palmer and Joan Sangster, eds., *Labouring Canada: Class, Gender, and Race in Canadian Working-Class History*. Don Mills: Oxford University Press, 2008, 373–394.

——. *Working-Class Experience: Rethinking the History of Canadian Labour, 1800–1991*. Toronto: McClelland & Stewart, 1992.

Panitch, Leo and Donald Swartz. *From Consent to Coercion: The Assault on Trade Union Freedoms*. 3rd ed. Aurora: Garamond Press, 2003.

Pattison, Jimmy with Paul Grescoe. *Jimmy: An Autobiography*. Toronto: Seal Books, 1987.

Parnaby, Andrew. "'The best men that ever worked lumber': Aboriginal Longshoremen on Burrard Inlet, BC, 1863–1939." *Canadian Historical Review*, 87 (March 2006), 53–78.

——. *Citizen Docker: Making a New Deal on the Vancouver Waterfront, 1919–39*. Toronto: University of Toronto Press, 2008.

——. "What's the Law Got to Do with It? The IWA and the Politics of State Power in British Columbia, 1935–1939." *Labour/Le Travail* (Fall 1999), 9–45.

Payne, Raymond W. "Corporate Power, Interest Groups and the Development of Mining Policy in British Columbia, 1972–77." *BC Studies*, 54 (Summer 1982), 3–37.

Penner, Norman. *Canadian Communism: The Stalin Years and Beyond*. Toronto: Methuen, 1988.

Persky, Stan. *Bennett II: The Decline & Stumbling of Social Credit Government in British Columbia*. Vancouver: New Star Books, 1983.

———. *Son of Socred: Has Bill Bennett's Government Gotten BC Moving Again?* Vancouver: New Star Books, 1979.

Petter, Andrew. "Sausage-Making in British Columbia: The Creation of the Land Commission Act, August 1972–April 1973." *BC Studies*, 65 (Spring 1985), 3–33.

Phillips, Paul, *No Power Greater: A Century of Labour in British Columbia*. Vancouver: BC Federation of Labour/Boag Foundation, 1967.

Plecas, Bob. *Bill Bennett: A Mandarin's View*. Vancouver: Douglas & McIntyre, 2006.

Porter, Ann. *Gendered States: Women, Unemployment Insurance, and the Political Economy of the Welfare State in Canada, 1945–1997*. Toronto: University of Toronto Press, 2003.

Price, Charles A. *The Great White Walls are Built: Restrictive Immigration to North America and Australasia, 1836–1888*. Canberra: Australian Institute of International Affairs with Australian National University Press, 1974.

Prudham, Scott. "Sustaining Sustained Yield: Class, Politics, and Post-War Forest Regulation in British Columbia." *Environment and Planning D: Society and Space*, 35/2 (April 2007), 258–283.

Rajala, Richard. "The Forest as Factory: Technological Change and Worker Control in the West Coast Logging Industry." *Labour/Le Travail*, 32 (Fall 1993), 73–104.

———. *Up-Coast: Forest and Industry on British Columbia's North Coast, 1870–2005*. Victoria: Royal BC Museum, 2006.

Rebick, Judy. *Ten Thousand Roses: The Making of a Feminist Revolution*. Toronto: Penguin Canada, 2005.

Resnick, Philip. "Social Democracy in Power: The Case of British Columbia." *BC Studies*, 34 (Summer 1977), 3–20.

Richards, John. *Retooling the Welfare State: What's Right, What's Wrong, What's to Be Done*. Policy Study 31. Toronto: CD Howe Institute, 1997.

Richmond, Ted and John Shields. "Reflections on Resistance to Neoliberalism: Looking Back on Solidarity in 1983 British Columbia," *Socialist Studies/Études socialistes*, 7/1–2 (Spring/Fall 2011), 216–237.

Robin, Martin. *Pillars of Profit: The Company Province, 1934–1972*. Toronto: McClelland and Stewart, 1973.

Roy, Patricia E. *Boundless Optimism: Richard McBride's British Columbia*. Vancouver: UBC Press, 2012.

———. *The Oriental Question: Consolidating a White Man's Province, 1914–41*. Vancouver: UBC Press, 2003.

———. "The Preservation of the Peace in Vancouver: The Aftermath of the Anti-Chinese Riot of 1887." *BC Studies*, 31 (Autumn 1976), 44–59.

———. *A White Man's Province: British Columbia Politicians and Chinese and Japanese Immigrants, 1858–1914*. Vancouver: UBC Press, 1989.

Roy, Patricia E. and John Herd Thompson. *British Columbia: Land of Promises*. Don Mills: Oxford University Press, 2005.

Ruff, Norman. "Social Credit as Employer." In Warren Magnusson, William K. Carroll, Charles Boyle, Monika Langer, and R.B.J. Walker, eds. *The New Reality: The Politics of Restraint in British Columbia*. Vancouver: New Star Books, 1984, 152–64.

Salazar, Debra J. and Donald K. Alper. "Beyond the Politics of Left and Right: Beliefs and Values of Environmental Activists in British Columbia." *BC Studies*, 121 (Spring 1999), 5–34.

———. "Reconciling Environmentalism and the Left: Perspectives on Democracy and Social Justice in British Columbia's Environmental Movement." *Canadian Journal of Political Science*, 35/3 (September 2002), 527–566.

———. *Sustaining the Forests of the Pacific Coast: Forging Truces in the War in the Woods*. Vancouver: UBC Press, 2000.

Sangster, Joan. *Dreams of Equality: Women on the Left, 1920–1950*. Toronto: McClelland & Stewart, 1989.

Schwantes, Carlos A. *Radical Heritage: Labor, Socialism, and Reform in Washington and British Columbia, 1885–1917*. Vancouver: Douglas & McIntyre, 1979.

Scott, Jack. *A Communist Life: Jack Scott and the Canadian Workers Movement, 1927–1985*. Ed. and intro. Bryan D. Palmer. St. John's: Canadian Committee on Labour History, 1988.

Seager, Allen. "Socialists and Workers: The Western Canadian Coal Miners, 1900–21." *Labour/Le Travail*, 16 (Fall 1985), 23–59.

———. "Workers, Class, and Industrial Conflict in New Westminster, 1900–1930." In Rennie Warburton and David Coburn, eds. *Workers, Capital, and the State in British Columbia: Selected Papers*. Vancouver: UBC Press, 1988, 117–40.

Seager, Allen and Adele Perry, "Mining the Connections: Class, Ethnicity, and Gender in Nanaimo, British Columbia, 1891." *Histoire sociale/Social History*, 30/59 (May 1997), 55–76.

Seager, Allen and David Roth. "British Columbia and the Mining West: A Ghost of a Chance." In Craig Heron, ed. *The Workers' Revolt in Canada, 1917–1925*. Toronto: University of Toronto Press, 1998, 231–67.

Sethna, Christabelle and Steve Hewitt. "Clandestine Operations: The Vancouver Women's Caucus, the Abortion Caravan, and the RCMP." *Canadian Historical Review*, 90/3 (September 2009), 463–495.

Simon, Gordon. "A Comparative Historical Explanation of the Environmental Policies of Two Woodworkers Unions in Canada." *Organization & Environment*, 16 (September 2003), 289–305.

Sinclair, Bertrand W. *The Inverted Pyramid*. Vancouver: Ronsdale Press, 2011 [original 1924].

Slinn, Sara. "Restructuring Reality So That the Law Will Follow: British Columbia Teachers' Quest for Collective Bargaining Rights." *Labour/Le Travail*, 68 (Fall 2011), 35–77.

Smith, Andrea B. "The CCF, NPA, and Civic Change: Provincial Forces behind Vancouver Politics, 1930–1940." *BC Studies*, 53 (Spring 1982), 45–65.

Stanbury, W.T. *Environmental Groups and the International Conflict Over the Forests of British Columbia, 1990 to 2000*. Vancouver: SFU-UBC Centre for Study of Government and Business, 2000.

Steeves, Dorothy. *The Compassionate Rebel: Ernest Winch and the Growth of Socialism in Western Canada*. Vancouver: J.J. Douglas, 1977.

Teeple, Gary. *The Riddle of Human Rights*. Aurora, Ontario: Garamond Press, 2005.

Tennant, Paul. "Vancouver Civic Politics, 1929–1980." *BC Studies*, 46 (Summer 1980), 3–27.

Thompson, John Herd and Allen Seager. *Canada 1922–1939: Decades of Discord*. Toronto: McClelland and Stewart, 1985.

Thomson, Ann. *Winning Choice on Abortion: How British Columbia Feminists Won the Battles of the 1970s and 1980s*. Victoria: Trafford Publishing, 2004.

Tinker, Hugh. *A New System of Slavery: The Export of Indian Labour Overseas, 1830–1920*. London: Oxford University Press, 1974.

Umeek (E. Richard Atleo). *The Principles of Tsawalk: An Indigenous Approach to Global Crisis*. Vancouver: UBC Press, 2011.

Vogel, Donna. *Changing Politics: COPE, Electoral Politics and Social Movements*. Halifax: Fernwood Publishing, 2003.

Warburton, Rennie and David Coburn, eds. *Workers, Capital, and the State in British Columbia: Selected Papers*. Vancouver: UBC Press, 1988, 117–140.

Warburton, Rennie. "The Workingmen's Protective Association, Victoria, BC, 1878: Racism, Intersectionality and Status Politics." *Labour/Le Travail*, 43 (Spring 1999), 105–120.

Warburton, Rennie and David Coburn. "The Rise of Non-Manual Work in British Columbia." *BC Studies*, 59 (Autumn 1983), 5–27.

Warner, Tom. *Never Going Back: A History of Queer Activism in Canada*. Toronto: University of Toronto Press, 2002.

Wasserman, Louis. "The Essential Henry George." In *Critics of Henry George: A Centenary Appraisal of Their Strictures on Progress and Poverty*, Robert V. Andelson. Cranberry, NJ: Associated University Press, 1979, 29–43.

Watkins, Mel. "A Staple Theory of Economic Growth." In W.T. Easterbrook and M.H. Watkins, eds. *Approaches to Canadian Economic History*. Toronto: McClelland and Stewart, 1967, 49–73.

Webb, Patricia G. *The Heart of Healthy Care, The Story of the Hospital Employees' Union: The First 50 Years*. Vancouver: HEU, 1994.

Weyler, Rex. *Greenpeace: How a Group of Ecologists, Journalists and Visionaries Changed the World*. Vancouver: Raincoast Books, 2004.

White, Howard. *A Hard Man to Beat: The Story of Bill White: Labour Leader, Historian, Shipyard Worker, Raconteur*. Vancouver: Pulp Press, 1983.

Wild, Paula. *Sointula: Island Utopia*. Madeira Park, BC: Harbour Publishing, 1995.

Wilson, Jeremy. *Talk and Log: Wilderness Politics in British Columbia, 1965–96*. Vancouver: UBC Press, 1998.

Wilson, Judy Tyabji. *Daggers Unsheathed: The Political Assassination of Glen Clark*. Surrey: Heritage House, 2002.

Wilson, Kevin. *Practical Dreamers: Communitarianism and Co-operatives on Malcolm Island*. Victoria: British Columbia Institute for Co-operative Studies, 2005.

Wiseman, Nelson. *In Search of Canadian Political Culture*. Vancouver: UBC Press, 2007.

Wiseman, Nelson and Benjamin Isitt. "Social Democracy in Twentieth-Century Canada: An Interpretive Framework." *Canadian Journal of Political Science*, 40/3 (September 2007), 567–589.

Wotherspoon, Terry. "Occupational Divisions and Struggles for Unity Among British Columbia's Public School Teachers." *BC Studies*, 107 (Autumn 1995), 30–59.

Wright, Robert. *Virtual Sovereignty: Nationalism, Culture and the Canadian Question*. Toronto: Canadian Scholars' Press, 2004.

Young, Walter D. *The Anatomy of a Party: The National CCF, 1932–61*. Toronto: University of Toronto Press, 1969.

———. "Ideology, Personality and the Origin of the CCF in British Columbia." *BC Studies*, 32 (Winter 1976–77), 139–162.

Zelko, Frank. "Making Greenpeace: The Development of Direct Action Environmentalism in British Columbia." *BC Studies*, 142/143 (Summer/Autumn 2004), 197–239.

UNPUBLISHED MATERIAL

Hak, Gordon. "On the Fringes: Capital and Labour in the Forest Economies of the Port Alberni and Prince George Districts, British Columbia, 1910–1939." PhD dissertation, Simon Fraser University, 1986.

Hill, Patrick George. "A Failure of Unity: Communist Party–CCF Relations in British Columbia, 1935–1939." MA thesis, University of Victoria, 1977.

Isitt, Ben. "The Search for Solidarity: The Industrial and Political Roots of the Co-operative Commonwealth Federation in British Columbia, 1913–1928." MA thesis, University of Victoria, 2003.

Johnson, Ross Alfred. "No Compromise – No Political Trading: The Marxian Socialist Tradition in British Columbia." PhD dissertation, University of British Columbia, 1975.

Keeling, Arn. "The Effluent Society: Water Pollution and Environmental Politics in British Columbia, 1889–1980." PhD dissertation, University of British Columbia, 2004.

Martin, Eryk. "When Red Meets Green: Perceptions of Environmental Change in the B.C. Communist Left, 1937–1978." MA thesis, University of Victoria, 2008.

McDonald, Ian. "Class Conflict and Political Factionalism: A History of Local 213 of the International Brotherhood of Electrical Workers, 1901–1961." MA thesis, Simon Fraser University, 1986.

McDonald, Robert. "Modernity and the Political Left: Robert Strachan, Thomas Berger, and Leadership of the Provincial NDP, 1963–69." Paper presented at BC Studies Conference, Kelowna, 6 May 2011.

Moore, Joseph G. "Two Struggles Into One? Labour and Environmental Movement relations and the Challenge to Capitalist Forestry in British Columbia, 1900–2000." PhD dissertation, McMaster University, 2002.

Parker, Stuart. "From Social Experiment to Electoral Entity: The Transformation of the BC Green Party 1988–99." Paper presented at BC Studies Conference, New Westminster, 2 May 2013.

Price, Christine. "'A Very Conservative Radical': Reverend Robert Connell's Encounter with Marxism in the BC CCF." MA thesis, Simon Fraser University, 2006.

Roberts, Dorothy June. "Doctrine and Disunity in the British Columbia Section of the CCF, 1932–1956." MA thesis, University of Victoria, 1972.

Roussin, Della. "Political Legitimacy and Regime Change: The 1972 British Columbia Election." MA thesis, University of British Columbia, 2012.

ABOUT THE AUTHOR

Gordon Hak was born and raised in Prince George, British Columbia. He earned degrees from the University of Victoria, the University of Guelph and Simon Fraser University, before going on to teach at Vancouver Island University, formerly Malaspina University-College, in Nanaimo. His research and teaching interests include the Canadian histories of labour, business, politics, immigration, human rights, and post-1960 social and political movements. He has published two scholarly books on the BC forest industry, one of which won the Canadian Historical Association's annual prize for best book on British Columbian history, as well as numerous articles. He lives in Victoria with his wife Joanne.

INDEX

Citations of photographs are in bold